George lectures fervidly on as we eagerly group around him

"Gravity is bullshit, a lie we believe collectively. If we could release ourselves from this illusion, we would be able to fly around the room like they did in the movie, *Mary Poppins*. Remember when they floated up and had a tea party on the ceiling?"

An unanticipated surge of rage rises from deep inside my chest, reddening my cheeks. I tilt my face downwards to hide, but George catches my reaction and makes an example of me. "Elizabeth, do you have a problem with what I just said?" He glares, rising from his seat and approaching me threateningly.

"Y-y-y-yes," I stammer, cursing myself for wearing my emotions on my sleeve, as usual . . . now forced to admit my lack of faith publicly.

"See everybody," he turns to face the rest of my comrades, "this proves my point. Elizabeth is defending the lie that we can't fly, and that lie is precisely what holds us all on the ground."

I recede into my chair in humiliation. His accusations make me feel personally responsible for keeping the entire human race weighted down on the Earth's surface. Soon, another surge of rage passes through me, commanding me to jump up and argue, even attack him, but I suppress it, gluing myself to my seat. Nonetheless, George senses my continued opposition and glares, filling me with terror. . . .

"I thank the authors for illuminating the subtleties of cult involvement along with the agonizing struggle to break the spell. An incredible story."

Frederick J. Berle, Ph.D., Clinical Psychology
Author: "Cults and Abusive Religions"

"Insightful, thought-provoking and fascinating. Ms. Burchard and Mrs. Carlone help us to understand how an intelligent, well-read, and insightful individual could be manipulated into accepting the bizarre doctrine of a sociopath."

Bill Goldberg, M.S.W.
Board of Directors, Cult Information Service of NY & NJ

"An intriguing story . . . reveals how devious individuals can take advantage of good people in a vulnerable moment. Bottom line—a book everyone should read!"

David R. Cole, Vice President
Leo J. Ryan Education Foundation for Cult Awareness

"Burchard and Carlone, in the revelatory *The Cult Next Door*, have rendered an invaluable service. All of us *must* be alerted to the consummate devastation that may be perpetrated by an enslaving, malevolent predator. Wake up America! Read this book!"

Evelyn Ortner
Executive Director, The Unity Group, Inc.
A non-profit advocacy group for battered women & their children

"A painstaking, sometimes painful, insightful, case study—the surprising part of this tale is that, despite two decades of mind control, the author was able to be deprogrammed. The grit, patience, and determination displayed by Judith Carlone (the "deprogrammer") had me mixing metaphors—describing her as an avatar of St. Michael."

Dayn DeRose, Psychology Dept., Drew University

"A captivating story that illuminates the insidious nature of destructive cultism. Interweaving the authors' two viewpoints offers a unique counterpoint into this often puzzling phenomena.*"

Paul Engel, LCSW, Executive Director,
Queens Counseling Services,
Foundation for Religion and Mental Health

"This story clearly reveals how currently popular spiritual principles can be manipulated by a power-hungry individual concealed behind a benevolent facade; how the lives of innocent people can be utterly destroyed—entirely permissible within the bounds of our legal system. A testimony to true friendship and the resilience of the human spirit."

Judy Chapman
Editor and Founder, Garden State Woman Magazine

"*The Cult Next Door* is a testimony to human weakness and the ability of love to conquer evil."

Al Sullivan
Senior Staff Writer, The Hudson Reporter

The Cult Next Door

A True Story of a
Manhattan
New Age Cult

*Elizabeth R. Burchard
and Judith L. Carlone*

Ace Academics, Inc. New Jersey

This is a true story.
Some of the names have been changed to protect
the privacy of the persons involved.
Conversations were composed from memory
and presented to reflect the speakers' intentions
with the greatest possible accuracy.

The Cult Next Door
©2013 by Elizabeth R. Burchard & Judith L. Carlone
Print ISBN 9781576333006
eBook ISBN 9781576333013

cover art by Jared Phillips ©1998
title by James Foley, Esq.

Published by Ace Academics, Inc.
Bergenfield, N.J.
phone: 201-784-0001
fax: 201-784-7704
e-mail: info@TheCultNextDoor.com
www.TheCultNextDoor.com

To each of my great teachers: Rachael, George, Mike, Matt, and Cynthia; amidst your opposition, I found my inner strength.

To the friends I left behind: I pray for their eyes to open, that someday they will reach for the light. . . .

To my two friends who left "The Group" before me: thank you for your support, and the healing we shared together.

To those generous of spirit who, knowingly or unknowingly, gave me light and shelter in the dark night: Franco T., Addy R., Melissa G., Preston Y., Nestor S., Hal D., Val M., Robert C., Tom P., Lee G., and Rich B.

To Bill and Lorna G., and the members of C.I.S.-NY & NJ for giving me a safe haven to learn and to heal, with others who have, in different places and times, walked the same path as I.

And finally to my angel, Judy, words fall short.

Elizabeth R. Burchard

To my mother for showing me how to love.

To my father, Eugene F., and Lucy C., for challenging my weaknesses.

To my husband Michael for enduring with boundless love, since the moment we met.

To Leslie S. for helping me overcome my personal battles.

To my animals for their unconditional love.

To God for selecting me to carry out His extraordinary mission.

Judith Lynn Carlone

I don't believe in secrets. Secrets protect sin, and sin enslaves the soul. With the assistance and encouragement of others, combined with my own naivete, I have committed terrible crimes in my life—mostly against myself. My journey begins here, through persecution, betrayal, miracles, and finding the strength to overcome.

I was a vulnerable young woman searching for love in all the wrong places. Perhaps, despite the strange circumstances, you will find a piece of yourself in me.

Foreword

The authors of *The Cult Next Door* make an extraordinary contribution to the literature on cultism and mind control. Elizabeth's story offers insight into her vulnerability, her manipulation into the world of the cult, the techniques used by the cult leader to control her, and the ways that Judith helped her to leave. By suggesting these insights, this book helps to dispel some of the common myths of cult membership.

The first myth is that individuals who are involved in cults are less bright than most people. Elizabeth is clearly an intelligent person. She is a class valedictorian, a graduate of Swarthmore, and a successful businesswoman. Her involvement with George Sharkman and his group was not caused by her lack of intelligence, but by the manipulation of a malevolent man who took advantage of her at a time of vulnerability in her life.

The second myth that this book helps to invalidate is the belief that individuals who join cults are always seekers by nature who look for someone to guide them. Although, in truth, the portrait she paints of her mother may suggest that the mother was looking for such a guru, Elizabeth was not. She was looking for relief from depression and overeating—complaints that are not uncommon. Had she found a legitimate therapist to help her to overcome these problems, chances are that she would moved on with her life. Unfortunately she was introduced to George Sharkman, a charismatic sociopath, who portrayed himself as a professional and who took advantage of her vulnerability.

A legitimate helping professional helps his or her patients to recognize that they have the power within themselves to overcome their issues. The therapist helps the patients to develop and use their own resources. An unscrupulous or cultist therapist (or, in this case, pseudo-therapist) indicates that only he or she has the key to help the patient and attempts to make the patient feel less strong, less able and less independent. The beginning place is the same—an individual who is in some kind of pain and who is looking for relief from that pain. It was Elizabeth's misfortune—not her wish or her personality flaw—that she encountered an individual who would use her desire to better herself against her and who would use manipulative techniques and interpretations to keep her dependent.

Another myth that the general public believes about cult members is that most of them join a cult because the cult's bizarre belief system somehow makes sense to the cultist. Elizabeth Burchard is not a person who accepts irrational beliefs without question. The reader of this book will recognize that she often questioned, and sometimes challenged, the outlandish beliefs promulgated in her cult. That fact may cause some readers to wonder why Elizabeth stayed in the cult, even though she recognized the invalidity of some of the doctrines. One of this book's virtues is that it honestly portrays the simultaneous repulsion and appeal of the cult.

In fact, most cult members do not adopt the belief system of the cult because it makes sense to them. Instead, they adopt it because the group seems to have something they want—a sense of belonging, a certainty, a feeling of sameness of purpose. The cult leader's manipulation is aimed only partially at convincing the cult member to adopt a new belief system. Even more significantly, the manipulation is aimed at convincing them not to trust their instincts and their own knowledge. Sharkman refers to the "old" (i.e. healthy, reality-based) way of thinking as "The Program." He interprets his followers' aversion to stealing, sense of loyalty to family or desire to decide for themselves with whom they wish to be intimate, as examples of their old, outmoded way of thinking. This tactic of denigrating pre-cult logical thinking is universal among cult leaders and is a necessary step in the process of destroying the cult member's sense of integrity and autonomy. Elizabeth never fully accepted the absurdities that Sharkman tried to get her to adopt. However, he was able to convince her to suspend her logic and beliefs just enough to accept the possibility that his world view may have merit. Once she accepted that possibility, she was able to rationalize her continued involvement with the guru.

Finally, and perhaps most importantly to anyone who has a loved one in a cult, it is enlightening to examine the way that Judith Carlone coaxed Elizabeth out of the cult. The myth involved here is that simply by identifying the absurdity of the cult's beliefs and doctrines, the cult member will be persuaded to leave. The mistake made by many parents of cult members is simply to confront the cultist with facts: "This is a cult...You've been manipulated... You're being harmed by your membership." Pointing out the validity of these facts, by itself, is rarely enough to bring about the self-examination necessary for a cult member to leave. Usually, a more efficacious approach is the patient watchful waiting adopted by Judy. If she had pointed out every inconsistency and absurdity each time she recognized them, Elizabeth may have been scared off early in the relationship. Instead, Judy focused upon building her relationship with Elizabeth. Then, by asking well-timed questions and pointing out discrepancies in the doctrine, Judy helped Elizabeth to bring to consciousness the doubts and contradictions that Elizabeth had recognized, but had taught herself to ignore. There is a lesson in Judy's patience for individuals who have lost a loved one to a cult.

This book is valuable for the honesty of its authors and for the insights it inspires, as well as for the story itself. It is a fascinating account of an individual's journey into an exploitive cult and the friendship that helped her, eventually, to find within herself the courage to leave.

William Goldberg, ACSW
May 2005

Introduction

The word "cult" draws a variety of responses from people: fear, disgust, fascination; thoughts like: *It would never happen to me. I'm too smart; I don't understand how the members can believe (or do) such crazy things; only an insane person would join a cult.* Yet, after my own formidable journey, an experience that robbed me of two decades, I have come to view my ordeal as a bizarre addiction, sustained by those who had much to gain from my exploitation, people who convinced me that I could trust them. The cost was heavy; I lost a sizable inheritance from my father, threw away childhood plans of becoming a physician, ruined my health, and severed ties to family and friends.

I began my life like most people: developed hobbies, attended college, planned my future, and looked for love. Every day I tried to make the most sensible choices I could, and yet, despite my conscientious efforts, one day I woke up to find myself entangled in an impossible web of lies—painful and confusing beyond anything I ever could have imagined. Low self-esteem, youthful idealism, gullibility, and loneliness all led to my entrapment. As a basically isolated person with few friends or family, once I had succumbed, there was no one present to protest or try to rescue me from the quicksand. But I am not unique. Most people possess at least some of the weaknesses that permitted my seduction, and although they may never enter a cult, these imperfections do emerge to foster much misery: failed relationships and businesses, self-destructive habits, or obsession with the wrong lover.

It was indeed my weaker self—insecure, unassertive, and demanding recognition—that tolerated my enslavement. In that bondage, I endured the evolution of "The Group," born from "stress reduction" sessions in the office of a Manhattan psychologist, but soon developing into an incestuous cultic religion, a small group of primarily women who served every whim of their idolized leader—a pathological liar and a malevolent genius.

It was my higher self, the part that craves self-expression, success, and wholesomeness, that eventually drove me to find freedom. This self relentlessly sent out an SOS, even as my brainwashed mind patently ignored its desperate pleas.

Cults like The Group meet every day, all around us, even in our own backyards. They share common characteristics: a charismatic guru who controls the minds and lives of his followers, and a worshipful assembly who willingly (or under duress and manipulation) donates its allegiance, energy, time, and money to its fraudulent spiritual leader-parent. The identities of group members might surprise you: neighbor, mayor, physician, or rabbi; perhaps your child's school teacher. . . .

The Search for Spirituality

"All of us have a sense of spiritual destiny, a
deep longing for eternity."

Dr. David Jeremiah, *What the Bible Says About Angels*

Many of us believe in the existence of a separate world, a
higher truth beyond our secular existence. Despite faithful
attempts to govern our personal lives, unanticipated events
occur, often for incomprehensible reasons. Intuition,
coincidences, and ultimately the keys to our destiny seem to
originate from this invisible realm that may both terrify and
fascinate us—our connection to eternity. Sometimes, especially
during crisis, we seek comfort in the knowledge that a higher
intelligence exists, a God who loves and protects us. We strive
to understand this divine presence with whom, when our fleeting
physical journeys are complete, we hope to ultimately find
happiness, peace, and a home for our souls.

Normally, as part of our upbringing, parents transmit a set of
instructions, both verbal and non-verbal—a personal rule book
on which to base future decisions. If we don't like what we see
and renounce our parents' way of life, how do we find a path? At
the dawn of a new century, more than ever before, humanity
seems to crave spirituality. Those not fortunate enough to find
stability during childhood may become seekers. I was an only
child and my mother a single parent. We were all each other had,
yet we never got along. Emotional conflict was perpetual and
resolution hopeless. As a small child I rejected my mother as role
model. Thus, I spent my youth longing for an adult mentor—a
source of strength, wisdom, and truth upon whom I could lean
when I felt lost.

George Sharkman, a man I met as a college freshman in
1977, seemed to be the answer to my prayers. He was merely a

biofeedback therapist, assistant to an Upper East Side psychologist, but he clearly had a calling; I had never heard anyone speak so passionately about higher truth. His powerful conviction awoke my yearning for spiritual wisdom. His charisma captivated me, and my intensely aroused emotions supplied irrevocable evidence that through him lay the keys to my "deep," "big," unanswered questions. He seemed to have uncovered a magical recipe to achieve perfection, and I sincerely believed that emulating him would afford me anything I could ever want. I took him at face value, assuming he was truly the person he claimed to be. Thus, I gave my allegiance to George and embraced him as my personal guide. I glued myself to him, drinking in his every word. With the goal of absorbing all that was in his mind and making it my own, I became his most faithful student. A furious desire for his knowledge overwhelmed me and immediately took priority over everything else. Each of George's lessons was taken to heart, and I carried his precious jewels of supernatural wisdom out into the world where I eagerly sought to verify them.

In the search for happiness and prosperity, many find New Age spirituality extremely attractive. This is evident at George's author signings at Barnes & Noble for his self-help book, *Biofeedback and Beyond*. There, much of the audience absorbs his concepts willingly—professed formulas for personal fulfillment, shedding illusions, and unlocking infinite potential. These concepts are the cornerstones of many best-selling self-help and New Age books. Although George's assertions are attractive, very much in line with Neale Donald Walsch (*Conversations with God*), James Redfield (*The Celestine Prophesy*), Dr. Deepak Chopra, and Dr. Wayne Dyer, in contrast, George possesses a personal, hidden agenda. Many of those exposed to his rhetoric, or the grandiosity of other cult leaders like Jim Jones (The People's Temple) or Marshall Applewhite (Heaven's Gate), respond as I did: they trust his pretense—an ardent instructor whose heart is focused on your greatest good—one who will share your joy as you grow spiritually.

Sadly, people have no idea what danger lies ahead should they take that fateful step toward the guru's inner circle.

Elizabeth R. Burchard—July 2000

I visit my mother's apartment on Manhattan's Upper West Side for the first time since the breakup. Entering the dimly lit hallway, I sense disembodied spirits of neglect and decay rushing through me, crying plaintively of unfulfilled dreams—a wasted life, now almost concluded. The place is beyond dirty; it is filthy. I am appalled by the sight of the kitchen floor, tiled black and white, now soiled completely grey and black. Splotches of some unidentifiable brown substance stain the sides of her freestanding, white metal cabinet—a dented off-balance monstrosity that holds her treasured collection of wonton soup containers and marred brown plastic vitamin bottles—some dating back thirty years. The face of a dish cupboard displays a large circle of grimy dirt that originates at the knobs and fans outward, covering much of its white painted wooden doors.

A nauseating stench emanates from a hopelessly scorched pot sitting at the back of the stove, filled to the brim with brackish water. My mother admits that the smell is repugnant, but she has "gotten used to it." I suggest gently that she throw it out, and she looks bewildered, as if the idea never occurred to her. The buildup of frost in the freezer leaves little room for her food; most of it is carelessly wrapped in wax paper and rubber bands, severely freezer-burned, much of it more than a few years old. Large balls of dust scatter on the living room floor as my steps disturb them. There are two rolled up, room-sized Persian rugs that once graced the floors of my father's ten-room Park Avenue apartment. They are still in brown paper, wrapped from a visit to the dry cleaners a decade ago. The cocktail party lifestyle that my mother shared with my father—designer clothes from the trendiest Fifth Avenue boutiques, gourmet recipes, and carefully applied cosmetics—faded long ago.

Today she reigns, the Queen of Polyester, over a kingdom of overstuffed closets. $10 pants and $3 shirts spill out onto the floor, treasures she has purchased at 14th Street discount stores.

My childhood bookcases are filled with $5 slippers; I spot six identical pairs varying only in neon color. Her short hair, burnt brittle from too many coloring sessions, is almost orange, with an inch of grey root forming the part at the top of her head. She has a slight cold and a bead of fluid glistens, clinging tenuously to the tip of her nose, but she seems oblivious to its presence. Her red polyester pants don't quite reach her ankles or the green slippers she wears with them, and her thermal underwear peeks out from under a partially buttoned orange shirt. The fabric barely covers her extended belly, extra weight she has gathered from lack of exercise and "eating too much chocolate cake, my favorite." She walks the rooms in a trance-like state, wearing the keys to her apartment on a thick green cord around her neck. They jostle below the undershirt and bounce on her belly button in rhythm with her step. On the street she has sometimes been mistaken for a bag lady despite the fact that at seventy-five years old she still holds a full-time job as research economist for the New York City Department of Housing, to which she dutifully commutes daily by subway.

My mother discontinued the weekly maid soon after I moved out; it has been fifteen years since the house was properly cleaned. Not that she can't afford the cost, it is simply not a priority. I offer to help her at least vacuum a bit, but she cuts me off defensively, "No Liz, you would just take over and boss me around. I don't trust you."

The shower curtain is green from algae growth, and I am afraid to sit on the toilet seat. There is dust on every surface, including the bathroom sink that has been unusable for over two years because it required some minor repair that she never got around to arranging with the building superintendent. This beautiful pre-war co-op apartment is huge for one person: three bedrooms, two baths, eat-in kitchen, parlor; yet, she has collected so many things that it is difficult to move about. Even my childhood toys still rest on a shelf in the third bedroom, her "storage room." There are piles of paper everywhere, fascinating newspaper articles, Ross Perot's *United We Stand America* propaganda, and devotedly safeguarded, manila folders filled with appetizing tidbits of material that once touched our former life together: "apple picking," "Liz's school report cards," "summer camp," "vitamins and health."

I am struck by the profusion of small slips of paper strewn everywhere; on these, my mother has preserved choice morsels of her personal affirmations. A Post-it stuck to the refrigerator door reads, "Talk to god—YOU." On top of the TV, dated two years ago, rests a bold statement: "I DO exist; I must learn to assert this." Next to the telephone lies another: "My daughter is a separate person from me." Under this, I discover the phone number to my former Hackensack, New Jersey apartment—disconnected eight years ago. Her bed is entirely covered with piles of additional, unattended folders that she believes she will someday need. To avoid spending the several necessary minutes to move them each night, she has been sleeping on the couch for the past five years.

I realize that surrounding herself with thoughts fills the emptiness, that the senseless logic that springs forth from her mind defines her identity. Sadly, I see an old woman who has thrown away her self-respect, dignity, and her only child for a life of rubbish and denial.

Amidst this disarray, my mother has three havens: her computer, her microwave oven, and her television. I visualize her filling lonely days rotating her attention from one machine to the next, deriving a cherished sense of vitality from her interactions with these inanimate offspring of our modern technology. My heart breaks for the barrenness of her soul. How did this ever happen to her? Always at the head of the class, my mother skipped three grades and graduated college at the age of nineteen. She obtained a master's degree in the early 1940's, a time when many of her peers had left school after the eighth grade. If only I could rent a Dumpster, park it on 98th Street, and throw her papers and dust out of that fourth story apartment's front windows. *How did I ever come from a place like this?* I wonder. I yearn to rescue her from this decay and sweep her away to a safe place, but I know she will not reach out for my extended hand . . . that although momentarily I can force her with my stronger will, when I let go she will inevitably return, like an over-stretched rubber band that regains its natural shape as soon as the tension is released.

My Past
October 1940 to September 1977

In the fall of 1940, my mother, Rachael, married her professor of psychology, Edward Burchard, after graduating from Philadelphia's Temple University. She was nineteen and he was thirty-one. She went on to earn her Master's Degree in Research Economics at Boston University. My father graduated magna cum laude from the University of Pittsburgh earning a Ph.D. in psychology. A quiet, modest intellectual, he had a high I.Q. and numerous professional awards to his credit. My parents spent the first years of their marriage in Washington, D.C. There, my father served in the United States Navy during World War II, decoding enemy intelligence. Eventually they ended up in New York City, where my father accepted a position as a psychology professor at Queens College.

Rachael: My mother

After nineteen years of marriage, in December of 1959, I was born at Mount Sinai Hospital on the Upper East Side.

I don't remember much about my first three years but according to my mother, my parents fought all the time. One day, just after my third birthday, there were big, strange men moving things out of our East 96th Street, Park Avenue apartment. Wandering around confused, I bumped into my mother who informed me curtly, "We are leaving your father."

That day we moved directly across town to West End Avenue and 96th Street. Many years later my mother explained her decision to divorce: my father was a selfish baby who ignored her, and she could no longer tolerate feeling unappreciated.

With my father out of the way, I became the center of my

mother's focus, and soon the battling began. Impulsively, she focused unyielding wrath upon me, accusing me of bad intentions and misbehavior that she seemed to invent randomly and that I never understood: "You are rude and defiant. You never listen to me. You don't respect me." A monster lunging without warning from darkness, she would react to something I said and slap me full in the face, in public, sometimes in front of one of my little friends. Her scorn and humiliation stung much

Elizabeth: Age 3

worse than the blow. Although I tried to be cooperative—to avoid punishment—it seemed I never could predict what would set her off.

I also found myself continually frustrated by her frequent embarrassing displays. Unpredictably, she threw public tantrums, shrieking irrationally at bewildered waiters to complain about food that had not been prepared to her expectations. Mortified, I longed to crawl under the table, to reassure the shocked onlookers that I didn't know this woman—she was no relation of mine.

When I learned to write, she disciplined me frequently with the assignment of writing two hundred times, "I will not be rude to my mother." I spent many evenings, pencil in hand, forcing myself through this drudgery. And during the night, I relived my conflict-ridden days as nightmares delivered an ugly, cruel witch who persecuted me. From beneath a black hat my mother's face sneered with contempt and the pleasure she took in keeping me prisoner.

Lonely and unhappy, I became fascinated with some of my female teachers and baby sitters, in fact, anyone who was nice to me. When my mother sensed my allegiance to this new person, she would go crazy: "How can you look up to that woman? She is so unsophisticated—*downright dumb*. Besides, you are rude and bossy. No one could stand spending too much time around you. You'll never be able to keep friends for very long."

The unnegotiable message that she didn't want me to love anyone but her—ever—made me fear that even when I grew up, she wouldn't want me to leave, that we might remain each other's sole companion forever. Knowing how she felt filled me with dread. Living with Rachael, I felt completely desolate.

Precious Saturdays spent with my father were my only break from my mother. He never punished me, so I felt free to be myself. We had a subscription to the Lincoln Center Ballet and visited museums and restaurants all over Manhattan. Our trips to FAO Schwartz were frequent, and my father bought me almost anything I asked for. He also stashed several Beatles' records in his phonograph cabinet especially for me. In my happiest memories I am whirling around his living room in a spontaneous dance inspired by *The Magical Mystery Tour* or *The White Album*. Frequently, we visited his well-heeled Westchester colleagues, spending lazy, summer afternoons on their luxuriously manicured lawns, sipping lemonade or swimming in a nearby lake. The world was sweet and gentle with my oppressor miles away from me. Edward bragged about me to his friends, and they lavished attention on me; he was so proud of his smart, vivacious daughter. Most Augusts we vacationed in Provincetown, on Massachusetts' Cape Cod. Alone with my father I felt safe, loved and happy. At the age of eight I knew in my heart that I wanted to follow in his footsteps, so I selected a future career similar to his. I decided to become a psychiatrist and committed myself to my precious dream of entering medical school someday.

December 7, 1971 was three weeks before my twelfth birthday. It was the day of the seventh grade Christmas PTA

Edward: My father

Bazaar, and I spent my lunch hour buying handmade gifts for my mother, my father, and numerous cousins. When the school bus dropped me off, I rushed into the apartment to find my mother sitting on the couch. I grabbed my school bag, about to pull out the little treasures I had obtained just a few hours earlier. Christmas gift buying for our large extended family was one of the few things we enjoyed together. However, just as I was about to display my first item, she stopped me in mid-sentence. In an instant, I perceived that something was terribly wrong. My stomach fell to my shoes seconds before unimaginable words came. "Elizabeth, your father died today."

All in one profound moment the significance ripped through me. As if my life force was being sucked out of my body, I stared in shock, unwilling to believe, unable to understand, refusing to accept. My mother seemed to feel genuinely sorry for me, but she was now a distant entity in another universe. My father had just abandoned me, dooming me to the unsupervised jurisdiction of my mother—my enemy—a woman who let me know every day that she hated me, a woman whose irrational rages arrived without warning and focused on me. Our cleaning woman, Annabelle, a kind and warm colored woman from Brooklyn who had been with our family for over twenty years, had found my father that morning in his bed. He had passed away during the night of congestive heart failure—completely unexpected. It was two weeks before his sixty-fourth birthday. An hour later I found myself pacing the hallway outside my mother's bedroom door while she telephoned my father's two half sisters in Oil City, Pennsylvania, and her two brothers who lived near Philadelphia. She repeated the same short message over and over, "I just wanted to let you know that Ed died today."

With those words, a gong rang sadness through my soul, and from that day forward, a shadow of grief accompanied me everywhere—throbbing loneliness. Life no longer held importance, and I cut myself off from everyone and everything. After my father's death, I received my inheritance: a profound need to replace him and a small fortune ($183,000). The money meant nothing; I just wanted my father back.

During the two years prior to my father's death, my mother developed an obsession for health foods. It all started when a busybody neighbor from down the hall approached her by the elevators. While chatting casually, this woman glanced down and commented on my complexion. "Your daughter looks a little peaked. I suggest that you give her some wheat germ. If you wait here for a moment, I'll fetch you my extra jar."

She sprinted back to her apartment and returned a few moments later, offering my mother an ample container of this, according to her, miraculous substance. On that fateful day Rachael found a guru—prominent nutritionist Adele Davis. Her book, *Let's Eat Right to Keep Fit*, became my mother's personal bible. It was filled with bookmarks, underlining, and paper clips, and she could quote the vitamin or mineral solution to almost any ailment; she spoke of nothing else. She started shoving health foods into my mouth and her new religion down the throats of our friends and relatives.

During the fall of my tenth year, we moved to Riverdale, a middle-class section of the Bronx. That first winter, despite her health food diet, my mother's symptoms of hypoglycemia (low blood sugar) began. The frigid December air would hit her lungs, causing them to spasm into an asthma attack. A two-block walk took 30 minutes. She would take a few steps and then stop to clutch a lamppost for several minutes, bent over, gasping for breath. To me she looked as feeble as a ninety-year-old. Concerned passersby would stop and ask if she needed help. My mother would look up at them with pale face and feeble gaze, murmuring, "I'm just having a little trouble breathing. I'll be OK in a bit after I rest."

I felt something awful was happening to her, but Rachael clung tenaciously to the belief that her faith in Adele Davis' theories would cure her. Therefore, she refused to consult a doctor. Meanwhile, her symptoms continued to worsen, almost completely disabling her for days at a time, obliging me to fill in with shopping, cooking, etc.

Organic foods and vitamins filled my mother's thoughts and our kitchen, and they drained her wallet. After her start with Adele Davis, she soon met Dr. Seidler, a Manhattan chiropractor-nutritionist. He prescribed "living vitamins" (that shipped direct from Ohio) and enchanted her with detailed narratives of the vitamin factory where they "pull the carrot out of the ground and immediately grind it into a capsule for you to swallow." These garden stories justified in Rachael's mind the exorbitant costs, in 1971, of more than $250 a month for those pill-shaped carrots. Twice a week she dutifully visited his office where he put her on a weird machine with a small wheel that went up and down her back. After leaving the room for fifteen minutes he would return, stating encouragingly, "You're doing very well; you can add more oranges to your diet."

His advice extended, my mother would write him a check for $55. Dr. Seidler's consummate answer to good health was—the potato. He claimed potatoes were nature's perfect food because "they are starch when raw, but when you bake them they turn into protein." This "logic" felt wrong to me, but I was only eleven and had not yet studied Introductory Biology. However, Rachael viewed his word as scripture. Everywhere we went my mother's potatoes, packed lovingly in a plastic container, accompanied her. She ate at least four per day, cold, with the skin on, holding one up and biting into it as if it was an apple, even while we rode the public bus or subway. In addition, we were both required to begin each day with a large glassful of the doctor's special concoction: tomato and lemon juices, living vitamins, lecithin, brewer's yeast, and tiger's milk—a blender cocktail. My mother jokingly referred to it as "Witches Brew"; it was so gaggingly vile that I held my nose to choke it down. I begged her repeatedly not to force me to drink it, that my health was fine, but my pleas fell on deaf ears. Rachael had no mercy and I resorted to pouring it down the sink behind her back whenever I could.

At meals a small saucer rested next to my plate containing my vitamin pills, at least twenty. To get past this distasteful ritual as swiftly as possible, I learned to down them all in one gulp. Dr. Seidler told her that the vitamins would be more effectively absorbed into her bloodstream if she actually chewed them, so she spent each meal painstakingly wrapping all of her 30 individual pills in morsels of food—one by one. They tasted so awful, she said, that she "wouldn't wish it on a horse," yet she persisted. However, after three years of faithful attendance, the good doc was no longer satisfied with his $110 per week plus $3,000 per year in vitamin sales. In the sanctuary of his office, safely concealed from his wife's watchful eye, he began slipping his hands toward my mother's breasts. He even tried to steal a kiss while she was lying on the table with that strange wheel machine rolling up and down her back. After a few such incidents, although she definitely seemed flattered by his interest, my mother concluded analytically that he was "probably not acting in her best interest." Therefore, she decided to abandon Dr. Seidler, his potatoes, and his living vitamins.

Out of the frying pan and into the fire, Rachael soon discovered a new guru, Dr. Mark Winston, a chiropractor who had written a book on nutrition, destined to become my mother's next bible. She purchased a dozen copies to distribute among friends and family, and every month we made our two-hour pilgrimage to Stamford, Connecticut. The doctor's strategy for better health confused me. During each $125 visit, I sat under a red lamp for fifteen minutes and then a blue one for another ten. Then, Dr. Winston pulled a little on my arms, legs and neck (but not too much, he was a doddering eighty-year-old). At the end of the session he evaluated our current diets and added a few new items. "This month you may eat ten grapes *twice a week*, and next month we'll add *half a cantaloupe* every other day."

His prescription delivered, Rachael would gaze adoringly, her eyes shining with gratitude. Like a kindergartner anticipating milk and cookies, on the drive home she would chatter ecstatically about her new permitted foods. After the first visit, where I observed his methods and heard his fee, I hit the roof. When we returned to our apartment I confronted her, trying to wake her up to the truth—that Dr. Winston was taking advantage of us—that his diet was simply a ridiculous excuse to collect large sums of money (over $2,000 a year for each of us). But my efforts were wasted. I screamed and begged, crying in frustration for a long time that day, but I could not break down Rachael's mental brick wall. She was convinced; she knew what she was doing and was going to follow every single instruction of Dr. Winston's, no matter what.

Her new doctor's miracle foods were lemons and grapefruits, and he prescribed the "grapefruit fast" (twenty-four hours of grapefruit exclusively), three days a week, to detoxify my mother's system. The rest of the week she was to drink the juice of two lemons, three times a day, and eat nothing but fruit until dinner. (During this period, my mother squeezed more than sixty lemons per week, by hand, for the two of us.) For her only real meal of the day, she could select a fowl or fish protein, steamed vegetables and more fruit. No fat or dairy was permitted. Rachael followed this regime religiously for over a year, a diet that was perfect poison for a hypoglycemic—the equivalent of feeding sugar to a diabetic and taking away their insulin. Her post nasal drip (a symptom of hypoglycemia) was constant, and by bedtime, her lungs had become so filled with mucus that she spent more than two hours in the middle of each night coughing it up. Her asthma was perpetual and she had no energy. For days at a time she would be bedridden. She lost weight— eventually shrinking to an emaciated eighty-nine pounds.

Two of her girlfriends, Judy, a teacher, and Ruth, a psychologist, begged her to stop. They knew enough about proper diet to advise her with confidence that this extreme regime was endangering her well-being. But my mother was oblivious; under Dr. Winston's spell, she followed like a zombie, defiantly ignoring the life-threatening symptoms she was suffering. Then it got worse. Her blood sugar crashed so low that she began to have seizures. In the middle of one night she fell in the hall outside my room and I rushed from my bed, terrified to see her convulsing on the floor. She was so thin that I, now a ninth grader, was able to pick her up and carry her back to bed. During these seizures she would foam at the mouth and let go of her bladder and bowels. I thought she was going to die.

My only emotional support came from Addy, a Manhattan social worker my mother and I had started seeing during my early teen years. Every Saturday my mother and I drove down the West Side Highway to Addy's East 81st street apartment-office off Lexington Avenue. Addy, an empathetic woman with a healthy dose of common sense, developed a special place in her heart for me. This weekly three-hour therapy session was supposed to assist mother and daughter in building a better relationship. My mother's crazy diets were often a topic of discussion, and much to my relief, after a few years with Addy, without explanation, almost as if she had become bored with one hobby and had decided to focus on another, my mother gave up Dr. Winston. Apparently, just like his predecessor, he had made a pass at her one day while she sunned herself under his precious red lamp. Rachael changed her diet and quickly reversed many of her hypoglycemic symptoms.

Addy became her new focus. Under Addy's tutelage, she mounted a xerox of Dr. Winston's face on the bottom of a cardboard carton. This creation sat on the floor next to her bed, a sacred altar to my mother's commitment toward personal growth. As a nightly exercise she stabbed the paper with an ice pick, uttering obscenities to vent her hostility toward her former mentor whose negligence had almost killed her. (Dr. Winston, despite his miracle, cure-all diet, died of cancer a few years later.) In addition, my mother woke herself up several times during each night to write down her dreams. Cardboard cartons overflowing with paper covered her bedroom floor, scribbled records of her involuntary thoughts and analyses of her personal problems. Like a diligent doctoral student, she delivered numerous pages of her insightful revelations to Addy every Saturday, hundreds of words that our therapist could never have possibly had enough spare time to read. My mother also took notes on our daily fights so that she could report my transgressions as well. She scrutinized and analyzed my behavior with friends. She pointed out that I was dysfunctional and self-destructive and she didn't approve of my choice of boyfriends. Instead of vitamins, my diet now consisted of perpetual therapy. "Liz said this; Liz did that; I don't think Liz should like this boy or have that friend."

Addy labeled my mother as "socially defiant," a woman who did and said whatever she wanted, without regard for the feelings of others. During the early seventies, short skirts were in and Addy was horrified to hear my mother's description of a job interview where she wore no underwear, shamelessly offering the office manager a full view of her private parts as she sat across from him. Addy spent several sessions trying to convince Rachael that this and some of her other behavior, such as leaving the bathroom door open while using it, was my mother's attempt to control people by upsetting and offending them. But my mother never saw her point. Addy felt genuinely sorry for me and eventually Rachael began to denounce her as an enemy who was influencing daughter against mother. She concluded that Addy had "very serious problems" and nothing to offer us. Rachael ended their relationship by running up a $2,000 tab and then quitting without paying, an action she justified because "Addy was behaving unprofessionally."

I earned valedictorian in junior high school, and my mother scheduled me to take the Bronx High School of Science entrance exam. I passed and soon began my sophomore year. Early that first semester, I noticed a handsome, blond boy with glasses two desks in front of me in French class. One day, when he turned to pass back some papers, I found myself intensely drawn to him. My classmate's name was Joe Radic, and apparently he felt the same as I. Two years later (senior year) we began dating, and for those twelve short months we were together constantly. Inside our bubble, we were safe and content; we knew we would always be together. For the first time since before my father died, I experienced an oasis of happiness.

I graduated from high school in June of 1977 and moved that fall to Swarthmore College in Swarthmore, Pennsylvania to begin my freshman year. I had to leave Joe behind, but I knew that our separation was only temporary. Joe had his sights set on becoming a mechanical engineer and continued to live at home in the Bronx, where he attended Manhattan College. I was terribly lonely without him, as if a part of me was missing. And despite the distance between us, our feelings for each other remained strong. Although phone calls were infrequent, my commitment to him and our future was always with me; we would finish college, each become a professional, get married, and have kids. Our lives would be perfect.

That fall, a friend recommended biofeedback therapy to my mother—an innovative method of stress reduction. My mother yearned to fill the void that had formerly been occupied by Addy and eagerly pursued this fresh path toward self-improvement, starting weekly sessions with Dr. Keith Rogers, Ph.D., a psychologist who specialized in biofeedback and breathing relaxation exercises. Twice a week my mother reported to his office on East 79th between Park and Lexington, only a two-block walk from Addy's office. To begin the therapy, she was seated in a comfortable brown leather chair while the doctor strapped three electrodes mounted to a nylon band onto her forehead. For the next half hour she sat in a darkened room and listened with headphones as the biofeedback machine translated the degree of muscular tension into a low buzzing sound. By practicing the doctor's exercises, she relaxed and the sound slowed. Thus she learned to loosen those tight muscles and reduce her stress.

The doctor had an assistant, George Sharkman, a licensed biofeedback technician. One day, George substituted while Dr. Rogers was on vacation. My mother expected the same instructions as Dr. Rogers', but when she asked him, "What exercise should I do while I am on the machine?" he replied to her surprise, "None, just leave yourself alone." For some reason, this permission to "do nothing" impressed my mother tremendously. It triggered a rare and special lift, a sense of delicious freedom that she associated with the man who had made the suggestion. Over the next several weeks, George became my mother's favorite topic and she insisted that I must have a session with him during my Thanksgiving visit home. Instinctively, I had a bad feeling about George. All my life Rachael had adoringly paraded what seemed like a never-ending stream of weird men in front of me, and now I feared that George was next in line. But sharing my mother's avocations was the only way I could feel a sense of family. So, although I really didn't want to meet George, I agreed to go.

My Present — November 1977

I am one month shy of my eighteenth birthday on the day Dr. Rogers conducts my orientation interview. He asks me why I have come and I describe the demons that torment me. Despite my relationship with Joe, I have frequent bouts of suicidal depression. The previous year I had locked myself in my bedroom during a three-day internal battle. The conflict was so intense that I missed school. With an enormous, crushing weight on my chest, I couldn't even speak to tell my mother what was wrong. A relentless voice in my mind commanded me to consume the entire bottle of my mother's prescription sleeping pills and end my life. However, another part of me couldn't permit that. I did sneak out to her medicine cabinet, but only swallowed three pills and slept eighteen hours until mercifully, the persecution finally lifted.

In addition, I am obsessed with food. I can't stop eating carbohydrates, even when I am so full that I am bursting out of my jeans. As a result, after always having been slim, I am terribly distressed over a recent gain of 30 pounds that has forced me into size 13 clothing.

Unbeknownst to me, George is eavesdropping from the adjacent office. Without warning, he enters, interrupting our conversation. Barely introducing himself, already an expert about me, he declares with assurance that I am exaggerating my problems to get people to feel sorry for me. They really aren't such a big deal, hardly worth the air time. My gut responds; I practically detest him. First impressions are often correct, but I feel vulnerable and confused and I still want to please my mother. So, I muster the willpower to push my instincts aside, and not for the last time. . . .

Soon George puts me on the biofeedback machine. Dimming the light he exits, advising me to "have a good time." Half an hour later he returns and slips into an armchair facing me. Together again, I give him the once over. George Enoch Sharkman is a six-foot, slim, rather handsome, thirty-eight-year-old man with curly, brown hair. His style of speech reveals his New York Jewish background. Aside from his abrupt introduction earlier, his demeanor is easy on the eye. George caressingly inquires what I have experienced on the machine and I reply that after several minutes I dozed off. I anticipate forthcoming advice about relaxing during the coming holiday week, but instead, from this moment on, the unexpected is destined to become routine.

Sitting at the edge of his chair he leans toward me and delivers my first dose of his true spirit. Completely intent on reaching for and discovering some "new information" through his conversation with me, he lectures, referring to incredible feelings, spiritual love and uncovering the ultimate truth in a sea of confused thoughts. His passion for this "truth talk" fascinates me. I have never heard such rhetoric and it captives me. What attracts me more than what he seems to be saying is the fervor of his performance and his charisma. After spending my last seventeen years watching Rachael chase one quack doctor after another, paying thousands of dollars, making a fool of herself, alienating friends and relatives with her obsessions, and never gaining anything of value, I am starving for a person who can deliver results. I yearn for a sense of purpose and I am desperate for a role model. I crave a mentor who will help me develop a stronger personality and a life different than my mother's. I want to accomplish big things: to be a mover and a shaker—to change the world. George juggles his interpretations of life like balls in the air. He weaves together universal "truths" he has absorbed from books on Eastern religion, self-help and popular psychology into a patchwork quilt that compels me into a state of intellectual euphoria. This feeling sweeps me away.

George explains his working concept for achieving personal growth, overcoming the "fight or flight" reaction. "Animals operate by instinct alone. They are totally controlled by this reaction. We start out like animals too. For example, when someone insults you, you either want to punch their lights out, fight, or run away with hurt feelings, flight. Either way, their insult affects your physiology. Our bodies react as if we were about to be eaten by a saber-toothed tiger. Of course this is a big lie because we no longer live in the jungle where a challenge from another means our survival is at stake. There is only one way to get rid of these outdated reactions. When you are triggered, sit through them; neither fight nor run. It will be painful at first; you must endure the uncomfortable adrenalin rushes and a burning desire to distract yourself from the sensation. However, it gets easier, and when you finally triumph, you will be a bigger, more grownup person and closer to your true spiritual self. Pursuing personal growth consists of seeking situations that will trigger you to react and then facing your fears. I call this 'search and destroy.' Every time you confront the programming you absorbed from your parents and society and refuse to let it control you, you break a barrier in yourself; you reclaim another small piece of your freedom. The more reactions you break, the happier you'll be. These reactions also separate us from our true potential, locked inside our brain. Scientists have proven that we only use *three percent of half the brain*. Imagine what a wonderful life we are missing out on! This is our mission: to merge into oneness with each other and the universe, to realize our genuine, innate capacities. Instead of being separate, *alone*, we will become *all one* together."

He ends our session with these fervent words, "I don't care if it's a book or a chair, we relate to everything and everyone as if it was mother. We have never matured beyond our first and most significant relationship—the person who gave birth to us. Everything is mother!"

I am impressed by the simplicity of this statement. It seems to cut through all possible entangled, intellectual analyses, right to the core nature of relationships. To me, these words hold great meaning, and I am determined to go out into the world and verify them. My mind becomes ablaze with abstractions, contemplations, and seemingly logical deductions. After my short conversation with George, I am hooked, and the painful first impression I experienced just one short hour ago is forgotten. It is incredible how such fleeting minutes can drastically alter the entire course of your life.

By the time my boyfriend, Joe, picks me up in front of Dr. Rogers' office, my mouth is a river of new ideas and theories. From the passenger seat of Joe's older brother's yellow Sebring, my mouth shifts into automatic pilot, and I can't shut up. I am overwhelmed and speak unceasingly about the incredible man I have just met. Infected with a virus of motor mouth babble, every word that springs from my lips is terribly significant, and I know that I have a future ally, George, with whom to share these revelations. I beg Joe to find a way to meet him. He *just has to* experience the exhilaration I feel!

I return to college and stay until Christmas break. I think about George a lot. From that single, one-hour session, he has quickly become larger than life. I spend hours filling the ears of my roommate, Pauline, with George's wisdom, to reinforce my ebullience. My mouth races to keep up with my mind as I strive for new heights of creative thinking, stemming from the seeds that George planted. As I attempt to make discoveries about "truth" myself, I anticipate our next meeting where I will run my ideas by him.

That month, Joe schedules an appointment with George. Because Joe has neither money nor physical problems, George concocts some phony ailment to justify billing the insurance company. With Joe, he is man-to-man and begins his new student's lessons about the "female game" and "female program." According to George, all females have the same intention—to manipulate men. They do this through sex and by creating emotional dependency. "All females" includes me, the person who was, up until that moment, the love of Joe's life and his best friend. Joe begins to question our relationship, and when I return for winter break, the man I love so much, to whom I am totally committed, rebuffs me coldly.

Sitting in George's waiting room, listening to him joking with Joe on the other side of the wall, rage explodes in my chest.

Faithfully parroting George's logic—"hostility and anger are all lies stemming from the fight/flight reaction"—I struggle to disqualify my negativity. Thus, I rationalize, *This reaction must be evidence of my immaturity—possessive insecurity that I must conquer. After all, Joe has the right to enjoy a relationship with someone other than me.* But, despite my attempts to quash my conflict, it remains, just the same. During that vacation Joe and I are estranged from each other for the first time. He accuses me of playing childish games and manipulating him. Finally, he refuses to see or talk to me until I "grow up." He has absorbed George's attitude like a sponge and is projecting it onto me, and worse, George is encouraging him to do so. I am hurt and confused. I have done nothing to earn this rejection, and I feel powerless to repair the rift. Since the first day Joe set eyes on me, he has loved me more than anyone. Now, I have lost what is most precious to me, and I can't understand how, or why. . . .

January 1978

My eighteenth birthday passes during Christmas break, and in mid-January I return to Swarthmore to begin my second semester of freshman year. About a week later I go to bed early, about 8:00 P.M. At the end of the previous semester I had joined the swimming team, and tonight we have just returned from a swim meet. Feeling exhausted, depressed, and strangely empty, I welcome an escape into the cocoon of sleep. The communal hall phone rings and a few moments later, a neighbor knocks on the door and calls my name. I walk to the phone half asleep. My mother's voice speaks from the other end of the line and she sounds upset. I ask her what's going on. She sighs, takes a deep breath, and forces terrible words past her lips, "I'm sorry Liz, but Joe is dead."

Anguish floods my chest. *It can't be. . . . We had plans; we were going to get married. . . .*

Joe was not happy living with his parents and had sought a school with a better engineering program. Two months ago he was accepted as a midyear transfer student at a New York State university (SUNY, Stony Brook) on Long Island. On his first day at the new college, he took a walk that led him along some railroad tracks. It was a windy, frigid, January day and he kept his jacket hood securely fastened. He didn't hear the train coming. In an instant he was killed—the week before his nineteenth birthday. My childhood friend, Jeannie, also a Stony Brook student, read about the accident in the school paper. She called my mother with the news. My mother immediately consulted George about how to break it to me, and he commanded—general to private—"Don't procrastinate; call her and get it over with. Tell her to move past it right away. We must focus on bigger and better things."

Disbelief engulfs me. Joe was neither suicidal nor stupid. He didn't drink or take drugs. He was intelligent, sweet, and alive with a bright future ahead of him. What was going on in his head that day? How could he not have sensed the thunderous approach of an oncoming train? Now I will never know. . . .

I remember the last time I saw him. We were standing on the corner of Fifth Avenue and 78th Street after one of George's sessions. In my mind I see our parting, he walking south and me, north. I had looked back over my shoulder sadly, watching him retreat. We had just had another fight about the "games" I was playing. If only I could have pulled him back from George and made him love me again. Maybe then Joe would have heard the train coming.

I travel by bus from Swarthmore to New York for the funeral. That first night my mother lends me a black dress and takes me to the viewing. I am a sleepwalker, moving automatically, too numb to feel. Joe's parents greet me indifferently and then drift away. I can't understand their strange, detached behavior until one of their relatives explains that their doctor put them on tranquilizers to separate them from their overwhelming agony. As I enter the room, despite the presence of Joe's family, I still hope that this is all a big mistake, that when I finally make it to the coffin it won't be him.

Joe is dressed in a brown suit. Funny, I have never seen him like that; I only remember his casual clothing: jeans, corduroys, sneakers, T-shirts, and his smiling face drinking me in. Joe is not here; this empty shell no longer holds my best friend and I wonder where he is—if he still exists in some form at all. I hope that he knows how much I loved him, how devastated I am by his loss. I pray that somehow, from the other world, he will be able to help me go on with my life, because I don't know how I am going to make it. The face is unscathed because the blow that took Joe's life was to the back of the head. I stroke his cold, lifeless hand thinking of all the warmth we felt together, planning our future. I remember how perfectly he understood and accepted me as no one else ever had, how we both believed that we were destined for each other alone. Harsh reality crushes my heart; what I have lost today, I can never replace. I am alone again.

My mother schedules a "therapy session" with George for the day following the funeral. I arrive at his office hoping he can help me and sink down into the big, brown leather chair next to the biofeedback machine. Staring at the floor, my throat suffocated, I can't even speak. I wait for George to start the dialogue, to help me cope with this unbearable sadness.

His opening line, "What's going on?" is simply matter-of-fact. George acts as if this is a day just like any other, and I look up at him—astounded. In fact, although his face is blank, I sense that he is content, as if some mission has just been accomplished. I had expected George to understand, as Addy would have, perhaps to hug me supportively—human to human. Instead, he is cold and composed.

Trying to respond to his question, I stammer, "Well, I feel so terrible, you know. . . ." My voice falls off as tears fill my eyes and my head drops again.

His response comes quickly. "Well that's all over now. It's time to move on. What else is going on?"

I feel as if he has just kicked me in the stomach. He neither grieves the loss of his new friend, nor shows any empathy toward my devastating loss. For his unforgivable insensitivity, I despise him. In this moment I want to walk out of the office never to return, but my depression won't allow me the strength to lift my body from my seat. Therefore, I retreat into numbness and try to follow the professional advice being given by this older, more experienced man whose recommendations *must* be valid because after all, he works in the office of Dr. Rogers, psychologist on the Upper East Side, a man who has worked long years to earn his Ph.D. and many more helping patients.

To end the uncomfortable silence, I ask George why he didn't attend the funeral, since he cared about Joe, too. He replies with authority, "I don't need to go to those things to impress other people. My feelings live in here." He points to his chest. "I know what I feel, and that's all that's important."

Leaving the office, drowning in sadness, I realize that I must try to get past this, as George has advised. What choice do I have anyway? *George can handle the death without falling apart, so he must know how to help me cope*, I conclude.

Joe's passing is much worse than my father's—half of me has been ripped away, and my bright future destroyed. I return to college in deep depression and roam the campus as if drugged, apathetically dragging myself though lectures and term papers, praying for night when I can escape into sleep's temporary solace. I interact with no one; in fact, my three roommates generally avoid me now; my grief is so enormous that I make them uncomfortable.

Haunted by the specter of Joe's memory, I search for him daily in the crowded cafeteria. The back of a blond head turns, powerful male thighs bulge in familiar corduroy pants with a tiny Gap label on the back pocket. Mentally, I reconstruct him from pieces of other young men. During evenings I gaze dejectedly at embracing couples between the library stacks, thinking to myself, *If only they knew how lucky they are. . . .* In my mind I hear his voice calling, or laughing at some silly joke. Yet with each day these images fade just a tiny bit more. Resolutely, I clutch at the vanishing shreds of my dearest friend, as if by sheer willpower I could pull him back to Earth, back into my arms to stroke my face and tell me it's all OK now.

I lose interest in my future plans, and my grades slide. Anguished thoughts scream, *I want to leave this Earth. There is nothing here for me.* If I could, I would end my life, because I know no other way to escape my suffering. But I am unable to do myself harm. The only promise I can conceive is that my participation in George's mission for higher truth will lift me out of my despair. I grasp this hope and wait.

My return to the city for a month of spring break brings relief from academic demands and also, twice-weekly appointments with George—pre-scheduled by my mother. George never mentions Joe; it is as if he never existed. However, he is remarkably friendly and enthusiastically shares his recent revelations. His positive energy supplies a welcome distraction. George introduces the concept of "real love" and it comes up in most conversations. "This is not the stuff they write all those dumb romantic songs about. Oh no, that's just a cover for co-dependent babies mothering each other. This begins with caring about yourself first and then spreading that to everything around you. Boy, when you get practice, you'll feel connected to the whole universe and—what ecstasy! It's worth all the work to get to that feeling."

That first day back, just as I am about to leave the office George approaches, and without explanation, kisses me lightly on the cheek. He tells me I'm doing very well. No one has touched me with affection since the last time Joe held me. Spontaneous joy floods me as I experience a personal connection to George. I float from the waiting room out onto East 79th Street with clouds under my feet. My emotions catapult me upward; I am surely in love.

The following week, during our talk-session that always follows my half-hour stint on the biofeedback machine, George surprises me. With a glint in his eye he inquires lightly, with almost childlike innocence, "Would you like to try an experiment?"

"What do you want to do?" I respond with genuine curiosity.

"I wonder how it would be if you took your shirt off," he states scientifically, "you know—to break a social barrier. In Europe, women go topless on the beach and it's no big deal; they are much freer over there. We uptight Americans were trained to be ashamed of ourselves. We should learn to accept our bodies.

After all, everyone has one and we are not born wearing clothing!"

A surge of adrenalin flushes my face with heated embarrassment, but also excitement. I feel trapped, as if he has just ever so politely forced me into a corner, but I do see validity in his logic. Inside, I squirm and panic, because I have never been put on the spot like this before. I don't want to do it but I can't say no; George is the boss. So I comply, removing my shirt and sitting bare-chested in the big, brown, leather chair next to the biofeedback machine, giggling like a little girl, nervous and ashamed, and yet happy, because George seems pleased with me. In fact, from the smile I see on his face, I think he is beginning to love me. Within a few minutes, George invites me to sit on his lap. After I calm down, he gently places a hand on my breast. "See Elizabeth, it's really no big deal, just a new experience to adjust to," he reassures me.

Soon my hour is over and I am gratefully released. When I leave his office, I keep it all secret. Anyway, who do I have to tell? My mother? She would only get mad that George chose me instead of her for his experiment. . . .

A couple of sessions later, George pushes me again, asking if I would like to take another step into the unknown—but only if I have "the courage."

"How about if you try to masturbate in front of me?" he suggests with sweet caress and curiosity in his tone.

Danger! Danger! My adrenalin surges instantly. But again I feel trapped, and again excited too, anticipating challenging this taboo. With such contradicting emotions, I don't know what to do, so I let him decide for me. I follow his suggestion and remove my panties. George positions himself in an armchair across the room, a voyeur, studying my every motion. I am nervous. I hate what I am doing, yet somehow I push through it, relieved when it is finally over. When I have dressed again, George praises me and then offers a lesson for "advanced students." He will now train me to "focus."

"Just look directly into my eyes and try not to blink. . . . No, don't move your eyes back and forth, just straight ahead, both eyes at once. Focus hard and the whole room will come into view."

After about ten minutes, he asks me what I feel.

"Well, I was nervous at first, but that passed, and now I feel like I'm floating. I have no more thoughts; I feel calm, as if the room around us, all the sights and sounds, have receded into a distant background. Now this is really weird, but I see white and green light around your head, and it keeps getting more intense. What is that?"

George grins proudly, "Very good, you are really coming along. That light is the energy that flows through everything. It is all around us, but most people are too distracted to notice it. When you connect with the light, you get in touch with your real, living self, not the programmed, robot self. You connect to the universe—and everything in it."

"I see light around the chair too, why is that?"

"You see, all things are alive, not just people and animals; everything is made of energy—all one interconnected mass. Only our minds break things into parts—post-office boxes. Actually, that chair is more alive than we are, because it doesn't have controlling, know-it-all thoughts that get in the way of just yielding to the universal energy field and existing."

"I've never tried it, but this must be like meditation . . . ?"

"Not at all; this is way beyond. People who meditate put themselves into a state of stagnation by repeating a mantra. They make themselves even more dead than they already are. Focusing makes you alive and advances you spiritually."

My mind races from his explanations. I would never have believed that a chair was alive—certainly my biology textbook wouldn't agree—but I didn't imagine this light I just saw for several minutes. So, although this doesn't feel right, I must keep an open mind; maybe I have more to learn.

As I am leaving, George praises me for my courage to break today's barrier; I will be rewarded with personal growth from our session. He also warns me that "the others," (Dr. Rogers, my mother, and his other patients) aren't advanced enough to understand. "This must be our secret until they can grow to our level. Understand?"

I agree to comply.

These barrier-breaking episodes bond us, and I soon become George's protege, his partner in discovery. Among all of his patients, he has selected me, and I feel special. I finally have a mentor; more than anything, I want to be just like him. In my mind I give birth to the new me, "Little George," and my commitment solidifies. Another bonus, my mother and I now have something to share, something about which we are both excited, (as long as I keep certain secrets from her). Over the next several months, George, my mother, and I become the originators of a new and exciting mission. Although I am only able to see him on vacations, when I am home he usually shares any new information with me first. George reads copiously, and he often references the authors' ideas in his discourse. But he assures us that this pastime just gives his mind "something to play with"—his true information is delivered directly from some higher, spiritual source. George becomes divine in our eyes, and we can think of no one else.

By the end of the year, George has self-published a book. Its plain, brown cover sports the title *Biofeedback and Beyond*. All of his innovative strategies for personal growth lie within. My mother purchases two dozen copies from him to distribute to friends, relatives, and co-workers, people who she is sure will benefit from George's wisdom. And she urges any and all to "have a session" with this "unique genius"—she will even pay for their first visit as a gift.

As George continues to break subsequent "social barriers," during our sessions, the biofeedback machine frequently remains untouched; instead, we find ourselves lying on the office carpet, locked in intimate embrace. George directs our activities with such conviction that I now comply unhesitatingly with every suggestion. It feels good to have someone guiding me, especially because I believe that George really cares and wants to watch over me. Naturally, the possibility of being caught is ever-present, but our fear from shared risk only fuses us more tightly. George seems to trust me to keep his secrets and begins to let me in on just about everything. For example, Jackie, the office receptionist, has been flirting with him, so one day after closing, they release their passions, writhing under Dr. Rogers' desk while he is across town seeing patients at Saint Vincent's Hospital. George is also sitting naked with some of the other female patients. I am not jealous; I don't need to be the only one. I just want him to pay attention to me—anything to fill the emptiness from Joe's absence.

"Elizabeth, how about if I stop by your apartment this afternoon before your mother comes home?" George suggests after one of our sessions.

His gently delivered, "How about if . . . ?" the preface to all of his propositions, leaves me with a sense of personal choice every time. In my mind, this is merely another innocent, curious experiment. So, later that day, his professional commitments complete, George heads uptown toward West 98th Street to visit. I am so excited. . . . I can't wait to give him the grand tour of my home, especially my room—to share another piece of myself with him. My favorite hobby is photography and I have set up my darkroom in a spare bedroom. But George has his own plans. Immediately upon crossing the apartment's threshold, he strides swiftly down the long hallway, past the livingroom's French doors and finally into my bedroom. Uncannily, as if reading my mind, he plops down on my bed and abruptly states, "And don't show me any photographs; I *don't* want to see them."

He squashes my spirit instantly with a giant invisible fist. I don't understand why; most people enjoy viewing my images—I'm pretty good. Command delivered, George moves on, soon noticing my baby picture on the bureau, an appealing image of a vivacious one-year-old. He disapproves and begins his lecture. "This whole, stupid society is lost. Everyone lives in the past—hanging onto memories, distracted by thousands of thoughts—instead of experiencing *the now*. Whatever happens should be enjoyed fully and then let go. Why must we use photographs, diaries, and old letters to bring back experiences that are dead? People only save mementoes from insecurity. They don't have the courage to *just be alive*. I don't hold onto anything; I travel light and live each moment to the fullest, then, onto the next. *My home is under my hat*. I threw out my old photographs years ago, and I feel free."

Seating myself next to him I reflect on his words for a moment and then purposefully make my sacred commitment: From now on I will find the means to drag myself out of the stagnant thinking patterns into which I was conditioned. I embrace his controversial, yet exhilarating, perspective. George is clearly a man ahead of his time. It will take hard work and dedication on my part to attain the lofty, enlightened station he now occupies, but I intend to give it everything I've got. We remain on my bed a while longer, chatting. Today we have crossed another barrier from professional to personal. Our relationship is maturing, and George E. Sharkman has become the most significant person in my life. Of course, this visit must be another secret I keep from my mother and Dr. Rogers.

A week later I force myself past my resistance and take the necessary action to prove my new commitment. While my mother visits the local grocery, I place two treasured albums of my baby pictures and more than 100 rolls of black and white negatives—pictures I've developed in my darkroom since high school—into a brown grocery bag. Exiting our apartment, I walk halfway down the hall. With a resolute, deep breath, I open the door; I wince as the heavy books bang against the incinerator walls, making their final journey into a pile of ashes four stories below. Hating to give it all up—hundreds of hours of heartfelt dedication to my craft and irreplaceable childhood mementos—I attempt to reassure myself. *Now I am one step closer to freedom. I must expect this personal growth to be difficult, but the rewards will be worth the pain, and George will certainly be proud of me!*

Soon, I am challenged again. One day I return home from work to an empty apartment. *My mother told me she'd be home, but where is she?* Calling her name, I search the rooms, until finally, standing in the hall outside her bedroom, I hear a faint reply. "Is that you, Liz?"

"Where are you?" I move toward the voice and soon discover it is coming from behind the closed door of her bedroom closet!

"What are you doing?" I demand, confused and upset.

"Oh, I've been here all day." Her sing-song voice responds nonchalantly. "George has given us a new exercise to break resistance. Our focus on distractions: working, watching TV, talking on the telephone, shopping. . ., must be overcome in order to be open to growth. Sitting in a small, dark place will force us to drop our thoughts and make room for new information."

Disgust floods me, but Rachael is aglow—a model student who has completed her assignment with flying colors. My aversion holds no validity for her, and she repeats the exercise several more times during the weeks that follow. Her unswerving dedication wears on me, and I begin to feel like a traitor for not following suit. So finally, one Saturday I relent; while Rachael is out doing errands, I spend five hours in her closet. After a period of irritated boredom, I fall asleep. Eventually waking refreshed, I am otherwise untransformed. My mother soon returns home to discover me, and she is pleased. I smile weakly with relief. Sometimes, rather than fighting, it is easier to give in.

Within a few weeks, George informs my mother of his visit to our home, and trips to our apartment become a regular event. My mother is thrilled. It is company—something she hardly ever has. She feeds him hamburgers, and he talks and talks. . . . His presence fills our lives. We learn about his family, his past, his personal philosophies, and his dreams for the future. During these hours in our living room, the three of us solidify our relationship. As if we possess the seeds of some special spiritual gift that we are about to sow and water, we are sure the harvest will be unimaginably wonderful. Like intimate friends, hungry for details about each other, we share our personal histories. Among many other things, my mother gives him the particulars of my father's death and my inheritance—now worth about $200,000.

George also tells us about his past. He was the middle of three boys. His father was a kind, although weak-willed, man who developed a lucrative, family business selling breathing apparatus to hospitals. In fact, he invented machinery that is still in use today. In contrast, his mother, George claims, was the most evil woman in existence. Abusive and nasty, she once force-fed baby George his own vomit when he threw up in his high chair. His mother threw irrational tantrums without warning, often chasing her son around the house with a butcher's knife. George adds that he found it amusing when she went crazy; he often laughed at her, escalating her reaction to even higher levels. In addition, he knew exactly how to trigger her. Sometimes he purposely "heated her up." He brags that his mother was so good at manipulating others, she could "intimidate and control anyone on the planet," bullying them to their knees in terror whenever she wanted. But George would never let her control him. No way! While the other kids were outside playing, at three years old, George was sitting in the kitchen scrutinizing his mother and her female friends while they interacted. He analyzed their behavior so that he could learn how to avoid the psychological traps they set. At that tender age, he began to intensively study "The Female Game." Now, he insists, no woman will ever get over on him with any type of seduction or control. He is an expert at spotting all female manipulation.

As a child George developed grand mal seizures. A frequent occurrence, they prevented him from being a successful student or holding down a regular job when he got older. One day, as a man in his early twenties, he decided to use his willpower to force himself to remain conscious during a seizure. At one spectacular moment within this experience, he perceived a new path of total bliss. Like a seminary student who has just been called by God, he perceived his destiny: to pursue this ecstasy. Soon after that incident, his seizures ended. In college he mastered the art of hypnosis. George could hypnotize "an entire room full of people." One time he put himself and two other boys under. All three wandered around the school for a few days doing and saying strange things, until the dean finally found out and demanded that George remove the post-hypnotic suggestions holding them captive. During his undergraduate years, he discovered that his body put out an inordinate amount of energy, so much so that when he carried batteries in his pocket, they discharged themselves. George never graduated from college. A psychology major, he left school just three weeks before he was due to earn his diploma. He quit on purpose to prove to the world that he did not need "society's approval" to succeed in life. After that, he earned only one professional credential, a biofeedback technician's license.

At the time of these intimate meetings in our apartment, George is in financial straits. He earns $18 per hour assisting Dr. Rogers part time and drives a beat up white VW Beetle. He has two children, Serena, age ten, and Christopher, age eight. His family is crammed into a two-bedroom apartment on the Upper West Side. His wife, Doris, adds what little she can to the family income with part-time bookkeeping jobs. Up until recently, George worked in sales for his father's business. However, he, by his own admission, was lazy, and would often slip into X-rated porno movie theaters during the afternoons, rather than making the rounds of his father's customers. Eventually, a breakup occurred, and his spiteful mother disowned him and cut him out of the will. George seems to be proud of his role as family black sheep. Nonetheless, he is left to his own devices, and although he acts cocky and confident, my mother senses that his money problems terrify him.

One day George invites me to sit in on his session with someone new. Sara is a heavyset, thirty-something African-American who lives on the Upper West Side near my mother. Possessing an unshakable positive attitude, she is always jovial, and George finds her weird and fascinating. In fact, he seems almost obsessed. George makes frequent visits to Sara's apartment, bringing me back tales of tarot cards, incense, strange homemade wine, and occult relics she has collected from all over the world. Sara claims to be able to channel spirits, and the two of them spend hours immersed in her special powers, meditating, focusing, and brainstorming. George seems to want to suck all of the knowledge out of her head. Unexpectedly, during one of their intimate sessions, something miraculous occurs. According to him, "My head just started shaking side to side on its own!"

George is out of his mind with excitement; he talks about headshaking and nothing else. Almost immediately, he trades his interest in Sara for the headshaking. And Sara soon disappears from the scene.

The three of us are engaged in an evening session at my mother's apartment when George first introduces us to his new found skill. Seating himself in one of our stiff-backed, living room chairs, he commences his routine, shaking his head slowly and purposely from side to side. Faster and faster he goes, until it looks like he *must* be hurting his neck. Soon, his legs begin to levitate, and then his arms rise as well. What a bizarre creature George seems, all four limbs suspended in the air, as if on the end of a puppeteer's strings, throwing his head back and forth violently. As my mother and I continue to concentrate on his head movements, we feel somehow mesmerized by the motion, and I slip into a state of relaxation. My thoughts float away, rendering me mentally and emotionally sluggish. Pausing after several minutes, George explains, "You know how a dog shakes his head to change his mood, well now we can do the same; we can control and change our emotions."

After several more minutes of shaking, George asks us what we are experiencing. I tell him that I am calmer, and he explains why. "The energy pouring out of my body can relax, even heal, any person who is willing to give in to it. Soon we won't need to use the biofeedback machine anymore. We'll be able to release our stress just from the headshaking. When I shake, I feel a switch turn on in the back of my head that releases my special energy—The Energy. No one besides me has to shake, they can just sit near me and experience what I am putting out."

His eyes glow, and his passion escalates, as George feeds us the incredible significance of what he is just now discovering about his special powers. "For some reason, I have been chosen to pass The Energy through my being. I see now that *it* is the answer to every problem ever made. It can heal our bodies and minds; it will get us to freedom—out of The Program forever."

"What's The Program?" I ask.

"It is a universal rule book that they handed us at birth. All people in society follow it like dead robots. Because they are too stupid to notice they are only chasing their tails, they never get to live their real lives. Look at everyone around you. People celebrate holidays that don't mean anything and give gifts to family members they hate, because they were trained to feel obligated. I never bring a gift when I pay someone a visit—holiday, birthday, or otherwise; *I am the gift*, not some meaningless object that the person probably doesn't even need. And funerals, look at how ridiculous a coffin is, fancy satin and mahogany, useless speeches to a lifeless body that couldn't care less. If my mother died, I wouldn't waste one moment of my time; I'd stick her in a pine box; she wouldn't know the difference. . . . And men, I don't care which house you pick, the husband is controlled totally by the wife—but he acts macho to cover it up and then defies and punishes her on the sneak. Now take the woman, she has contempt for her baby husband and then withholds sex to get what she wants. Every interaction is no more than a parent-child game, 'Mommy, I will perform for your approval.' This starts at birth, and we never grow out of it. No one has the courage to go for themselves—to become their own person. I broke The Program in myself years ago, when I studied my mother's games, and I can teach others to do the same. Feeling The Energy forces people out of The Program temporarily. Then they must make a decision to work toward their freedom. It's all about breaking distractions, resistance, reactions, and fears—the strong wiring that connects you to The Program. This defines our mission; it is why we are all together."

My mother is all applause, but I am not. George's focus on the headshaking feels overblown. I don't like the fact that he is doing it several hours a day, and his talk about his new experiences leaves me feeling ignored.

"When I shake my head, I have wonderful feelings," George declares. "They are the ultimate and surpass all others."

He also tells us that the shaking evolves his brain and propels him into another dimension. In fact, once it fills him, he becomes invisible to the people in The Program. "I could walk down 42nd Street stark naked, and no one would pay any attention to me," he professes.

This outrageous declaration makes me sick, but my internal coach reminds me, at times like these, to keep an open mind. *Our journey of discovery could lead to amazing things, if we find the courage to challenge programmed thinking patterns.*

Intensely curious about everything George does, I try the shaking myself. The resulting calm from the exertion feels the same as when I exercise. True, I feel relief from anxious thoughts, but this is not my definition of joy; I want what I felt with Joe—personal love. I refuse to believe that these headshaking feelings are the ultimate; they are certainly not my goal!

I have tested his theory, and now my gut instincts scream to wake George from the spell that he *must* be under. Uncharacteristically, I confront him angrily, my face reddening in frustration as I exclaim, "No. Headshaking feelings are only physical, no more. There is something else out there—something real that happens between people, and this is not it. What you are saying is a lie!"

I expect that my fervently delivered feelings will affect them, but I am sadly mistaken. Instead, my words fall on the deaf ears of George and my mother, and they continue to praise his wonderful new discovery. I try harder, begging to be heard, until my voice is hoarse and my throat sore. "This is all wrong; I despise you for ignoring me."

I cry, yell, plead . . . but my efforts are futile, and George just stares at the wall, cut off from me. When I have finally given up from pure exhaustion, he thanks me sincerely. "Elizabeth, I really appreciate what you have just done. You have helped me to become even more sure than before that I am right."

In the months that follow, George's headshaking becomes his trademark. He shamelessly performs his act in restaurants, on airplanes, at movies, parties, and family dinners. In public, embarrassed, confused strangers try to avoid looking at him. Without our inside information, they usually conclude that he has an affliction to his nervous system, some sort of palsy. His wife, Doris, is mortified. She calls him a weirdo and begs him to stop. Defiantly, he responds with pride, "Hey, I'm a weirdo. That's pretty cool. I like that name."

George seems to relish the attention people pay him and the discomfort it causes them as well. He enjoys their confusion and the fact that the truth behind the shaking is his coveted secret—to be shared only with a select few. His visits to our apartment, after office sessions, continue to be frequent, and we spend hours simply staring at the shaking, trying to feel some shift in our physiology and mood. George's movements are so drastic that the window panes rattle and the chair joints squeak painfully, threatening to become unglued. The irritating repetitive sound drives me crazy, and I sit there hating him, wishing he would stop. However, George doesn't care; nothing else in this world exists for him but that shaking.

January to December 1980

I spend the spring semester of my junior year in France, attending the University of Grenoble. During my absence from the continent, George seduces my mother (twenty years his senior). When I return to the United States in June, it doesn't take me long to figure it out. My mother is acting like his wife, as if she owns him and he has made a commitment to her. Within a week George tells me anyway. However, he explains that he obtains no pleasure from these intimate encounters. "It's just an experiment for growth. I really find her body repulsive, but I must break this barrier, free myself from reactions of disgust toward an old woman," he smirks. "You see, all people are filled with reactions. Because they are cowards, they avoid situations that will trigger them. Therefore, they only live ten degrees out of a possible three hundred sixty-degree life. To grow, we must sit in the environment that sets us off, until the reactions pass. I know this works because I have trained my body not to need a coat in winter. I used to stand outside and shiver, until my body adjusted and made more heat. It's like getting infected with chicken pox; the body builds immunity in response. Only now, we are building our emotional and spiritual immune systems."

I get his logic, but I am still terribly distressed about him and my mother. Feeling powerless, I try to convince myself that in time I will learn to accept the larger truth to which George alludes. Regarding his reaction to the cold, even today you may see George striding confidently down a Midtown Manhattan street, in twenty-degree weather, sans jacket; he doesn't shiver in the slightest.

At about this time, a female patient reports George to Dr. Rogers for inviting her to sit naked with him during a biofeedback session. George denies it and accuses the woman of insanity. Nonetheless, his boss threatens to let him go if there are any more incidents. And a few months later, Dr. Rogers indeed lets him go. George withholds the specifics of the breakup, simply proclaiming the doctor to be "a fool who never appreciated my unique abilities." My mother feels sorry for him; she knows he is scared because he has lost his source of income, and she volunteers to leave Dr. Rogers' office and follow him. They can continue private sessions in our apartment.

Like us, three other patients also quit. Beatrice, a fifty-something dark-haired woman of average height and nondescript visage, is married to a wealthy, Manhattan insurance broker. She has four grown children who live in other states, and three grandchildren. Beatrice explains that her relationship with her husband has never extended beyond the superficial and behind his back she ridicules him mercilessly. A former librarian with a Master's Degree in Library Science, she hasn't worked for many years. Beatrice has nothing but time on her hands. To fill his wife's empty calendar, her husband foots the bill for her "stress reduction therapy."

Next there is Bess. Pretty and petite with straight, long, dark hair and complexion, her European-Jewish features almost resemble those of a Native American Indian. Bess is about thirty and manages the office of a Midtown lawyer. She is single and friendless and mistrusts men because she has been badly burnt in a recently ended, long-term relationship. A self-taught singer/songwriter/guitarist, she has spent the past decade floating in and out of country-western bands. Currently, Bess is developing a demo tape that will open the door to a record deal.

Finally, there is Laura. A never-married, thirty-something, registered nurse at Columbia Presbyterian Hospital, she is tall and could be attractive if she chose to emphasize her female attributes—which she does not. In fact, her behavior is quite unappealing. Prone to immature outbursts, she also proudly proclaims that she "hates everyone," especially men. Her nastiness makes it virtually impossible to relate with her.

George sees his five new clients for $25 an hour wherever and whenever he can. Sometimes we meet in a downtown diner during lunch where he'll teach and shake his head over hamburgers. A bench in Central Park might serve as an outdoor office for the day. My mother and I receive him at our apartment a few times a week, and he soon insists that we recruit others. Thus, some old friends are quickly added to the mix: Rachael's girlfriend of seventeen years, Judy, and her two daughters, Jeannie, age twenty-two, and Karen, age thirteen. They live on Long Island and can only come during the evening. To accommodate them, George creates a Wednesday night group from 7:00 to 9:00 P.M., for which my mother donates our living room. We each pay $10. It is here that I first meet Laura, Beatrice, and Bess, the patients George took from Dr. Rogers. A sense of kinship develops, and we soon begin to refer to ourselves as "The Group."

George preaches that we must work toward personal growth every waking moment; time and energy invested in work, hobby, or relating with others, will serve to "lay another brick on the foundation of our future homes."

"You can do anything you want, as long as it helps you evolve. The goal is not to *need* anything to make us happy. Really, everybody has the entire universe inside, a shining star fed by its own fuel. People, the problem is that we're trained to focus on the outside, to put other people first and deny ourselves to satisfy them. Now, do you know who is the most important person in this world? It's you, of course! Only *you* are responsible for your life—the good things and the bad. But you don't owe anything to anyone, and we must learn to stop caring what others think, or if they approve. Just remember, your only job is to *go for yourself.* Just learn to be selfish, and you'll be able to give yourself a happy life. In fact, one day in the future, we'll be able to sit in a rocking chair *doing absolutely nothing* for eternity and feel totally content."

George gives himself a bear hug and mugs some smooching sounds, "Mwah, mwah. I love you so much George. You're the greatest." We giggle at his theatrics.

Although I force myself to embrace the lesson, secretly I

despise the "Rocking Chair Theory" with everything I've got, but I have no idea why. . . .

In December, my mother throws my twenty-first birthday party in our apartment. Of course George, our newly-adopted patriarch, is the guest of honor. My mother also invites Ruth, her close friend since they were college roommates together in the late Thirties. Ruth's two sons, Jake and Ben, are close to my age. Jake, about to graduate from Swarthmore College, is studying to become a rabbi, and Ben has his sight set on a legal career. The brothers are remarkably well-read and never fail to offer their opinions on most topics. At the party, George corners them and embarks on a vigorous discourse about religion. Despite the fact that he himself is Jewish, he begins to make controversial remarks about the Jewish people. As the discussion progresses into an argument, their voices gain volume . . . and then George crescendoes . . . "The Jews pissed off Hitler—antagonized him with their obnoxious greed. You know they controlled the money and the German economy. Their selfish behavior drove Hitler to destroy them. They should take responsibility for the Holocaust rather than throwing a pity party. Now take Jesus Christ—another dumbo! He defied the Roman authorities until they said 'Screw you!' and hung him out to dry. What a jerk!"

These pronouncements delivered, George's eyes roll toward the ceiling, his upper lip curling into a contemptuous sneer. Jake and Ben go crazy trying to convince him to take it back. Their mother observes from the couch, clearly outraged, a stern look freezing her face. Even my mother is angry at George because he has taken center stage at my birthday party, and worse, he seems to enjoy the disturbance he has created. The following week, Ruth phones my mother to tell her in no uncertain terms that she dislikes George, and not only for his remarks about the Holocaust. My mother doesn't seem to care what Ruth thinks, but from that day, the forty-year friendship between Rachael and Ruth begins to cool.

January 1981 to September 1984

I return to complete my final two semesters of college, bringing a biofeedback machine with me. On my dorm room door I publicly declare my new identity by displaying a photograph of myself sporting the machine's headphones on my head. Its caption reads, "Do not disturb. Biofeedback in session." Now I'm a weirdo too, just like George. At the same time, I begin to experience enervating symptoms. Brain fog throws off my balance and vision. During class, often, I can barely read the blackboard. Some days, intolerable fatigue drives me to sleep more than fifteen hours. I am anxious and speed when I talk, my hands frantically jerking in front of me as I struggle to communicate through my mental confusion. Bouts of suicidal depression continue to grip me. George has told us that our bodies will resist the spiritual changes. This anticipated reaction is part of the price we must pay to grow. In fact, according to him, the worse you feel, the faster you are progressing.

Thus, I find ways to cope and press on, convinced that eventually this trial will end. Yet, despite my faith, my feelings for George cause conflict. I am entranced by his philosophy; his mission gives my life special meaning. But I despise him for seducing both my mother and me. I am trapped between fury and fascination, as if two opposite souls, locked in mortal combat, fight to control my body. When I adore George, he is larger than life, greater than God . . . but then, sometimes, the memory of my visit to his office after Joe's funeral haunts me, and I loathe him. Acidic, violent emotions inundate me, threatening to explode. But I must stifle them; neither their perpetrator, nor my mother, would ever sympathize. . . . These thoughts surge frequently, and yet, once the adrenalin has calmed, I experience amnesia. Blind to the contradiction, I live only in the moment, embracing whichever part happens to be dominant—never seeing that the two halves of my mind are diametrically opposed.

In June 1982, I earn a Bachelor's degree in biochemistry with a French minor. True to my career plans, I have taken the MCAT and applied to about twenty medical schools. Even so, my paltry 3.2 GPA is miles away from a 4.0, and after numerous interviews, I fail to gain admission. My roommate, Pauline, an English major, has been applying for teaching jobs, so I decide to do the same. I have a plan; I'll teach science for a year and then reapply to medical school. After several interviews, I finally obtain a position at the Fieldston School, in Riverdale, N.Y., as high school chemistry and eighth grade physical science teacher. To save money, I move into my mother's apartment on 98th Street. That fall, I begin my new job.

My two college roommates, Lisa and Pauline, also decide to move to New York City. They have no immediate plans but prefer to settle in a large city, where there are more well-paying positions available. Soon, they rent an apartment a few blocks from my mother's, at 103rd Street off Broadway. Both originally from other states, they have no roots in New York, so they rely on me, the native, for guidance. Also, my enthusiasm for George has infected them and they eagerly anticipate their first meeting. When that day finally arrives, they are star struck. Pauline speaks for both, as if grateful to be breathing the same air as George. "I feel so honored to finally meet you; I have heard many wonderful things about you."

I am so glad they are going to join our exciting mission.

My mother offers the use of our apartment for their semi-weekly sessions. My friends arrive together and George sees them in my bedroom; he always closes the door. One night they emerge after their hour, looking terrified. After George leaves, I ask Lisa what's wrong, and her mouth trembles in a face white with shock. "He forced us to kiss each other on the lips to break a barrier. I'm not a lesbian; I'm not attracted to Pauline. I didn't want to do it, and I hope I never have to again!"

I know how she feels and I am sorry for her. . . .

George also teaches them the Spiritual Law of Reciprocity, "You must be willing to sacrifice anything for the mission. Only a total commitment—letting go of all that is familiar—will bring us home. Now, the more hours with The Energy, the faster the progress. Trust the process; the money you release will come back like a boomerang, multiplied many times over!"

Lisa has financial resources from her family, but Pauline is always broke. When we eat out, she calculates her portion of the tab down to the closest nickel. The two roommates fight over grocery costs—Pauline refuses to pay half the $1.50 cost of a box of brownie mix, because she claims to eat fewer than Lisa. Still, Lisa frequently covers Pauline's portion of the rent until pay day.

My own life away from teaching is filled with George. 7:00 A.M. Saturday morning the doorbell rings, our Schnauzer, Schnapps, barks, and I hear my mother running past my bedroom, down the long hallway toward the front door. She greets her guest enthusiastically, naked under a half-open bathrobe that threatens to slip from her shoulders. Burying my head under the pillow fails to drown out George's long, confident strides echoing in the corridor. He heads down the hall, past my closed door, and further on into my mother's bedroom. Cursorily he swats the door shut, but it doesn't catch. They quickly disrobe, and George mounts her. I sense my mother gets no pleasure from this union—that she is simply cooperating like an obedient student. I hear her thoughts speak in my mind: *Sure George, take it all: my money, my dignity, my soul . . . my daughter; just keep coming by to fill me. . . .*

Trapped in my room, I can't go to the bathroom without passing her doorway and witnessing this degrading scene. So, I hold it in, thrusting my head under the bed clothes even farther to escape their sounds. I pray for sleep to rescue me, but it never does. The minutes drag by as I grit my teeth, pleading with the hands of the clock to please hurry—for him to finish—but only until tomorrow, Sunday, when it will all start again. Some days I throw on my clothes and run from the apartment, aimlessly wandering nearby streets until I'm sure their time is up. Rage fills my chest as if my heart would explode, and I fantasize calling the police or blowing his head off with a gun. When George senses my rebellion, he lectures me; I am dysfunctional and have work do. "Get over it. I don't have time to follow social rules for good behavior. I focus my energy on more important things—getting us out of jail. You should know that."

I try begging my mother to stop, but she only responds with indifference.

Some days, after George has taken what he wants in her bedroom, they retire to the living room. Perched on the sofa, partially dressed, he shakes his head for awhile, only interrupting his exercise to pontificate about his latest discoveries. When their two hours are up, Rachael writes him a check, often having served him eggs and bacon as well.

Soon I am commanded to join them after they spend their bedroom hour together. My mother remains in her skimpy night clothes as we all settle on the couch. I carefully avoid looking her way, revolted at the thought of glimpsing her partially exposed private parts. George, seated in the middle, puts his arms around us both and begins the headshaking. His entire body quakes violently, and I try to move to his rhythm so he doesn't slam painfully into me. Sometimes, out of my mother's line of vision, he slips his hand between the buttons of my pajama top or under my panties. I'm too ashamed to tell him to stop; I wouldn't want my mother to know.

Soon, I am told I must pay for my time with George from my teaching salary. Meanwhile, my mother mercilessly adds more weekly sessions to our schedule, until one day I calculate my annual bill at $5,000! I plead with her to reduce the number of sessions, "I *won't* give him half my salary," I shriek in frustration. "I only make $10,000 a year, and I work too hard for that money!" But she turns a deaf ear. I have neither the strength to continue railing against them, nor the courage to throw myself from the nest; Besides, where would I go? If only I had gotten into medical school; I wouldn't be here at all. . . .

With his new paying entourage, George manages to save a down payment and moves his family out of Manhattan. He purchases a modest, three-bedroom home in Teaneck, New Jersey, about fifteen minutes from the George Washington Bridge. After settling in, his wife, Doris, opens a small gift shop in a local strip mall, and George seeks new avenues for delivering his message of truth and gathering more people. He begins by teaching an adult education course in "Stress Reduction" at the Englewood High School, a few blocks from his home. At the conclusion of an eight-week course, he hands out business cards and invites class members to private and group sessions at his home (if they "want to go to the next level.") Soon, the Wednesday night group at my mother's apartment ends, replaced by a Thursday night group filled with newcomers, from 7:30 to 9:30 P.M., in George's den. My mother, Lisa, Pauline, and I drive out once a week to participate. Rachael is very excited to see that George is progressing so quickly.

Quickly I become acquainted with the new members. There is Caroline, a forty-something, slightly heavyset, Italian housewife with two teenage children. Blond, attractive, and passionate, she lacks self-confidence and is looking for answers. Nora, an intellectual, grade-school librarian, has an empty, childless marriage. To us, she degrades her husband constantly. In her late thirties, she has short, dark hair, and a muscular, almost masculine build. Her favorite hobby is photography, something I have in common with her. Helen, a sweet, retired, school secretary, is in her seventies. Plagued with severe migraines, she hopes that George's classes will help her. Max Stavos is the token male. Unlike the women, he isn't a recruit from the adult education class. His parents live just a few blocks from George's new home, next door to Doris' sister, Joanne. Max first meets George at a Halloween party given by his neighbors. George, dressed like a "Cone-head" from the Dan Akroyd movie, pulls Max to the side and immediately captivates him with rhetoric. Max's body reminds me of a chimpanzee: large head, small gut, long arms and torso. His face is hidden behind a dark beard and mustache, and at twenty-nine, his hairline has already receded significantly.

As sessions with George continue, Lisa and Pauline drop their plans of pursuing graduate degrees. After an expensive education at prestigious Swarthmore College, they find work as legal secretaries, earning salaries that barely pay the rent. Always together, they begin to dress, walk, and talk alike. In our circle they are referred to as "The Girls." Lisa confesses, with anguish, that she's afraid she has lost her identity, that she and Pauline have become the same person. After renting a series of studio apartments, they eventually purchase a two-bedroom co-op in Queens and commute by subway to their Manhattan jobs. Lisa purchases a 1983 Honda Civic, and twice a week they make the grueling three-hour round trip drive, frequently fighting heavy traffic, to George's New Jersey home. George also opens a small office in Manhattan where he receives them, and several others, as well.

George's influence extends more deeply into all of our lives. He teaches the rest to "focus," and soon we have all developed the skill of perceiving colorful auras around each other and various objects. Often, after several minutes of focusing, arms, legs, and heads begin jolting spontaneously, and George explains that we are becoming "electrified with The Energy"—proof of great progress. For us, this physical display is evidence indeed that a genuine transformation is occurring in George's den, and in our bodies and lives.

George seems to possess solutions to our present struggles and a prophetic view of our futures too, all of which he connects to his shaking, the light we see, and the electricity we feel.

One day, after he has just completed an hour of headshaking, George advances into uncharted territory, with Max Stavos faithfully by his side. "It's time to start practicing relationships in the new way. You can have any woman here; which one do you want?"

Max rubs his chin thoughtfully. "Well that girl, Elizabeth, the young teacher, she intrigues me."

George says nothing and begins shaking again. After a few minutes he stops abruptly. "Done. She's yours in the other place."

Max believes him. . . .

With a hectic teaching schedule, sessions with George, and free time spent with Lisa and Pauline, I am still lonely and lost. I have spent the last three years looking for someone to love me—to replace Joe. So, when George informs me, "that guy in The Group, with the beard, is interested in you," I am seized with hope and anticipation. Perhaps the throbbing ache in my chest will finally cease. I know very little about Max, but I feel terribly lucky to have been chosen by the only man in our circle. George adds that I might "end up having a relationship with him." A relationship! That sounds just wonderful. Since I lost Joe, I have dated about twenty men, mostly one-night stands that left me feeling cheated and used. I can find no one with a genuine interest in me, and I often feel desperate—Diane Keaton in *Looking for Mr. Goodbar*. So, following the next Thursday group, Max and I end up walking and talking in front of George's house. Surges of excitement bring welcome relief after my endless, fruitless searching for Mr. Right. I want so much to find my other half. This time it will work; *it has to.*

We decide to experiment with a date, to "see what will happen," and George approves.

Max is the only child of Adrianna, a Greek fur saleswoman, and Tom, an Irish-German printer. Thwarted by personal battles with dyslexia and paranoia, he has only just recently earned his college degree, four years later than his peers. After college, his girlfriend/roommate dumped him in order to marry a doctor. (She wanted a man with a secure financial future.) And since that betrayal, Max has retreated from the apartment they both shared to his childhood bedroom in his parents' Teaneck home. There he hides, filling his days with TV movies, unable to leave the house due to agoraphobia and seizures. He has made the rounds of most of the major psychiatric hospitals in the tristate area, attempting to get himself committed. However, he has had no luck; the doctors claim there is nothing wrong with him. Thanks to meeting George, Max has decided to turn his life around, and for the past few months he has been diligently sheet rocking his parents' basement in order to build an office suite for his nascent enterprise, "Artmarketing Advertising." Between hammering and painting, he invests countless hours designing business cards and brochures, but he has neither clients nor income. Max views himself as highly spiritual, and he pauses frequently to interact with balls of light and energy floating in the air, while he practices the focusing exercises we have learned in The Group. George praises him for doing this additional "homework."

Max and I were put together to experiment with "having a relationship." But George lets us know, like choosing a lab partner in chemistry class, who you are with doesn't matter. "Everyone is interchangeable. The goal is to use the relationship to discover your weaknesses, so you can eliminate them and grow." George explains.

But I want love so much. Regardless of Max's displeasing traits, I have faith that, with my encouragement and support, he will eventually evolve into something better.

George shows The Group something new. As he shakes, his arms float up over his head spontaneously. They undulate lethargically before descending back to his lap. Soon he rises from his chair to wander aimlessly around the room, eyes closed, waving his arms and swaying like a drunkard. Leaning against a wall, his body slides slowly and laboriously to the floor. Regaining his seat again a few moments later, he recommences his headshaking and his legs rise slowly until they are both sticking straight out in front of him, in midair, parallel to the floor.

"I am being moved by energy from the 'other place.' My mind is not doing this. Although my legs are straight in the air, my muscles aren't holding them up. It feels like there is invisible Jell-O underneath supporting them. Everybody, you know we have to be loose and mushy to go to the other place. All the crazy people out there are obsessed with exercise, but they are really breaking down their bodies from the stress of tensing their muscles; it just makes them old fast. Exercise is a total waste of time."

I peer at his thighs and see an outline of tight bulging muscles, but I don't dare to contradict George. He encourages us to seek this new experience and begins headshaking. As the shaking intensifies, others join in. Nora's arms sway proudly in an invisible breeze. Pauline leans forward, as if pulled by some unseen cord, until she falls gently from her chair. She remains on the floor, face down in a heap, for several minutes, allowing The Energy to navigate her jolting limbs in a bizarre, modern dance. Helen rises from the couch, slowly crossing the room. George, who has moved past his shaking, rises to intersect with her, and they fall against each other gently, arms encircling backs, to conclude in some sort of impersonal embrace. Max rolls from the couch to the floor and drags me with him. He hovers his body over mine, rubbing against me suggestively, and I am mortified, yet not permitted to oppose him. Any protest would cause an interruption in the holy atmosphere of our sanctuary where, no matter what The Energy commands, you must acquiesce. Choked by rebellious feelings, I am immeasurably and secretly guilty.

Most evenings my mother voyages through our apartment, waving her arms rhythmically, eyes tightly shut, bumping into doors and furniture, duplicating the dance we do in The Group. One night, about 2:00 A.M., for some unexplained reason, I jolt from my sleep. Peering through the dark, I hear my mother down the hall, a few steps from my slightly open door. In the next few moments she applies the necessary force to push it open, and to my horror, gains entrance. Street lights through my windows dimly outline her nakedness under a skimpy, sheer nightgown. Approaching my bed, her arms float toward the ceiling, buoyed by The Energy. Spooked, I lie stock still, afraid to find out what she is up to. Slowly she continues toward my prone body and then makes her way toward my head. Her arms wave languidly as she bends down closer. Paralyzing fear explodes into outrage as one of her hands comes to rest, with seemingly arbitrary intent, on my breast. I hold back a violent desire to throw her off me and slam her body into the wall. She withdraws her hand a little while later and leaves the room, heading back down the hall toward her bedroom. It is as if some shadowy specter has just paid me a visit; if I didn't feel so violated, I would almost wonder if I had made the whole thing up.

The next night, I confront Rachael and ask her why she did this to me. She replies lightly, in a singsong voice, "Oh, no reason, I just felt like it. It doesn't mean anything. You know what Georgie-Porgie says," she chirps, "It's what's inside that counts; the outside is meaningless, just flesh against flesh."

After that night, I don't want to live with her anymore. . . .

I am able to escape from my mother's place a few nights per week by staying at Max's parents' house in New Jersey. He has a single bed; I am crammed against the wall and wake up stiff. In addition, his parents do not really welcome our presence and there are frequent fights.

To make matters worse, Max has been sharing my car for several months. His ten-year-old burgundy Fiat has been sitting in the driveway for close to a year, because repairs are unaffordable. He keeps promising that he'll "bring it to the shop next week," but he never does. Finally, Max asks for a $600 loan to fix it. I resist at first but then figure, *Maybe if I give him the money, I'll finally have my car to myself.*

"Come on," he encourages me, trying to push me over the edge, "George says we have to learn to let go of money. Hanging onto it only keeps you small. This is an opportunity for you to grow."

Walking to the bank to withdraw the cash, my mind repeats Max's logic over and over, to drown out my reluctance. Finally, I convince myself that breaking this barrier of possessiveness about money will be good for my personal growth. And I am sure that even before Max is able to pay me back, The Law of Reciprocity will reward me for my courage. Besides, I'm helping one of my fellow soldiers; George would definitely approve!

It is my second year teaching at Fieldston. As weeks pass rapidly, I begin to feel lost. I have never reapplied to medical school, as I had planned, and somehow, my motivation has slipped away unnoticed. Symptoms of brain fog and fatigue are ever-present, and it takes everything I've got just to make it through each day. As much as I hate to admit it, I would never be able to survive the rigorous schedule of a medical student. However, I do realize that I don't want to pursue a career in teaching, as much as I enjoy it. I couldn't support myself on such a salary. So I decide that this year will be my last. In addition, I begin searching for an apartment. With my priority to be near George, I scan listings of North Jersey papers, finally renting the upstairs of a Hackensack Cape Cod. With three hundred square feet of living space and seven foot ceilings, this tiny hotbox costs me an unaffordable $400 per month. Having just ended my viable employment, I must borrow from my inheritance. Max and I have been seeing each other for about nine months now, and the relationship has become a significant part of my life. Therefore, I don't hesitate to take him with me. There is no discussion about paying expenses. Unstated, it is mutually understood that I will take care of bills until he can conquer his emotional phobias and "get back on his feet financially." Both he and George reassure me that with Max's dedication to The Energy, this will happen very soon.

Fall 1984 to Summer 1987

Max and I begin our new life together. I am so relieved not to have a regular work schedule, because the only thing I want to do is sleep; most days I count the time until I can lie down and gain a few hours of relief from the stress of constantly forcing my body to stay awake. Between sleeping, I worry about what I will do with my life, because now I have no direction. To make some money, I take a job with an agency, tutoring high school students. For the next three years, I visit several homes each week, teaching chemistry, biology, math, and French. In addition, I find part-time jobs in photography: at Sears Portrait Studio, as a wedding photographer's assistant schlepper, and finally, as a wedding studio manager. I pick photographers' brains about equipment, posing, and pricing. But I live only moment to moment, always struggling, barely able to make it through the deep water of my confused emotions and physical fatigue. Migraine headaches that often compel me to vomit from the pain, are frequent.

"All part of your resistance to personal growth," George reassures me. "The more pain; the more gain."

Months turn into years, and much to my distress, no solid plan of action for my future emerges. I try to convince myself to enroll in a graduate program in biochemistry, but I can't find the energy to motivate these well-meant thoughts into action. Each day I float farther and farther away from my original career plans toward . . . I don't know what.

I make the best home I can, purchasing essentials to furnish it. I shop, cook, and clean. Max toddles behind me in the supermarket. He lights up like a Christmas tree each night during dinner, oohing and aahing over my choice of spice for the side dishes and beaming down contentedly upon our freshly ground coffee and dessert. Occasionally he takes out the garbage. . . . I keep asking when he will pay back the $600 I lent him for auto repairs.

"I have *just started* to make a little money; I can't do it yet." He is annoyed that I won't get off his back and trust him.

Soon the Fiat breaks down for the final time, and Max realizes that it's time for a car that will impress the important advertising clients he anticipates to be courting presently. He finds a two-year-old, light blue, 1983 Honda Accord sedan in the paper, and one evening, we take a drive to inspect it. After circling the car a few times and opening the four doors and trunk, Max makes a $4,000 deal on the spot. Then he turns to me for a $2,000 loan. I am confused, not sure what to do, but I feel obligated to support his efforts to improve his life. I don't want to appear controversial and embarrass us in front of strangers, but my hand trembles as I write the check. The following week, Max applies for a part-time job at a Formica furniture store, Room Plus, in Paramus. He works eight hours per week and his paycheck is typically $55. After a few beginner's luck sales that yield additional commissions, the rest of his deals fall through. He blames the customers for not appreciating his talent. I entreat him to ask for more hours and to try to learn from his manager, a top salesman worthy of Max's regard and study. But Max doesn't like the manager's personality—too egotistical—and besides, he is not strong enough yet to throw himself in; his agoraphobia still plagues him. However, he points out that George is really helping, and he knows he'll soon be able to work full time. Too bad he can only afford George's $25 session fee once a week. "If only I could pay for additional sessions with him," Max complains.

Hoping that my investment will yield fruit in the form of Max finding some serious work, I offer to pay for two additional hours per week.

Every day, I try so hard to make us work, writing checks to fill in for Max's lack of contribution, promising myself that this is the last time, that next month I will make sure things are different. Yet, despite my dedicated input, our life is anything but improving, and I often feel helpless. As if trapped in a nightmare, miserable vignettes repeat themselves over and over:

such as, Max is on his way to the Bank. "I'm going to cash a $15 check. That is all I have in my account," he complains. "I can't even afford to buy a coffee and donut." Max looks up at me like a lost, helpless puppy. "I'm a little tapped out today, would you lend me $5 for breakfast?" I hand him the bill and drop him at the diner. Driving away, I wish I could dump him there forever. *I hate my life*; I deserve more. . . .

Life in the bedroom is no better.

"Elizabeth," Max demands sternly, "I want some sex. You don't give me enough."

Having jolted me with his command, he changes to a softer, more convincing tone, "Come on, I'll make you feel good too. You don't know how to let yourself go and let me please you. You're too rigid."

Immediately, my skin begins to crawl. I want to be anywhere but next to him. I grope for excuses. "I'm too tired. I have to work tomorrow."

I try to change the subject, to distract him with the proposal that we rent a video and then go out for ice cream. This cozy suggestion works for that evening, but a few days later the demand returns again, with additional intensity. This time, slipping away is more difficult. Blocking my escape, Max grabs my collar, shoving me to the floor, declaring me an ungrateful witch. "You have such an intelligent, gifted man—a person who sees George and is going for himself. You won't find another man out there courageous enough to last on the mission. You are so lucky, and this is how you show your appreciation!"

His eyes bug out in rage as he raises his voice and approaches me again. I fear he is on the edge of hitting me. He outweighs me significantly; I won't be able to protect myself. Repressing this injustice I comply and enter the bedroom, quickly removing my clothes. I lie down and don't move; I have learned to detach my mind from my body to the point where I can almost believe that this isn't really happening.

In The Group, George touts us as "the couple that is staying together and making it work." The approval from the rest makes me forget what Max is really like. Safe inside their familiar bosom, I am hopeful that we can indeed work it out. I must continue trying to reach Max, to convince him to change. Behind the scenes, I beg him to be fair and take on his share of the financial responsibility. When I'm not complaining, I explain like a dutiful teacher. He assures me that he is well aware of the problem and just needs a little more time, that our happiness is "just around the corner."

"Elizabeth, I know I haven't always been able to contribute, but I have been trying to play catchup football for all the years I lost being ill. Last week some new clients told me they're seriously considering my proposal. This deal really looks good. You know I always give you money when I have it. Don't be so hard on me. I had a very rough childhood and it's taken me years to recover. All my friends from high school have houses by now, and I don't have anything. Don't forget, George says to be patient. I am getting so much better every day."

I feel guilty about being demanding. He is right. We are learning about patience in The Group, and I had forgotten that The Energy will bring all things in due time. Once again, for the time being, I let him off the hook.

Nonetheless, occasionally my sense of injustice rises from deep inside, like a geyser. Frustration commands me to pack my suitcase and leave forever. Like a child who knows he has finally pushed his mother too far, Max, galvanized from his sense of danger, fills the next few weeks with unusual attentiveness. He transforms into a gourmet chef, filling my plate with my favorite foods. Under my pillow tiny gifts appear with loving notes attached. He throws me his warmest looks and biggest smiles, amusing me with jokes and long drives through the Saddle River countryside. He lavishes hugs and squeezes, quelling my starvation for affection. His efforts court me back into my comfort zone, where I forget my unhappiness. The voice of truth that testified to my feelings, is slowly silenced, and my rage at his injustice flies back into a locked, basement trunk for another long vacation.

By the mid-1980's George's inner circle consists of thirteen, eleven women and two men. In addition to my mother, Lisa, Pauline, Bess, Laura, Nora, Helen, Max, Beatrice, Caroline, and myself, there are two newcomers: Jan is a divorced, thirty-something, eighth-grade special education teacher from Manhattan. Short and slim, she has black hair and an easygoing personality. Carl, generally nasty and critical, is short, almost bald and fortyish. Aside from a stint in the Peace Corps fifteen years ago, he is careerless and lives off a generous monthly allowance from his mother. With a new man available, George asks Lisa and Pauline which one of them would like to try a relationship with Carl. Lisa says she would prefer not to. Pauline, by default, is left to begin the experiment. George continues to gain additional, outer-circle members from the Englewood Adult School, or through referrals from other group members. At any one time, there are a dozen or so of these short-term clients. George reminds us frequently, "I have been given special knowledge and strength; I am the motorboat, and you are the water-skier; just follow in my wake. But if you leave, you will be lost. You can't make it without me, so don't even try."

George encourages us to socialize together. "You will learn more by spending free time with each other, than with ignorant outsiders. You should only be with family and friends from the past in order to learn how *not* to live."

Bess responds with zeal, "I am the luckiest person on Earth to have met you. There is no hope for billions of people on the planet, unless one day they find you. When I spend time with others, I see how far I have evolved beyond them. They will never understand unless they do all the difficult work I have done."

George nods his head, absorbing her adoration, smiling with pride at his brood of devoted seekers, "That's right, and the more time you invest, the faster you'll learn."

Thus, we all schedule more frequent sessions. Entering George's den, we seat ourselves purposefully, looking up expectantly like baby birds waiting for mother to place life-giving food into our mouths. Craving George's input, instead of "feed me," we say, "lead me, fill me." Our nourishment is derived from the "new information" presented each day that we hungrily ingest and then compete with each other to cultivate. Our group discussions are lively—an orgy of abstract wisdom that saturates us with a marvelous sense of empowerment. As we struggle to fill ourselves, George unnoticeably, but steadily, withdraws. It is as if, a little at a time, he is pinching the air hose that contains our oxygen, leaving us teetering at the edge of suffocation. Thus, our drive for his approval magnifies, rendering us ravenous, emotional beggars with no other goal than to strive for the most coveted prize: a morsel of George's recognition.

The world in George's den obliterates everything outside—the "crazy world," as George refers to it, inhabited by "crazy people" or "dead robots." The Energy, solely from George, is our only frame of reference. It has an independent personality and will. The Energy brings good fortune. If you get a raise at your job, The Energy made it happen. If people smile at you on the subway, they feel The Energy. If your cat slept next to you last night, The Energy attracted her to you. Good weather means The Energy has broken through, while bad weather means we are resisting The Energy. When the stock market goes up, the world is feeling and yielding to George's Energy. In a bad economy, the world is afraid of "the good stuff" he is creating. When another secretary in Pauline's office offers to do her xeroxing, we are told that The Energy is using people to do her work for her. After all, we have a much more important job to do. George explains, "When you people grow past your resistance, you won't have to work anymore. Others will be attracted and give you what you need, just like Jesus Christ was taken care of as he journeyed through the land."

Pumped with George's hype, enthusiasm explodes as we rush forth to spread the word. Our efforts are boundless; like Jehovah's Witnesses handing out bible tracts, we appeal to family and friends, coworkers, ex-lovers, bus drivers, repairmen, librarians . . . , just about anyone with whom we come in contact. We hunger to enlist new members, and our willful zeal frequently ignites the interest of some polite stranger as we explain, "It's something special and unique, but you have to experience it to understand." One at a time, visitors flow into our Thursday Night Group. George spends the entire evening teaching the newcomer to focus and explaining the awesomeness of The Energy. Sometimes they get it and begin to attend sessions. Max receives kudos from George when he brings his friend Richie. A local security guard, fascinated with metaphysics and psychic powers, he seems to fit right in. Soon Richie's girlfriend, Janet, participates. She merges her mastery of Transcendental Meditation with George's Energy, and assuming the lotus position, floats in blissful dissociation for hours. The Group is growing as we know it must, and George's delicious praise for each new recruit fuels us to try even harder.

The Energy is our invisible guardian angel, a constant companion who will never abandon us, who will award us our heart's desire . . . provided we trust, practice patience, and respect its authority.

"People, I am the custodian of The Energy; we are one and the same. It has evolved me beyond a human man."

The Energy speaks to us only through George, and we must consult him about all decisions. Besides, now that we are seriously committed, every move is critical to our well-being; disaster threatens with even the slightest misstep. . . . Should I look for a new job? Attend a family dinner? Buy this dress? Take my dog to the vet? Purchase health insurance? How should I have sex with my husband?

Everything relevant to our lives is discussed in The Group. We know more intimacies about each other than we ever could have wanted to.

"My body is being used as a refinery because the raw Energy that enters is too painful for you people to handle." George never says who or what has chosen him as the channel. He has no idea.

"All I know is that someone, a long time ago, made a big mess out of the whole human race by creating resistance and a universal crazy thought process. Why the hell am I, George Enoch Sharkman, responsible for putting an end to this stupidity? I wish I weren't, but I have no choice."

George strives perpetually to piece information together, to solve a riddle whose answer will illuminate the escape route from the sticky web of The Program. He also receives frequent, profound messages about an impending spiritual catastrophe. "We must all begin to prepare—*today*. There is no time to waste." His wide, frightened eyes instill terror, making us desperate to continue training before it is too late.

"The human species is headed toward extinction if we don't do something fast. We are destroying the planet with pollution. It is only a matter of time until The Earth says, 'Next species,' and wipes us out, just like the dinosaurs. Respecting The Energy is our only hope. All the Crazy People are doomed unless they smarten up fast. I have been getting messages that we're nearing the end. Next year we might not be here anymore. By then, The Energy ship will have landed and carried us out of this crazy thought system into total joy."

I believe that George has special powers. I believe that he will live forever. Only he can understand The Energy—our only source of hope in a necessarily dark and horrible future.

I enter the den one winter day and sit quietly. George shakes his head vigorously while Bess stares out the window at falling snowflakes, reporting how his headshaking is affecting the snow. "Yes, The Energy is getting stronger. Snow's letting up a little."

George replies gravely, "That's good." Keeping his eyes closed to concentrate, he doubles his headshaking speed. I stare out along with Bess, following her reports closely, my chest soon swelling, now soaring as if swept away on a magic carpet, propelled by Bess's confidence. Soon she widens her eyes and smiles winningly, "It's really disappearing now, thanks to The Energy. In fact, it's almost gone and I see a glow in the trees behind your back yard. You are glowing too! George, you did it again!"

"It's going to get warmer now. The Energy broke the resistance in the weather," he answers.

"We sure are lucky to know you, George."

"This is really exciting," he utters with misty-eyed awe.

There are new and wonderful things like this happening every day. George's den is the best place to be, as long as you are willing to cooperate. . . .

George lectures fervidly one sunny Saturday afternoon as we eagerly group around him in the den.

"Gravity is bullshit, a lie we believe collectively. If we could release ourselves from this illusion, we would be able to fly around the room like they did in the movie, *Mary Poppins*. Remember when they floated up and had a tea party on the ceiling?"

An unanticipated surge of rage rises from deep inside my chest, reddening my cheeks. I tilt my face downward to hide, but George catches my reaction and makes an example of me. "Elizabeth, do you have a problem with what I just said?" He glares, rising from his seat and approaching me threateningly.

"Y-y-y-yes," I stammer, cursing myself for wearing my emotions on my sleeve, as usual . . . now forced to admit my lack of faith publicly.

"See everybody," he turns to face the rest of my comrades, "this proves my point. Elizabeth is defending the lie that we can't fly, and that lie is precisely what holds us all on the ground."

I recede into my chair in humiliation. His accusations make me feel personally responsible for keeping the entire human race weighted down on the Earth's surface. Soon, another surge of rage passes through me, commanding me to jump up and argue, even attack him, but I suppress it, gluing myself to my seat. Nonetheless, George senses my continued opposition and glares, filling me with terror. . . .

"You still seem to have a problem. What is it?"

"Nnnothing," my voice squeaks from the depths of my throat.

"You're lying," he bellows, "I can see it in your face. . . . See what I mean people? Elizabeth is showing us something very important—how *not* to live. Gravity was created by our minds and our minds make it real. If we would release the true potential of our brains, we could do anything. We could fly; we will fly; I will find a way, you'll see, and when I do, it'll be too late for Elizabeth. She'll miss out on the fun, because she'd rather hold onto her stupid thoughts."

Bess, seated on the floor near his feet, looks up at him in gratitude, experiencing once again how fortunate she is to be part of it all. Stinging from his public scolding, I try to examine his viewpoint. *What if George is right, and there are things I don't know about yet? I learned the Law of Gravity in eighth grade, but science is always developing—existing theories are modified, and new laws defined. Isaac Newton had the last word, until Albert Einstein came along. Perhaps there is more beyond Einstein, and maybe George has the vision.*

The following week George reasserts that we will be able to fly soon. Again, that familiar rage swells automatically. Right away I correct myself. *There's the resistance again—a reaction to stop progress. This always happens when someone has a new idea. People fight change from fear. I must get rid of the anger, so I can be open to new ideas. After all, a hundred years ago no one would have believed that we could visit the moon, or fly in an airplane! They say whatever man can conceive, he can achieve. If all scientists possessed my negative attitude, they would never accomplish anything. Someday, what George predicts . . . could happen.*

When George mentions flying again later that week, the rage is still there, but I push it back down, so deep now that it's almost out of view. Nevertheless, these rages are regular companions in my life with George. When they erupt, I try to squelch them, but they reject silencing. My stomach twists as I attempt to distract myself with the conversation in George's den or office. Unable to believe many of his extraordinary claims, I feel like a traitor. He stresses almost daily that we must all be in agreement—on the same wavelength. As a team, focused on our collective commitment, we will cut through resistance like a laser beam and break free of oppression. Basking in delirious visions, George rarely notices my trouble being a team player. But when he senses my opposition I am reprimanded. "Elizabeth is making the intention, on purpose, to impede the mission and destroy the rest of our lives."

My other friends jump on board, adding support to his accusations. With the entire group against me, I believe that my negative thoughts are wrong, although try as I might, I remain powerless to evict them from my mind. . . . I sit through their castigations, adrenalin pumping, hands shaking and mouth parching. George criticizes me further for these physical signs of defensiveness, accusing me of receding because I am cowardly and refuse to grow up. Trapped, I focus only on surviving these minutes. Retreating into numbness, I wait for the session's end, when thankfully I will be released.

Having successfully seduced me and my mother, George begins to break in the others. Lisa and Pauline don't seem to question his motives when he first suggests they sit naked with him during a session. They are agreeable girls whose priority is to please others and to be perceived as nice. They have spent their lives in classrooms and libraries and believe like me that cooperating with the authority is all that is necessary to succeed in life. Also, like me, they accept his concept—breaking barriers leads to personal growth. Soon he is sitting between them, kissing and fondling. Nora gives in willingly as well. She and her husband share no intimacy and she enjoys viewing herself as a sensual being, ready to explore new territory. Beatrice, although married and old enough to be George's mother, would do anything for him. He is her protege and she praises him constantly. Her husband unwittingly pays thousands for her "therapy," unaware that while he conducts business at his Manhattan office, his wife is playing hostess to George at their Westchester vacation home. He's never there to see her therapist standing on the deck behind the house and shaking his entire body, stark naked. He never hears George encouraging his wife's hostility toward the man who supports her lavish lifestyle. In The Group she speaks of her spouse with open contempt, emasculating him with references to his emotional insecurities and his woes over erectile dysfunction.

Bess's insecure, little girl personality is easily manipulated by George, and he engages her in sexual encounters whenever he pleases. Caroline is the only one who turns him down. Besides defending her commitment to her spouse, she doesn't understand what sex has to do with stress reduction therapy. Nonetheless, George, intolerant of disobedience, persists in trying to convince her. For more than a year Caroline resists him, and finally he gives up, informing us behind her back that she was "very stupid to give up the opportunity of a lifetime."

Finally there is Mary, one of George's students from the Englewood Adult School. From the first moment they meet, a magnetic attraction engulfs them. Mary attends The Group on Thursday nights, but after a few months she disappears and George begins to visit her house several times a week, in the late morning after her husband leaves for work. He recounts their glorious sexual sessions that often last over four hours. "Incredible discovery is happening when I make myself totally vulnerable to the female program at the most intimate level."

He doesn't charge her for all of his time; she could never afford it; he's willing to sacrifice the money to take advantage of this exceptional growth opportunity.

George's children, Christopher and Serena, now in high school, know all about his relationship with Mary. George trains them to hide it from their mother. He has taught them about The Program and his wife's Female Game since they were old enough to speak. "Your mother is too stupid to give up her destructive relationships with her family and go for something real. You kids must make your choice: to live like her and ruin your lives, or to go for the good stuff and become big."

One Thursday night, after several years of failed attempts, George finally convinces his wife to attend The Group, so she can "understand the importance of our work." For an hour Doris rocks in her chair, silent, shaking her legs restlessly, a stern look frozen on her face. Halfway through the session, she sighs with frustration and leaves the room, never to return. The following day George brands her hopeless. "She's too dumb to get it."

In fact, Doris hates The Group with a vengeance. She avoids the house whenever sessions are held and passes a law forbidding their children to take part in The Group's activities or to have contact with us. But each Thursday night, the kids join our meeting after Doris leaves. At 9:25 P.M., when the headlights of her returning car shine down the driveway, he motions them silently, but urgently. They catapult from their seats, sneaking from the den, noiselessly closing the door behind them. In the adjoining family room, they dive toward the couch. From my seat, I hear the remote click on the TV as the front door opens.

"Hi Mom; can we help you with your packages?" They greet her politely with feigned sincerity. "We were just watching a really good show. Do you want to hear about it?"

One day George asks Christopher to explain to the rest of us how he handles the conflict of living with such contradictory parents.

"I was following my mother for a very long time. My father was trying to warn me about the danger, but I thought I had all the answers. Finally I realized he was right and quickly changed direction. I was so stupid; I almost destroyed my life; but I'm OK now. My father is special, and I'm sticking with him. My sister was always smart, she knew my father had the right way and my mother was way off base. George is not only my father, he is father to us all, and we are a family."

According to Serena, "My mother is stupid; she just never learns that Dad knows what's going on for real, and she should give up her games and let him lead."

As group members crave more time with George, he begins to invite us to sit in on each other's private sessions. On a typical Friday evening, I take bus and subway to reach his office on 71st Street between Park and Lexington Avenues. The heavy metal street door, swollen in the jamb, squeaks and groans as I throw my entire body against it and force it open. I bound into the narrow waiting area where I seat myself expectantly. There are two offices opening off this room, both sublet by practitioners in the mental health field. George's tiny office is on the left. About fifty square feet, a love seat and two chairs leave little floor space. Muffled voices leak through the wall. George is expounding excitedly on a new discovery. I strain to listen to the dialogue; anything George has to say, I want to know. I also want to know where everyone else is at, the gossip, so I can evaluate my current status in our family. Soon the office door opens, and he beckons with a friendly "Come on in."

Mumbling goodbye to George, Laura, the nurse, rushes by, almost slamming against me, eyes downturned. She is out on the street in a heartbeat, and then I am invited into the inner sanctum. Brimming with anticipation, I seat myself quickly on the couch, snuggling gratefully into the comfort zone of my now thrice weekly ritual of two-hour stress reduction sessions.

George nods amicably, then immediately queries authoritatively, "What's doing?" I scramble to report a positive experience at work or expand on my growing awareness of one of his most recent truths. He nods his head continuously while I chatter excitedly, finally rewarding me with an encouraging—"Oh boy, you're getting smart."

Lisa and Pauline arrive shortly thereafter. Discourse between George and each of The Girls is similar to mine, although Pauline generally whines and then eventually sobs hopelessly over her inability to put our leader's teachings into effect. Lisa doesn't usually have a lot to say, but appears serious and very apprehensive. When his three young girls have finally settled in, George proceeds by inquiring suggestively, "How about if I take my clothes off?"

It is the same sweet voice he used that first day, about six years ago, when he invited me to try removing my shirt. Effortlessly undressing, he regains his seat, closes his eyes, and begins headshaking. His body shows no sign of sexual arousal. George has explained many times that the wonderful feelings he obtains from the headshaking are "beyond sex." He no longer needs nor desires this primitive activity. "However," he tells us, "because I care about you, and I am the only man on the planet who can do this, I will lend you my body. You can experiment with your feelings. Do anything that you want. This will help you grow."

We focus on his spinning head and soon perceive clouds of colored light floating around the room. Lisa's arm jolts with electricity, and Pauline's head leans awkwardly to one side, pulled there by The Energy. This familiar exercise slows us down, preparing us to concentrate on the work we must each now begin to overcome our personal resistance. Painstakingly, one of the three girls removes an article of clothing from her body. There is no cue from anyone. It is entirely up to each of us to choose what she wants to do and when. Nevertheless, we all feel that we must push ourselves in this direction in order to take advantage of the therapy. In fact, if you do not eventually strip and ultimately participate in the group activity by at least placing your naked body against the bodies of the others, you will be labeled as "holding back," which in our circle, where you only get praise when you "go for it," is a sin. I grit my teeth, close my eyes, and slowly unbutton my shirt. The silence in the room is deafening while George's chair squeaks relentlessly from his shaking motion. I want to know what The Girls are doing, but I don't want to know. . . . I strain to listen and hear more clothing rustle. I know that Pauline and Lisa, crammed next to me on the couch, are continuing their undressing. Internal conflict increases as the minutes lag, but leaving the room is not an option. Half an hour later, there are three additional piles of clothes on the floor, and three naked, slim young women in their mid-twenties sitting terrified, silent on the couch while the naked man, eyes closed, continues headshaking. The overhead light in the room burns bright, painfully exposing us.

There is only one thing left to do now—approach George—the prize. The air is charged with emotion: anticipation, competition, and confusion. Each of us focuses on George alone. We race against each other to get close to him. This contest takes nearly an hour to complete, and every agonizing minute feels like ten. One of the three girls drops off the couch and onto the floor. With total focus, she yields to The Energy that drags her body across the carpet, limb by limb, an inch at a time. It takes fifteen minutes to cross the seemingly infinite span of three feet between the couch and George's chair. The other two follow suit, and rivalry develops quickly as we sense each other's actions. The first girl finally reaches his chair and remains there for a while, her head resting on his feet. George continues shaking. The silence gets louder. The other two move along the carpet too, toward the oasis. Girl number two squeezes behind him, while the first girl lifts herself up toward his chest. The chair creaks in response, and she pulls back a little, shamed to have broken the silence. There is no room for the third girl, the competition's loser, to be right next to George, so she crouches on the floor behind the first girl. She must be satisfied with being next to the person who is next to George. The second girl now becomes a little more bold and lifts herself up toward George's face. Her lips find his mouth, and she rests them there. The head shakes relentlessly, while the girl focuses on moving her head with the same rhythm as his, so that their lips can remain together. Soon her mouth becomes irritated—red and sore from the constant friction of George's five o'clock shadow.

This action gives the first girl courage, and she slides her head slowly down his chest, finally resting it on his thigh. Her hand creeps toward his crotch, which she begins stroking softly, trying to convince herself that this is what she wants to be doing. Diligently forcing herself, a fraction of an inch at a time, toward the ultimate, about ten minutes later, she finally goes down all the way. George's rhythmic shaking doesn't miss a beat, but his body responds, betraying his frequent assertions that he is "beyond sex." Over the next several minutes, girl number one does what is required to finish him off, assisted by the third girl, who has managed to maneuver herself into a position where she can assist. Sometimes their lips even touch as they apply themselves to their task. When it is over, George always says the same thing, "Whew, that was really big." He refers to The Energy, released from his climax, which will propel him to the next higher spiritual level. During the entire time, he has not touched any one of the girls. According to him, the goal is to face uncomfortable feelings and learn from them—work, not play. Our infinitely patient tutor explains, "It was difficult for you girls to fight your resistance and move toward me and The Energy, but you did. Today you have made tremendous progress."

Soon, George turns scientific and asks us collectively, "So, what's going on? What did you feel?"

We each describe our reactions and thoughts, and it usually comes out that one, or more, of the girls was competing—game-playing. The crime admitted, George scolds. In addition, one girl is deemed the most courageous; she is envied by the other two. It is unimportant which one is girl number one, two, or three. We are all swimming in the same cauldron, exchanging roles and actions randomly. Pauline often ends up crying, "I can't stop holding back. I am a failure."

George encourages the person he has selected as winner to advise her—valuable suggestions such as, "Just go for it next time."

Pauline replies tearfully, "But I don't know how to stop resisting," and the helpful answer comes quickly,

"You stop; you make a decision and *do it*."

Sometimes George berates her further. "If you don't get wise fast, you will get left behind."

The competition we feel among ourselves, for a prize that none of us truly wants, rises like an angry demon, twisting our guts, asphyxiating our spirits. What rage we suppress! We, unlike Mary, pay for every minute that we spend with George, no matter how many times we pleasure him. . . .

Even beyond the sanctuary, in the Lexington Avenue diner where we three former college roommates share Swiss burgers, cheese omelettes, gyros, and coffee after our sessions, we no longer feel comfortable together. As if obeying some invisible dictum, we never discuss what occurred or how much we paid. Personal connections and our previous friendships are long gone. We monitor everything we say (and think), as if spies are all around. Although we want to desperately, we never dare to question George's actions. Any negativity will be uncovered and reported. Public humiliation, or worse, is what we fear above all.

These days, George's pants spend more time draped over the office chair than on his body. From 10:00 A.M. to 7:00 P.M., an almost hourly changing of the guard takes place. Beatrice visits first, replaced by Bess, then Jan, next Beatrice or Bess once again, and to wind up the day, a grand finale of me, Lisa and Pauline together. Sometimes, George even adds in Bess—a group of five. The additional female competitor escalates our distress. I shut my eyes tightly, and I am sure the others are doing the same. Bodies touch and hands probe with hesitation as we struggle to figure out how to win George's approval. We know we must push at the envelope; it is in our own best interest—the whole point of these sessions, but the terror of failure is ever-present, along with overwhelming confusion. It is in this blackness that one day I feel a hand on my wrist. There is intent in the grasp, and I shiver. Slowly it pushes down along a belly, inch by inch, until finally I reach the top of a feminine thigh. Revulsion bolts through my mind, freezing me in terror, but I am captive to momentum. When my fingers, shoved ever forward by George's decisive grip, finally reach the private parts of my friend (I soon realize it is Pauline), thoughts plead, *I don't want to be doing this. Please stop.* It takes all of my strength to stifle my aversion, but somehow I manage, praying for this thousand-year moment to end. When twenty minutes later George calls for a bathroom break, I say nothing to anyone. It will be several days before I can look directly at Pauline; I am so mortified. . . .

George has no problem sharing details about his intimate life with his wife either. "This is how I have sex with Doris. I put my cock into her, and stay motionless; then I focus. The Energy comes out of me. This should give her pleasure, but my wife is impatient. She wants me to thrust, like all the other dumb, jerk men who are just performing for Mommy. I refuse. Doris hates that she can't control me. Someday, if she decides to be smart, she'll learn how to have sex the right way."

But Doris *is* smart, smarter and more present than her husband thinks. . . . One Friday evening, Lisa and Pauline are in George's city office. All three are naked. Unexpectedly, George hears the outer street door opening. Doris was supposed to meet him at the end of their session, but she is very early.

"Holy Shit," he mutters under his breath as he hastily shoves his body back into his clothes, motioning for Lisa and Pauline to do the same. Unfortunately, they haven't sufficiently practiced subversive clothing removal and redressing, and they do not move as quickly as he does. Doris's footsteps echo up the short hall and into the tiny waiting room. While politely waiting for George to finish with his clients, a sound enters her ears—the jingle of her husband's belt buckle. Instinctively, she bolts from her seat, and without knocking, grasps his doorknob and turns firmly, opening the door. George has just made it back to his chair. Although he has missed a couple of buttons, he looks pretty much in order. The Girls, however, have managed only to put their slacks and bras back on. Their shirts still remain crumpled on the floor. Upon viewing the scene, Doris's face reddens with the rage of a woman scorned. "What is going on in here?"

George dons his Mr. Innocent mask and explains "sincerely," "Nothing. It's just that it was too hot, so the girls decided to take off their shirts for awhile."

As if dragging an unruly schoolboy out by his ear, Doris commands George to follow her to a private meeting in the waiting area.

"Did you have sex?" she asks directly.

"Oh no," he replies looking so sincere and grasping at explanatory babble that ends up contradicting his previous statement, "we were only experimenting, breaking barriers created by society's training."

Doris exits the office in an angry huff, and when George returns to The Girls, he lets them know that this is their fault. Lisa and Pauline guiltily accept blame; they apologize profusely for having been too slow. For weeks, they beat themselves up for committing that terrible crime. Due to their inadequacies, they have jeopardized George's marriage. Doris bans them from her house in Teaneck, and like disgraced outcasts, they must sneak in for therapy sessions while she is at work.

The encounter with his wife does little to interrupt George's schedule of creative experimentation. About a week later, he suggests that Nora and I remove our clothing and sit naked during an afternoon group session in his Teaneck den. "Society has programmed us to be ashamed of our bodies, but everything's natural. Sit through your embarrassment until it lifts, and you'll feel very comfortable in your own skin," he directs.

Dropping my head in shame, I stare at the floor, praying for my panicked thoughts to end while I imagine the others, Beatrice, Carl and George, ogling me. Nora, in contrast, comfortable with exhibitionism, continues her stream of intellectual chitchat. But it only gets worse, because a few moments later the doorknob turns, and I freeze. George's 16-year-old daughter, Serena, enters unannounced. She appears mildly surprised at the scene before her but hides her reaction with a slight smirk. George laughs at this unexpected intrusion while she quickly finds a seat. Conversation resumes with no explanation offered to the teenager. I can't understand how Serena can accept it all so nonchalantly. . . .

"Your mother has left The Group." These ominous words are thrown at me, without warning, as I enter George's office one afternoon. He goes on to predict her fate, "Rachael is a fool, but her life is down the tubes without The Energy. Guaranteed!"

I can't believe it. *How could she leave? Where else is there to go?* Rachael is now on the other side of the fence—a traitor. Stunned, I avoid telephoning her, and for a long time, we hardly speak. When we do, it never occurs to me to ask her why she left, or how she is doing without The Group. . . .

Several months later, Rachael shows up again. Confused, I finally probe, and my mother explains, "After George moved to New Jersey and stopped using our apartment for group meetings, I realized he just used me and never appreciated me. I didn't like how he was treating me since he'd built his harem with all those younger women. I'd had enough."

My mother's not making sense to me. "Then why did you come back?"

"Because I want to use his Energy to grow. It is unique and special, and there is nowhere else to get it."

"Don't you care about how he treats you anymore?"

"No; I am willing to put up with his personality imperfections to get The Energy."

Now that she has returned, I see my mother twice a week in George's den. She just blends in with the rest of the troops; we have no personal connection. Our sole focus is the same—The Group. About twice a year I visit her apartment, usually Christmas and Mother's Day. These meetings are awkward, and conversation always leads to George, the only subject we have in common. . . .

After four years of intense involvement, George breaks up with Mary. "She refuses to believe in The Energy. I can't have a relationship with someone who wants to die."

The immense importance of this hits each woman like a tidal wave. Now he will need a new partner! Each female silently prays that she will be selected. For my part, I am sure it will be me. After all, I was his first, and I am the best student—more dedicated than the rest. From the day George kissed me on the cheek in Dr. Rogers' office, I have had unrequited love for him. It is as if, in one decisive moment, a specter took permanent residence in my body. The yearning for George has become so familiar that I never doubt its continual insistence that I must, at all costs, find a way to one day make him my own. I would find completion, even ecstasy, if only I could fulfill my dream. And today the opportunity has finally arrived.

However, rather than waiting for him to choose, Bess takes the step and volunteers herself. And George agrees. Feeling betrayed, I complain to him, but he only derides me and praises Bess. "You missed the boat. You should have taken a shot, but you were too distracted with your female seduction. You wanted me to chase you, and *that will never happen in a million years!*"

Bess, in her new role, gets the same special treatment that Mary had. She is instructed to arrive half an hour early on

Saturday mornings, at 8:00 A.M., so that they can experiment with sex. Engaging ever so quietly on the den couch, they hide from the ignorant Doris who is asleep in the master bedroom literally over their heads. Bess also remains after the rest of us leave at 2:00 P.M. for more relating. Occasionally, on a Sunday when Doris visits her sister on Long Island, George invites Bess back.

One Saturday afternoon, Laura begins to gripe. Not that she wants George as her boyfriend, but she guesses that Bess isn't paying for the extra one-on-one time. "It isn't fair. Bess gets special treatment while the rest of us pay for every single second with you. You are always watching the clock and counting the money. Why do you need so much anyway? You tell us that you're going to a place where money doesn't even exist!" She raises her voice mockingly, "You just love Bess. Bess. Bess. Bess. She's your girlfriend; she's not so great!"

"Shut up," George hisses, "Do you want Doris to hear you?"

But Laura, forgetting with whom she is dealing, loses control and releases her uncensored feelings, "You're so greedy; you don't care if I starve as long as you get all of my money! And how come you're always the one criticizing *us*? Nobody ever corrects *you*! Are you perfect?"

"Oh believe me, you have it easy," George spits out, "You only have to interact with a human being, but I get disciplined by The Energy, and it's a hundred times worse; you wouldn't be able to last two minutes in my pain."

"Oh yeah; I think you're making it up."

"Sister, cut the crap and learn some respect, because you have no idea. . . . Last week I fell off track. One afternoon, this terrible stench started coming out of my body. It was so bad that I could have vomited. Then The Energy grabbed me and slammed my body against the wall. It let me know I'd better clean up my act, or else! Beatrice was there and saw the whole thing."

Beatrice nods obsequiously, but Laura doesn't seem to want to buy it. George, fed up with her insubordination, leaps from his seat. He lunges, grabs her collar, and shoves her toward the door bellowing, "You fuck; you've got to get out now."

I agree with Laura about the money, his frequent reprimands, and Bess's privileges, but I would never support her, lest he force me to share her punishment. Beatrice and Pauline glare judgmentally, condemning Laura for her disrespect. Beatrice adds, "Are you stupid? What if Doris was in the kitchen listening? Do you want to get George in trouble and screw everything up? You know she'll never understand."

Reacting to his rough handling, Laura instantly flips from confrontational to pitiful. "Please don't make me leave," she pleads as he slams the door behind her.

Laura drives home in a fog of terror, knowing that she can never survive without The Energy and George's guidance. That night she telephones him and apologizes. He accepts tentatively, permitting her to "try again," and the following day she returns. Sitting humbly silent in the corner, Laura is infinitely grateful simply to have been accepted back into the kingdom.

However, for Bess, there are consequences to being George's woman. . . .

It is a Tuesday afternoon. The phone rings in George's den, interrupting his shaking. Holding the receiver in silence for a few moments, his face soon twists into annoyance. He calls his daughter, Serena, to his side and whispers something in her ear, after which she exits immediately. About an hour later Serena returns, mission accomplished, followed by Bess. Bess' shirt and face are bloody. An ugly gash scars her forehead. She sits down miserably while George explains to the rest of us gravely, "Bess just screwed up big time. She was sitting at a traffic light up on Route 59 in Nanuet when a car crashed into her from behind. Last night she was playing her female games on me. They didn't work, so she decided to make this car accident to get me to feel sorry for her. I've told you a million times; I won't be manipulated! Not even if you stick a knife in your chest right in front of me."

George proceeds with his headshaking, tuning us out. Several others enter and exit during the next several hours while Bess remains in her corner, motionless and speechless, her face smeared with dried blood. Ever focused on George, many don't even notice her. The few who experience a natural impulse to reach out quickly stifle themselves, suppressing their humanness and averting their eyes in shame. The unspoken, invisible rule is sovereign—*Ignore Bess. She defied George and is now paying for her sins.* That endless afternoon no one inquires how Bess feels. No one asks her if she'd like to borrow a clean shirt, or if she needs to lie down and rest, or drink, or eat. . . .

Lisa and Pauline's schedule now includes lunch hours with George. Every Monday, Wednesday, and Friday they grab a taxi at noon, bringing sandwiches to share with him. Including round trip travel, they desert their offices for nearly two hours. This arrangement infuriates me. If their bosses realize they are stealing extra time, they could miss a promotion or even get fired! They are already seeing George two hours after work on those same three days, as well as Thursday night and all day Saturday. This behavior is obsessive and costs too much. They can't save for their futures, and they have no money for anything now. Nonetheless, George praises them and I feel rejected—Lisa and Pauline have replaced me as his model students. When George senses my distress, he scolds, "You people are all competing with each other instead of focusing on yourselves. The Girls are willing to invest in their futures. Why won't you do the same?"

Soon George is ministering to groups of three to ten people during the hours that used to be devoted to private sessions. Whether one has the rare fortune to be alone with him, or shares him with several others, the charge is the same—$40 per hour. He reassures us frequently, "The more time you devote, the more you'll progress. Don't worry about the money. The Energy will bring it back to you."

Finally Lisa, egged on by George, breaks the barrier of separation forever. She spends her entire vacation week at his office, arriving with him at 10:00 A.M., and leaving with him at 7:30 P.M. At noon she runs out to buy them lunch at the deli around the corner, and they share it in his tiny office so she won't miss a single moment. George reports to the rest with glee, "Lisa is my new wife; she's spending every day with me; she is really committed to her life!"

That week Lisa spends more than forty hours ($1,600 plus). Soon, despite the outrageous cost, others follow suit. We remind ourselves that letting go of money breaks our ties to The Program. We convince ourselves that this catharsis is healthy.

Pauline, ever the competitive sibling, monkeys her roommate by spending her next vacation week with George. But she has no money beyond her $25,000 legal secretary's salary, and is soon forced into debt. When her paychecks run out, she takes cash advances on credit cards.

Beatrice has nothing but free time. She spends three full days a week, every week, with George. Her husband's budget of $2,400 per month does little to cover her bill. To make up the deficit, Beatrice secretly sells antiques that she and her spouse have collected from thirty years of world travel. George brags that her proceeds exceed $30,000, money she'll use to invest in her growth.

Laura, the nurse, gives all of her salary that is not spent on a tiny studio apartment and minimal groceries. She frequently protests, "Why don't I just sign over my paycheck to you?"

George ignores her, changing the subject, and Laura keeps paying. Barriers of professional privacy dissolve and sessions, six days per week, alternating between George's New York office and New Jersey den, become open house.

The presence of a diverse assembly soon prevents the former nakedness from continuing. One day Laura joins a Friday evening meeting with Lisa, Pauline, and me—a session that for the past few years has consistently been the scene of intense erotic activity. This day, we all remain clothed. The following week Laura returns. The arrangement becomes permanent, and encounters between George, me, and The Girls end forever. George seems content to move on, as if he has outgrown a former hobby. But I feel dumped. The intense intimacy, as one-sided as it was physically, filled me emotionally. Our shared experiences reinforced that I was special to George. As separation anxiety grips me, I realize that to George we were only lab rats manipulated for his personal research. My outrage at George's betrayal reminds me of his indifference toward Joe's death. I battle these excruciating feelings privately, and they take more than several months to subside.

Money pours into George's bank account in truckloads, and not one of his patients (except me) takes the necessary thirty seconds to do third-grade math. . . . George's annual salary now exceeds a quarter of a million dollars. Having eliminated private sessions, yet charging the same per head for groups of up to ten people, instead of earning $40 per hour, he can now earn $400. From barely being able to maintain a VW Beetle, George now possesses a healthy stock portfolio. Yet, like a collectively denied dirty family secret, discussing George's finances is strictly forbidden. Several people, including Laura, Bess, and Pauline, have difficulty buying groceries, despite annual salaries of close to $50,000. Nonetheless, George ignores the severity of our circumstances by continuing to insist that money is meaningless. "What do you mean?" Bess asks one day, "We need it for rent and food."

"No; people only believe this lie because they buy into the illusion created by the universal mind," George explains. "It is possible to become hidden from the system and live for free, but first you must break your attachments to money. A few nights ago, Chris and I had some fun. While Doris was out, we burned cash in the fireplace. I began with a fifty dollar bill, lighting one corner and sitting through my reactions, watching the flames engulf it. At first it was hard, but we kept going until the resistance broke. After about two hours of burning all kinds of bills, one by one, Chris and I were having a ball, rolling around on the floor, laughing our guts out. And there was a big reward for our work because the next day I discovered something brand new."

George points to his kitchen screen door. "See that? I got it for free—a gift from the store," he states proudly.

"What? How?" we respond in unison, intensely curious.

He laughs knowingly, "I just carried it out the main entrance of Home Depot, right past the registers. In fact the stupid manager was in such a fog that he held the door open for me and smiled."

Bess looks distressed. "I really don't understand."

George continues, shaking his fist, gaining momentum. "Just think about the system, governed by stupidity and greed. People are trained, like good children, to give up their money to big business and the federal bureaucracy. But how do they end up? Screwed! Because those institutions waste and steal most of what comes in. It is time we stop cowering in the corner and take back what is rightfully ours. Money shouldn't exist anyway; if it weren't for the stupid Program, we would all just share. Someone has to write some new rules and have the courage to make a stand. I know I have the Truth, and I'll live it out, even if thirty million Frenchmen think I'm wrong."

As George reaches his climax, we rise emboldened—troops summoned to battle. We don't really understand, but his passion proclaims the validity of his assertions. George, having captured us, quickly switches to his mentor mode and explains the ropes. "People get caught stealing because The Program decrees they are doing something wrong. They hide the items and look around furtively to make sure no one's watching, and their body language rouses the suspicions of store employees. Here is the right way to do it: Suspend your thoughts and go beyond your training to the Truth—that everything belongs to us already, we are just too afraid to claim it. With total confidence in this Truth, you can exit the store invisible."

Soon, like it or not, we follow suit. Christopher, now a high school senior, is the superstar. His store of choice is also Home Depot, in Spring Valley, N.Y. There he obtains a microwave oven, dishes, paint, and power tools—stuff he hides from his mother in the basement, essentials he'll need when someday he has his own place. But I am hesitant, so one Saturday George sends me to train with his son. Upon entering the store, I immediately sense that Christopher has put himself into a state of deep calm. I ask, "Aren't you nervous?" and he hisses, as if

I'm an irritating third-grader. "Why should I be? Didn't you listen to my father? We have the right to anything we want."

Christopher is a chip off the old block. He selects several items, making sure there are no magnetic inventory tags attached. After about twenty minutes, we head toward the exit with a shopping cart full of unpaid merchandise worth more than $300. I follow on Chris's heels, focusing inward, desperately trying to calm my fluttering chest and shaking knees, praying no one will notice. To my great relief and awe, we are not stopped.

These days we enter George's den with avid reports about "shopping for free." George beams with pride when Max walks out of the Paramus Pier One Imports with a five foot in diameter "papasan" chair. Pauline brags about how she draped a sweater over her arm at Annie Sez, convinced herself that she had taken it from her closet that morning, and strolled past the register, throwing a friendly smile to the salesgirl en route to the door. Laura exits a local deli, around the corner from her nursing job at Columbia Presbyterian Hospital, without paying for her coffee. The most popular exercise is to obtain free meals from restaurants, particularly diners where the waitresses don't take up your check. Even the faint of heart among us muster courage. We grab the check, and with sufficient cash in one hand, head toward the register, take a deep breath and continue out of the establishment, acting as if someone else in our party is paying the bill. We also develop a backup plan, should we fail. One day Lisa, Pauline and I walk out of a coffee shop in Tenafly, but the waitress chases us into the parking lot. I am holding the check, and I turn to her with trained calm and feigned sincerity, "I'm really sorry; I got distracted and forgot."

Falsely humble, I expose our check, folded around a twenty-dollar-bill, and follow her inside to pay. We are three well-dressed, pleasant, young women, and the waitress suspects nothing. Later that week, Lisa points out to George that sometimes missing checks are deducted from waitresses' salaries. But he ignores her, and instead digresses to reiterate that "management in large corporations does little to eliminate waste." This leads to inflated prices and consumer ripoff. In light of this larger incompetence, like a drop of water removed from an ocean, loss from items we claim for ourselves could not possibly hurt the company.

Although it is exciting to get stuff for free, there are two greater attractions for most of us—what little money we save gives us a momentary sense of relief from the burden of paying George, and more important, each success story wins a coveted slice of his heartfelt approval.

Max Stavos has great bravado, and one day he tries to pinch a vacuum cleaner from the Closter K-mart. A manager spots and detains him. The police are called and charges pressed. A few weeks later he is fined in a Closter courtroom. In response, George reprimands him. "Asshole! You tried to do it from your mind instead of using The Energy." Max sorrowfully admits he made a mistake.

K-Mart serves our mission again when Serena shops, accompanied by her father. She approaches the checkout, planning to pay for a hairbrush and shampoo. She prefers to do things the old-fashioned way, not for moral reasons, she is simply too afraid of getting caught. George spots her on line, pulls her into an empty aisle, and scolds her. She is commanded to walk out with the items; she must not defy The Energy. Serena complies; she has no choice.

Several weeks later, my mother is stopped by the store manager of Sloan's Supermarket, on 97th and Broadway. She has a can of tuna wrapped in a newspaper under her arm. The manager, viewing her as a harmless, piteous, old woman, lets her go—but bans her from shopping there again. Rachael doesn't seem to care.

Wealthy Beatrice is fond of hiding items under the supermarket circulars at the bottom of her cart. One day, she too gets caught, and a court date is set. Her husband, an upstanding citizen of their Westchester community, is mortified. However, Beatrice explains to their lawyer that she is currently writing a novel that portrays the life of a thief. The shoplifting was merely an experiment to connect with her main character and improve her narrative skills. The court lets her off with a slap on the wrist, and George spends hours bragging about Beatrice's skill. "She knows how to use The Energy to bypass the system."

Christopher and George make weekly visits to the Westwood Grand Union Supermarket. They place open, brown bags in a cart and stroll the aisles, nonchalantly filling them. Once satisfied, they walk past the checkout confidently, acting as if they have already paid. They are never stopped. But one day, Christopher goes alone and is caught. He is handcuffed by the local police and later released into his father's custody. George brings Christopher home in tears, all the while excoriating him for ignoring the signals sent by The Energy that today was not the day to do this. George hires a lawyer, for whom Christopher must pay with his Bar Mitzvah money. But he never makes it to court. Because Christopher is underage, seventeen, the store drops the charges.

Thanksgiving Morning
9:00 A.M. *to* 1:00 P.M.
1987 to the present

Today is a national holiday and a treasured day off from work, but we all arise early. Lisa and Pauline wake at 6:00 A.M. Traveling from eastern Queens, N.Y. they will arrive punctually at George's New Jersey den by 9:00. My alarm jolts me to consciousness at 8:30. I wake Max; we pull on clothes, grab a quick coffee at the 7-11 around the corner, and head north. Speeding on local roads from Hackensack to Teaneck, we reach George's block by 9:05. George's white house is first on the left. Everyone else has already arrived, and their cars selfishly crowd the tiny, residential block. I spot Laura's white Toyota, Beatrice's green Jaguar, Acura Integras (the official Group car of choice) belonging to Nora, Lisa, Christopher, and Serena; Bess's light blue Honda Civic, and Carl's Ford Escort wagon. Walking up the driveway, with Max at my heels, my stomach twists in fearful anticipation. I wish I was anywhere else, not only because of the painful amount of money I am about to spend, but also because dissension almost certainly lies within. I push back these feelings and struggle to recall some positive event that I can recount when I enter the room and George throws out his typical "What's going on?"

While ascending three stairs up to a deck, I force a cheery smile and then make a quick left. Two final, long strides gain us entrance to George's den through an oak door. Standing on white tile just inside, I remove my coat and place it on the floor. There is a full house today, and the inadequate coat rack to my right overflows with garments. I pause to quickly scan the room. A wave of tension passes through me; I hate being here, but I push past these feelings again. To my left is a blue and green plaid couch on which Pauline, Bess, and Carl are squeezed. Daylight streams through a large picture window behind them. George is barely two feet away, his back to me, comfortable in an overstuffed armchair with matching fabric. A love seat across from him, occupied by Nora and Beatrice, completes the living room set. Laura sits in an oak rocker to their right, her eyes squeezed shut, and Serena occupies a white-cushioned, swivel-based, rattan chair next to her father, just to the right of where I stand. Her impenetrable visage always makes me nervous, and I avoid looking at her. Christopher is nowhere to be seen, probably in his basement office doing a graphic arts project on the computer. Lisa and my mother (who is now close to seventy) perch on green velveteen folding chairs behind the love seat. As usual, later than the rest, all of the good seats have been taken. Only the awful folding chairs remain. I hate those chairs, especially when I know I'll be staying for four hours. Max opts for one, but I slip as unassumingly as possible between George's chair and Serena's knees, and plop down on the carpet beneath the fish tank. I am right next to Jan (the 8th grade special education teacher), whose earthiness usually directs her to prefer the floor as seating. Having settled myself, I blend in with the other twelve eager students who feel they must obtain a healthy dose of The Energy before heading out to the family, holiday dinner war zone.

Beatrice and Nora, pasty-complexioned, have entered their personal trance states already. Carl looks nervous and twiddles his thumbs rapidly. Max, his simian resemblance seeming so much more pronounced as I view him from across the room, rocks back and forth on his tiny, folding chair. I can imagine him in the jungle, perched on a tree's limb, banana in hand, grunting at passersby—just going with the flow. Serena, as if she were royalty, observes her subjects tranquilly. Her coarse, wavy black hair, cut in a shoulder-length shag, contrasts with her bloodless complexion. Completely clothed in black (her favorite color), she wears glasses and long, silver, star-shaped earrings. With her coloring, she could easily pass for one of Dracula's wives, except that she isn't pretty enough. Her weak chin and puffy features are far from easy on the eye. Actually, she resembles her father in female form. Of George's two offspring, Christopher, who takes after Doris, got all the looks. Bess, next to Pauline on the couch, seems terribly worried about something, while Pauline is so close to George that their knees touch. As I glance around, trying to avoid being noticed, I realize that a conversation is already in progress. George confronts an upset Pauline energetically, "Why don't you want to grow?"

"I don't know how," she moans, her yellow-gray hands (with the bony fingers and dry, wrinkled skin of a much older woman) clenching the fabric of the couch's arm.

"*YES. You do.* You're just holding back. Why don't you just let The Energy lead you? It's your only friend."

Pauline's voice trembles, "I try and try, but I never get it."

Annoyed by her whining, George raises his voice. "Don't waste my time; you have all the answers inside, but you're too lazy to make an effort."

Pauline's face pales by the minute. "No, I don't know what to do. Can't you help me?"

George switches gears and explains like a supportive teacher, "I can only assist after you take the first step on your own." He adds vocal force. "Just drop your manipulations, get on your bicycle, and start pedaling."

Pauline whimpers, "I can't find answers inside of me like you say."

George flips back to exasperation. "You're lying. You prefer to play games with me—games I have no time for. I have an important job to do, and you're holding me back on purpose."

Pauline continues to insist, "I really can't do it; I need help; I'm just stupid, and I can't get it."

George rises menacingly with glaring eyes, conceiving fear in all of our hearts. "Only people who choose to cooperate belong here. I'm giving you one more chance, but you better switch your attitude now, or you're out."

Tears roll down Pauline's face as she pleads, "Please don't throw me out; I'll try harder."

"Do you actually think I'm stupid enough to fall for your fake tears? I don't understand you people. There is all this wonderful stuff to experience, and none of you want it. You'd rather stay in misery. Why is it that I am always alone in the end, the only one who wants the truth? All of you want to be taken care of—thumb-sucking babies."

Each of us silently checks her attitude, and each concludes she *does* want the Truth and will listen to George. Poor Pauline sobs outright, her head down and scrawny body shaking. She rocks, wringing anxious hands, her throat so tight she can barely speak. This display angers George anew, and he escalates into full -blown rage, thundering at the top of his lungs, "Fool! Drop it now! There are others here who want to move ahead. I can't make everyone else pay because of you."

Having had his fill of assassinating Pauline, George abruptly begins a round of vigorous headshaking. The rest of us have no sympathy for Pauline, except Bess. Last year, thanks to her, Pauline obtained a lucrative position in Bess's office. The two women now work closely, and Bess feels responsible for Pauline. She leans toward Pauline reassuringly. Sweet and patient, she also possesses an intimate understanding of the rebelliousness that Pauline is experiencing. "Pauline, you know, yesterday at work I was resisting and resisting. Then I decided to sit still and focus. I thought, *Why am I such a baby? I am part of this wonderful mission.* Then everything changed, and right after that, Arthur (her boss) stopped by my desk. He told me he had just gotten a new client and that I would get extra, overtime hours. In that moment, I put it all together—when I let go of small thoughts, everything works out."

George interrupts his shaking. "There. Exactly what I mean. Does everybody understand? Bess was all screwed up, but when she let the garbage go, good things came immediately. Now, why can't all of you do that too? It would make my job so much easier. Don't you realize that I can't focus on discovery if I have to constantly stop and change your dirty diapers?"

This scene has become our daily diet. Six days a week, ten hours a day, people come and go; most spend at least four hours. Faces change, but George's stance remains the same. He has incredible stamina, usually railing against our lousy attitudes for many hours. His voice rattles the window panes. The object of his rage, different almost every day, recedes until her face turns ashen. The rest, simply grateful to be excused from the hot seat, sit quietly, wearing pious and knowing looks, trying to impress upon George that we, unlike the person under fire, "get it."

Pauline apologizes, "I'm sorry, I forgot to appreciate what we have here."

And George responds sweetly, "See, that's all it takes; just admit you don't know and let The Energy take over."

George directs his eyes to hers, and she returns his gaze. Her sobbing fades and eventually dies away. After about five minutes, as the focusing progresses, she slips into a staring trance, her body jolting from The Energy. She reports that there is green light around his head, and George nods encouragingly. We all understand that now all is well. George continues with Pauline. His head shakes a little, and then quickly gains speed. Exhausted from the battle, we focus on George's spinning head, and soon we all experience some Energy. One by one, eyes close and we nod off. Christopher comes up from the basement, entering through the kitchen door at the rear of the den. He lies down flat on his back next to Serena's chair and falls under instantly. George himself, after half an hour of continuous headshaking, lets go. His head rolls back in his chair, his mouth falls open, and he slips into deep sleep. I find solace in our familiar state of nothingness—no thoughts, no conflict.

This den is my home, and I know every inch: the diagonal, knotty pine paneling; the white, Berber carpet; the tiny bathroom to the left of the entrance, with its inspirational poster, "Footprints in the Sand," posted on the back of the door; George's oak roll-top desk in the opposite corner, overstuffed with personal paperwork and our checks to him peeking out from a cubbyhole; the square coffee table where we rest our feet when we sit on his couch; the jingle of wind chimes outside on the deck. Total silence reigns as fourteen people and George's two cats, B.J. and Tyler, succumb to a drugged sleep. The doorbell rings and his black Labrador Retriever, Ben, barks in another part of the house, but no one hears a thing. Our bodies weigh a thousand pounds; we couldn't move our limbs if we wanted to. After an additional hour George comes to. It is 12:55 P.M., exactly five minutes before the time he has intended to finish. Gently he rouses us, "OK everybody, it's time to get going."

We all groan as we drag ourselves out of the oppressive sleep still engulfing us. Feet grope for shoes, and one by one, we rise slowly from our seats. George, watching over his flock, asks how everybody is doing, and Pauline replies first, "I feel much better. I think I understand more of what you mean."

George replies lovingly, "Now you're getting smarter!" and then coaches the rest of us. "You know we are all in this together, and we need each other. We have to be unified."

Pauline looks at him gratefully, her face shining. She thanks him and follows with a hug, which he receives without emotion. Then she writes his check, but cautions while handing it over, "Don't cash this until next week. I can't give you everything for today; I'll give you the rest after my paycheck next Wednesday."

He nods in acknowledgment and continues his lecture, "We all went up a level today and learned a lot. Now everybody, make sure you don't throw it away as soon as you go out the door. At your Thanksgiving dinners, just observe your families, but don't get involved. Learn from them; use them to grow, to break your connections to the garbage they are drowning in. If you can get strong then maybe you can lead them out too, if they want something better for themselves. Just remember that The Energy is always with you. Stop resisting and enjoy the ride!"

Beatrice kisses George on the cheek as she heads for the door, and he smiles sweetly. Bess follows suit and then asks, "What are you doing for Thanksgiving?"

George's face dissolves into contempt. "Doris has some crap planned. Serena, Christopher, and I have to drive all the way out to Long Island so that we can spend the day watching her sister and brother-in-law act like babies. The house is filthy and her cooking sucks. Well, that's the price we pay right now. Holidays are total nonsense."

"I know. I'm going to my brother's. His kids are nuts, his wife's controlling him with the Female Program, and he doesn't have a clue. Every time I try to tell him that he could have so much more if he came here, he ignores me and changes the subject. I don't know why he is so stupid when the answer is right under his nose."

"Yeah, I know what you mean. Parents in The Program are so crazy that it's amazing our mothers didn't put us in the oven instead of the Thanksgiving turkey! Hah. Hah."

"Right you are, George! Well, take it easy and I'll see you tomorrow, first thing in the morning when you start. I have the whole day off from work. How late are you going tomorrow?"

"Short day. 9:00 to 5:00."

"OK, I can stay the whole time; See you at 9:00. . . . I'll bring some bagels." Bess leaves smiling, anticipating tomorrow.

Laura shares her plans also, as she leaves. "I'm going to my brother's in Harrington Park for dinner. They just had a new baby."

"Well, just watch how they throw away their own lives to put the baby on a pedestal and worship her. If you can sneak to the side with the baby, hold her and get some of The Energy into her. It will build up and she'll come our way when she gets older."

"OK, I'll see you tomorrow. I'll be here from 10:00 to 2:00." Laura pulls a stack of twenties from her pocket and peels off one for herself. The rest she hands to George.

We continue to file out, handing him checks or cash, all of which he receives without expression and immediately pockets. Serena and Christopher, the crown princess and prince, remain seated. They silently observe The Group members' exodus and the transfer of cash—the growing fortune they will one day inherit. Today, this holiday morning from 9:00 A.M. to 1:00 P.M., George has scolded Pauline, eaten bagels and fruit offered by Lisa, Nora, and Laura (at a spontaneous break somewhere within his two-hour tirade), and then headshaken himself into a ninety-minute oblivion. He has earned $1,760.

"Lisa, Pauline and Carl have just gotten married." George smiles mysteriously at me one Friday evening as I enter his office in the city.

"What do you mean?" I inquire, not comprehending.

"They have just started a business—a corporate union."

I turn to see three faces glowing with anticipation. "What are they going to do?"

Lisa answers, "It is called New Life Design. We're going to sell custom Formica furniture, window treatments, and wooden cabinets."

I accept this without question. George always makes it seem like anything is possible . . . with The Energy. Soon, everyone in The Group seems to be starting a business. Our collective passion persists. Our idealism prevails, and we are convinced: Whatever we conceive, we will achieve—The Energy is the wind in our sails. Beatrice begins writing a novel about a girl afflicted with an eating disorder. Nora and my mother throw themselves into a children's book, *Dashiki*, about a young Afro-American girl. Bess and Pauline establish a resume writing and editing service. Max draws from his business experience at his father's printing shop. He advises us on the ins and outs, such as designing effective business cards and selecting the proper paper stock for stationery. Soon our wallets are filled with each other's business cards. We hand them out everywhere, to waitresses, shop owners, and pedestrians. . . . Visions of a future overflowing with guaranteed wealth, the fruit of our dreams, whirl in our brains and lift us upwards on a cloud of ecstatic expectation.

Of course, a business needs startup cash. So, one week following the birth of New Life Design, I enter George's office to find Carl, Lisa, and Pauline engaged in animated discussion. "You just got here in time. We are about to do something really big," they tell me.

A wave of uncertainty passes as I probe George's face inquisitively, but Carl explains, "I have a wealthy aunt in Australia who really likes me. I'm going to call and see if she can help us out with our new corporation."

I tighten immediately. Not understanding why, I cannot share their excitement—quite the opposite. Nonetheless, I try to hide behind a counterfeit smile. It doesn't work; as if he could read my mind, George senses that I'm not playing with the team. "What is wrong with you, dream crusher? You must be jealous. I know you love to fail in your life, but the others won't fail along with you."

I recede from his attack, but I muster the strength to lie, promising aloud that I will change my attitude right now. Still, I can't stifle my gut instincts that protest that there is something very wrong with this picture. Meanwhile, Carl picks up the phone. Using his calling card, he soon connects to his Australian aunt. My discomfort storms as he chats with her superficially and then slowly moves toward the subject of his exciting new enterprise. On the surface everything seems normal, so why do I feel so bad? His aunt is taken with the idea. Although it's been 15 years since she's seen her nephew, Carl still holds a special place in her heart. Finally, after much hyped-up description, he gives her the figure; they will need $20,000. He doesn't identify it as a loan, but that's understood, isn't it? Miraculously she agrees, and as he hangs up the phone a sort of cheer arises from the occupants of George's tiny office. My own smile covers a set of gritting teeth.

Over the next several weeks, Carl feeds some of his aunt's money into the new corporation. The rest he uses to pay George, because he, like the others, has begun to spend entire days in George's office. With additional funds from Lisa's father, they purchase a $15,000 computer, expensive stationary, and booths at several local trade shows. They have invested so much to give birth to their precious enterprise; yet they have no product knowledge, no clients, and no business experience. Soon their

The Cult Next Door

bank account runs dry, and Carl calls his aunt again. This time she refuses him. . . .

To join in with everybody else, I come up with my own product. Currently, I am tutoring about ten students a week in high school chemistry. To each I dictate the same vocabulary list, the same equations. My students could really use a set of chemistry flash cards for self-study. I visit Barnes & Noble but can't find any on the shelf. So, I decide to create them myself. I choose a name, *Chemistry in a Flash*, and grab my typewriter and textbook to begin writing. I hire an art student to create the package design. After investing all of my free time for the next several months, I finally complete prototypes of three science titles: *Chemistry, Biology, and Physics in a Flash*. But then I hit the brick wall, typesetting costs to create the cards exceed $6,000—way out of my budget. Sadly, my lovingly designed prototypes are soon retired to a shelf where they commence gathering dust. They beckon me each time I pass, "Elizabeth, you have to publish us."

"I know I must," I respond, "but I don't know how. . . ."

When Max and I first moved into the apartment, I cashed some government bonds worth $10,000. I planned for this money to cover me temporarily until I found a career path. Three years have passed, and I am no closer to an answer. Meanwhile, the $10,000 is gone. Wrenched with remorse, I realize I have failed myself. How could I have let this happen . . .? Now I must make a change. And although I don't know it yet, I will make one very soon.

It is a bright, November day, and a crisp wind swirls leaves around my feet as I find myself peering into a storefront window across from the Demarest Duck Pond (about a mile from George's house). The sign says, "For Rent," and for some reason, perhaps curiosity, perhaps desperation, I call the realtor's number. Surprising even myself, after I have inspected it inside, I inform him that I'm considering opening a photography studio. The idea springs out of nowhere, yet, for some unexplained reason, I truly want to carry it through. So, I go into business for real, and Expressions Photography is born. Ignorant of marketing and sales, to say "I don't know what the heck I'm doing," is an understatement. Photography has always been a favorite hobby, and I have done some part-time work in the field, but that's it. My only saving grace is that I don't require a loan; the startup capital will come from what remains of the inheritance from my father. Actually, I've never heard of a business loan, I don't know what an invoice is, and the concept of "cash flow" means nothing; they don't teach these things in Swarthmore College's ivory tower. I can write a mean term paper, but that won't pay the rent. Setting up the place takes two months. I eat, drink, and sleep with the studio in mind, often waking in the middle of the night to jot down an idea that has just hit me.

When his personal chef and maid ceases to focus on him, Max becomes disgruntled. Neglected, he accuses me of being obsessed. And he is correct. I am driven; I want to succeed more than anything.

January 1988 to December 1990

My photography studio opens February first. That first day I don't know what to expect. I pace in circles for hours, straightening this and moving that. I hope some customers will come in and start the ball rolling, but they don't. How do you get them to come in anyway? I have no idea. About two months later, my first paying customer finally walks through the door; I make a $45 sale. Every month cash flows out of my checkbook like a waterfall: rent, heat, garbage disposal, electricity, telephone, office supplies, equipment. I put in ten to twelve-hour days, and when I am not at the studio, I can think of nothing else. I feel helpless to change my lack of cash flow. My thoughts tell me to quit and get a real job, because I don't know how I will ever overcome the downward momentum of spending without earning. . . .

On a sunny, spring day, the bell on my front door jingles, and a stranger enters. Her name is Melissa Goldsmith, and she has lived in town most of her life. She seems to take an instant liking to me, although I can't imagine why; with my file of "paid" receipts still painfully empty, I don't think much of myself these days. As if she instinctively knows that I am in trouble, perhaps even better than I do, she unselfishly offers her help, with no request for compensation. For the next several weeks she hauls my portfolio around to local businesses and promotes me. Soon she escorts several local shop owners, their children, and their dogs into my studio for sample sittings. We hang their photographs on the walls in their stores, along with business cards and discount coupons for their customers. In October, Melissa offers me a booth at the "Demarest Oktoberfest," a local crafts fair that she happens to coordinate. I book a few sittings at the event, and finally, my phone starts ringing. I find the flow, or the flow finds me; I'm not sure which. I still finish that first year in the red, but I'm sure I'll do better next year.

My second year, I manage to break even, and in my third, I am finally in the black. But the walls of the retail space that seemed so ample almost three years ago are now closing in on me. I search for larger quarters and fall in love with a loft, over double the size, in the neighboring town of Closter. The final three months of 1990 and the entire year's profits are spent fixing up the new place. A little after the dawn of 1991, I move the business. The new suite is perfect. Gazing at the fruits of my labor, I realize how far I've come. Business is finally flowing, albeit slowly, and this coming year I should be able to take a salary for the first time.

February to December 1991

It is a late Tuesday afternoon. Dizzy, nauseous, and exhausted from stress, I am slumped miserably on George's den couch. I have an appointment to deliver proofs to a bride and groom that evening at 7:00 P.M., and I don't feel well enough to make it. Serena is seated in a chair opposite. She has become a regular in her father's groups since she graduated last June from SUNY New Paltz, with a B.A. in communications. I am now thirty-one, and she is twenty-three. For the past nine months she has held various part-time jobs. Currently she is a cocktail waitress at Medieval Times, an entertainment restaurant in Lyndhurst, and substitute teacher at the Teaneck Elementary School. The rest of the time, she hangs out at the house. Lately, her father has been annoyed with her lack of motivation. A radio station has just offered her a full-time job with a starting salary of $6 per hour. However, Serena and George both decide that this paltry amount would hardly compensate her for her value, so she has turned them down.

George notices my pale demeanor, and when I mention my evening appointment, he gently suggests that Serena might be able to help out. Surprised at his thoughtfulness, I agree. That evening Serena accompanies me to my office. Immediately confident, she insists on handling the appointment alone. I am hesitant, but my stomach is rolling and my head is banging, so I give in. After the couple leaves, she asks me if there might be a little work for her. Bringing another person into the business has never occurred to me, but here she is and I don't mind trying something new. I spend the next few days pouring my acquired knowledge into her head. She listens and absorbs. I offer a 5% sales training commission, to be increased to 10% when she's ready to go solo. Serena glares. "I'll handle sales myself now. Five percent will do nothing for me."

Intimidated by rage-filled eyes, I give in, convincing myself that later it will work out OK. Over the next few months Serena handles all sales in private. Relegated outside the closed door, I want to be sure she treats customers respectfully and has adequate product knowledge, but she balks when I approach and accuses me of putting her down. "Do you think I am stupid? Don't interfere. I know what I'm doing."

In addition, she reports to her father that I don't respect her, and during my sessions he chastises me for criticizing his daughter. I can't fight her, and I certainly can't fight him, so she wins free reign despite my better judgment. Soon George is bragging to The Group that his daughter has saved my business from failure because "when it comes to business, Elizabeth's personality sucks."

"Serena has drive and courage. She can take the business to the stars. In fact she could run five businesses at once if she wanted to!"

I protest, but George counters, "Without Serena, Expressions Photography will go down the drain. If you're smart, you'll climb on her back and she'll take you with her."

I don't want to climb on her back; I want to take care of myself. Each time he praises her, my stomach twists. I do not see how Serena is so great. However, in addition to George and his daughter, the rest of The Group encourages me to let her "save the business." Peer pressure finally forces me to question myself. I *must* know less than Serena. She *must* have advanced knowledge obtained through osmosis. After all, she's been with Daddy since she was a toddler.

One day in the summer, Serena notices my flash card prototypes on a high shelf in the office. "What's that?" she asks.

I tell her about my project and the unaffordable $6,000 typesetting costs. Within the next few minutes she is on the phone with her father declaring that *she* will get them published. True to her promise, she quickly secures an appointment at Prentice Hall in Englewood Cliffs. George brags to The Group that I am too intimidated by the "big people" so Serena will carve the path to success. The following week, Serena drives us there. Our meeting goes well. Euphorically ambitious, we infect an assistant editor in the mail order division. He schedules a followup meeting with other staff. We leave high on a cloud.

"This is really going to happen," Serena says confidently, "and we will split it fifty-fifty."

Split it evenly? This doesn't sound fair. This is my idea. How is she entitled to half just for setting up a meeting? Upset, I call George to complain. Instead of defending his daughter as I fear, he calms me, "Nothing has happened yet. Why don't you just wait and see?"

I let it go.

The following week Prentice Hall shows some interest and sends out for production quotes. The costs turn out to be too high, and we soon receive a gracious letter of refusal.

When Serena took those three-year-old prototypes off the shelf and dusted them off, my passion reignited. Despite our first disappointment, my mind begins to fantasize in dramatic proportions. I envision the product on the shelves of all 30,000 retail bookstores in the United States. I calculate the potential profits that could reach into the millions! Serena and George immediately jump on the bandwagon. Another assignment for The Energy! The three of us spend much of my session time planning our next move. There is so much potential: retail stores, mail-order, international sales. . . . We see ourselves taking on the entire planet. I even comment to Serena that the cards are the perfect vehicle to get her father's information to the public. We can write things about The Energy in the card sets, and with millions of boxes of flash cards out there, people will surely be attracted!

From my experience with the Prentice Hall meetings, I realize that I lack the necessary gumption to telemarket potential business contacts. In contrast, Serena is fearless. I watch in awe as she picks up the telephone again and again, insisting on speaking to store managers, chief editors, presidents of companies. . . . She applies herself to any strategy we concoct, no matter how outrageous. I have come to feel that I really do need her.

After the Prentice Hall turndown, we decide to publish the cards ourselves. We come to a verbal agreement that since this is my brainchild, I will pay the costs: production, travel, advertising, and so forth (from my inheritance), and Serena will donate her time to make connections and ultimately, sales. We will split the profits between us.

Within the next weeks she schedules appointments at several major book chains. I hire a printer to make an initial run of 300 copies. George is involved as advisor at every stage. And best of all, he is pleased with me. I register our business name, Flash Enterprises, as a sole proprietorship under my name.

I have high hopes for both of the businesses. However, Serena, now my almost constant companion, throws me a curve one day when I arrive at our office to find her seated at my desk and scowling. When I ask "what's wrong," she glares, spitting out righteous indignation, "I have helped you out because I *care* about you, but all you do is criticize me."

"Huh," I don't understand. . . .

Serena terrifies me. I have never met anyone like her. When the mood strikes, she is so vicious that I can't stand to be near her. Her accusations make me recede: my face pales, my mouth parches, and my hands sweat. I feel faint from fear, and she makes me feel like I have committed a terrible crime from which absolution is impossible. No amount of reasoning will halt her attack. And when I try to leave the room, she orders me to return, parroting her father's teaching, "Sit through the war until it breaks, and then you will be stronger."

Nevertheless, with acidic reactions coursing through every vessel in my body, escalating in intensity as she utters each new allegation, I feel as if I am being forced to keep my hand in a fire. Trapped, I learn to numb myself to these unbearable sensations.

Although eight years her senior and the legal owner of the business, today, as usual, I shrink from her.

"I'm leaving," she threatens, "You can fail on your own."

After she and George have repeatedly stated that I am a failure without her, I am beginning to believe them. Therefore, I sink from her threat. She makes me feel as if I have committed a horrible crime against her, although I can't figure out exactly what. In her ranting, Serena has offered no specific details. But I am sure that ruin is inevitable if I don't win her back.

During that afternoon's, stress-reduction session, I face George with terrified countenance, and he reinforces his daughter's position. "Serena is the best thing that ever happened to you, and you take her for granted. If she goes, you will lose everything."

The next few days I drown in a state of impeding doom. Serena is present at the office, but makes it clear that time is running out. At any moment I fear she'll pull out the rug. Not only will I lose my only chance at success, but I will incur George's eternal wrath for mistreating his daughter. I would do anything to resolve this, but I still don't understand exactly what the problem is. All I hear from both is, "You really screwed up this time, and you're gonna pay."

A rabbit in the middle of an open field pecked at by crows, I have nowhere to run for cover and no weapons to ward off the enemy. A couple of evenings later Serena calls me into a meeting. This is it; my life is over. Dispassionately observing the pathetic heap of woman trembling in her seat, Serena surprises me, delivering these magical words, "Elizabeth, I was prepared to leave, but I will stay on one condition; I want a 20% commission on photography sales from now on."

I almost cry out. The doubled commission, from 10% to 20%, seems unimportant. I am simply overwhelmed with relief as Serena presses the button that releases me from three days of total terror. However, in this moment I also make a vow. Despite the pitiful fool I have just made of myself, I must find a way to stop Serena from controlling me. The next time she strikes I will fight back. I carry this oath with me always; it is my private secret. . . .

During the next months I take no money, while Serena earns her generous commissions. In addition, I have no more say in the business, but George reassures me gently, "If you had been fortunate enough to be my daughter, you would have had Serena's strength. So, be smart and let her channel The Energy to run the businesses through her. It will bring customers and command them to spend lots of money."

That first year together, I finally manage to pay myself the first salary in three years ($9,000). But Serena earns $25,000.

I pick up a grey, striped kitten on the back porch of a local house overrun by strays. Pocket-sized, having barely opened her eyes, she fits in the palm of my hand. I feed her with a baby bottle and she accompanies me everywhere, sleeping in a cardboard box. When I drive, she sits between my legs. I name the baby "Flash," after the flash card project. Of course she attends sessions with George too. To show us how animals react to The Energy, George holds her out in front of his chest. Her back legs hang down while he shakes his head vigorously, never moving the hand encircling her belly. The Energy radiates and knocks her out. In a deep state of relaxation,

Pocket-sized Flash

her limp body begins to vibrate rapidly. It is a bizarre sight, but I don't think he's hurting her. George laughs knowingly as he taps her jolting paws. "The animals are smarter than us to start with because they don't have crazy thoughts. Now, when The Energy knocks out her 'cat program,' she is transformed into a free and intelligent being."

George also works on Serena's orange and grey cat, B.J. (named after songwriter Billy Joel). He holds her in his lap, seated like a small person. When she struggles to run, he restrains her until she gives up, having learned from experience that escape is futile. Thus, she sits for hours motionless. George praises his example of perfection. "B.J. is as wise as the Sphinx of Egypt. We should learn how to hear what she has to say."

The rest worship her, too. I try to follow suit, but I have a hard time accepting.

George also works on Christopher's black Labrador mix, Ben.

"Ben's 'dog program' makes him into a self-destructive lunatic. He doesn't care about himself. No wonder dogs only live twelve years."

George spends hours lying on the floor clutching the dog in a wrestler's hold, restricting Ben's motion each time he tries to free himself. At mealtime he teaches the dog not to bolt down his food by holding Ben's head and restricting his jaw so that he is forced to chew more slowly. The more George is able to control his animals, the more he lifts them up as examples, "I have forced my animals to drop their crazy program. Now, they are more alive than we are. We should follow the animals."

At my apartment, more and more, I can barely tolerate Max's presence. In the evenings, I avoid him, and when we retire to the full-size bed we share, I bury myself inside my red sleeping bag, left over from teenage camping trips, and zip it up tight, leaving a barrier of goose-down between us. One Saturday evening, we fight, for the hundredth time, over money. In our seven years together, Max has yet to tap into the stream of income he always promises is "just around the corner." He works part-time, at his convenience, occasionally lavishing a diner hamburger on me, while I continue to pay our bills. Tonight he opposes me as usual, drawing from a seemingly endless vat of excuses, ammunition he hurtles at me relentlessly. Frustrated, still trying to convince him to change, I am staring into his glaring eyes when unexpectedly, a vision comes to me. I see myself trapped in a cage in the basement. Max feeds me infrequently, and I am starving. As if I am his personal Barbie Doll, when fancy strikes, he unlocks the door and enters to play with my body. His cruel laugh scorns me. I realize that Max doesn't even like me. To him I have simply represented a set of female private parts and a checkbook with a pen. Max has nothing to offer and never will—his promised "corner" doesn't exist. After years of interminable efforts to make us work, on this night, I lose my steam. I have imprisoned myself with a fool—a huge mistake. Something powerful is happening. Through no choice of my own, I feel as if I am being propelled away from Max.

During my Monday session, I complain to George for the umpteenth time. George always responds the same way, "Granted, the situation isn't ideal, but you haven't grown enough to leave Max; you still have things to learn. I know it's frustrating to pay his bills, but view it from the positive; you are *paying for your education.* Don't forget, a problem takes two. If you don't correct what *you're* doing wrong, you'll be the same wreck in your next relationship."

I try to accept his logic, but the repellant from Max is too strong. That night, against George's orders I pack a bag and run away. I spend the night in my photography studio. I know Max will call George to tell on me, and my knees shake as I walk into the den for my 8:00 A.M. session. George is sternly silent at first, but when he opens his mouth, I know what is coming. "You just couldn't wait for the right time, could you?" he bellows, and then rises, grabs my collar, and shoves me against the wall with such force that two framed posters fall to the floor.

"Damn," he sputters, "Look what you made me do. The glass is broken on these pictures. I'll expect you to pay for it."

I can't take George's opposition, and that night, I go home to Max. Besides, I have nowhere else to go.

It is late November when I reach the end. Hiding in my office, avoiding Max at home, I can barely hold even a superficial conversation. I approach George once again, and this time he senses that I'm leaving Max no matter what. Aware that he has lost this round, that I am not "Max's in the other place" as he had claimed when he joined us together, George turns 180 degrees to support me, as if he had never promoted any other position. "It's time to move on to new experiences," he sagely explains.

Neither angry nor bitter, I am instead sad to have thrown away eight years of my life to a lie. In secret I begin an apartment search. The last weeks with Max are strange. I feel as if a spaceship is on its way to pick me up. Although I am so cut off, he suspects nothing! The realization that he is totally disconnected from me expels my final shreds of doubt. One afternoon at the office, I invite Serena to look at a few apartments with me. It turns out she'd love to rent a house, if she could find a housemate. At twilight, the realtor brings us into a modest house in Closter with a reasonable rent. The electricity is off, and we examine the downstairs by flashlight. Swept away by the moment, before I have a chance to consider, the two of us decide to sign a lease. Serena and I are merging our lives—out of the frying pan and into the fire. Regardless, the relief of leaving Max and the prospect of starting fresh in this wonderful house with a fireplace at the end of a dirt road, just like I dreamed of ever since I was little, uplifts me. A week later, Max returns home from a "business appointment" to discover empty rooms. Sneaking out was my only choice, because Max, as he always has before, would have employed brute force to stop me.

New Year's Eve 1991 to December 1992

Several Group members spend the last remaining hours of 1991 and the first few of 1992, with Serena and me, assisting us in unpacking and setting up our new house. Carl, Pauline, and Lisa paint my bedroom: white walls and blue trim. They hang lace curtains to complement my floral bedspread. Nora and Chris help Serena decorate her room: black mini-blinds, black sheets, and various medieval props—swords, wizards, dragons. . . . Our tastes certainly contrast!

Serena and I, involved in two businesses and sharing a house, are officially a team. With this achievement, I have finally managed to surpass my peers on The Group's hierarchy ladder. One rung beneath George's children, I believe I can earn equality with them—*if I work hard enough*. And finally, one blessed day in the future, with George. As for now, Serena and Elizabeth are really going places, and everyone envies our status. We give sage advice to the rest, still floundering in unrealized dreams of success. At group meetings, with everyone involved in some entrepreneurial project, business is generally the subject of choice. We rent booths at mall trade shows where our services are offered collectively. Promoting Group hype incessantly, we often hand an unsuspecting stranger at least a pound of promotional paper while proudly recounting our plethora of amazing enterprises: books, offset printing, Formica furniture, photography, stress-reduction, etc. All this activity makes George's the only place to be—official headquarters for expert guidance, whenever you can get there.

Because our photography studio operates "by appointment only," Serena soon arranges for us to close three afternoons a week so we can visit her father's city office. We spend hours there, brainstorming about our two businesses. Serena is not paying for this exciting time—but I am. My weekly schedule often exceeds thirty hours, and for this, I must pay George over $1,000. My previous concern has turned into alarm. I resent every check, wishing it was the last, but I try to justify as he has taught: *This is an investment in your future. The money will come back. The cake is still baking; be patient until it's ready to eat.* Yet, my life feels like a speeding train from which I cannot jump, even though I clearly see the brick wall ahead. These days the others follow a similar schedule, and often George's tiny office is so filled that there isn't even room to sit on the floor. We leave the door open, and the remaining few sit on the hallway carpeting. Serena and Christopher are usually there all day—and always for free. Everyone envies his kids. They don't have to drain their bank accounts and struggle over food bills. Worse, George always cites them as the best examples of the success of The Energy.

Yet, George claims he treats everyone the same. "I don't have any favorites; everyone is equal in my eyes," George states proudly one afternoon, spotlighting his unprejudiced nature.

Skeptical, I challenge him. "What about your children, you must feel something special because they are a part of you."

"No, I feel the same about everyone. That they share some of my chromosomes is only relevant in the physical world. It has no effect on our spiritual connections to each other."

"Then why don't you have sex with Serena or Christopher too, to break a social barrier, like you have done with us?"

I think back to the time my mother touched my breast in the middle of the night, how she used George's rationale—"it's just flesh against flesh."

George looks at the floor, silent for a moment. Finally, he mumbles, seemingly grasping at straws, "I have decided to let them have their own experiences."

What kind of an answer is that? *It doesn't make any sense.*

The relentless allergies take over a few weeks after our move into the house. Swollen sinuses force me to breathe through my mouth most of the time. A continual post nasal drip fills my lungs, and nighttime brings long bouts of coughing up congestion. Asthma begins to impede my breathing and sometimes at night, I shake my head like George to try to calm my constricted chest. It barely helps. Lying down brings feelings of suffocation, so I must sit up to get what little sleep I can. During the day, attacks of anxiety and indecisiveness plague me, and I am always so, so tired. Sometimes people ask me why I am always sick. Every day I do my best to survive with what I have; *going to a doctor is not an option.* Serena is omnipresent and watching. George would punish me severely if I ever sought outside help.

My relationship with my new roommate brings anxiety as well. One Friday night, about 8:00 P.M., I am reading in bed when I hear footsteps on the stairs. Serena appears, making her way toward her bedroom across from mine. She looks fairly placid as she waves a greeting. But in the next moment, something strange happens. I sense an intense buildup of electricity in the air and then, as if a hostile ghost has just invaded her body and seized control, Serena's face twists into crazed fury. Without warning, she begins ranting about a pipe in the basement that she has just discovered is dribbling onto the furnace. Standing in the narrow hallway outside my room she grills me, making no sense whatsoever, "Why didn't you know it was doing that and get it fixed? The house could blow up!"

She soon loses control and shrieks incoherently. I try to reason with her, but she *will not be silenced.* Increasing the volume of these accusations, her face turns beet red and her veins threaten to pop out of her forehead; it looks as if she might explode. After about ten minutes of insanity, she suddenly stops short and runs into the third bedroom, her office, across the hall. Dropping onto the couch, she buries her face in her hands and sobs. Despite hurt feelings from her unreasonable attack, my caring nature compels me to sit down next to her; I hope I can offer some comfort. She seems to be ashamed that I am witnessing this vulnerability. In a little while she lifts her face and whimpers, "Everyone only sees the outside of my personality. They don't know how horrible it feels inside when this happens."

I listen sympathetically, knowing that the storm has passed, and she will soon find relief. I do not understand what has just happened, but I do know one thing: Serena, with all of her bravado and intimidation, is a tormented person. . . .

After my farce with Max, I have no interest in male companionship. . ., until I meet Preston. He owns a business, Learning Dynamics, located in an office suite down the hall. Our first conversation is about whether or not he might be able to sell our flash cards, but it turns into something more when he invites me to lunch to discuss it further. Over six feet tall, he is definitely my definition of "tall, dark, and handsome." Recently separated and on his way to divorce, from the first time he winks at me, I am captured by his charm and self-confidence. We go out a few times and I begin to feel involved. Serena, however, disapproves and reports to her father that I spend all day dreaming of "the man down the hall" instead of working. George warns that I'd better change my focus to important matters, or else. I try to continue the relationship quietly, all the while guilty, as if I am committing a grave sin. I feel torn between The Group, where I have dedicated my life, and these new, enticing feelings of which I can't get enough. Serena continues to press the issue, claiming my obsession has made me irresponsible, and The Group soon chimes in, branding me a pathetic fool for chasing one of the Crazy People.

"He seems like a nice man," George observes, having met him one day at our office, "but if he doesn't come here to learn, you are not safe. One day he will hurt you."

I beg Preston repeatedly to visit The Group but he always refuses, so one afternoon, George lays down the law. "Serena's going to leave the business unless you get rid of Preston."

Torn in half, the fear of George's vengeance wins. Later that evening, I call Preston from my office, dialing his car phone to deliver the news. When he hears my voice he responds with pleasure, while I, in contrast, betray my real feelings and sternly cut him off. "Preston, I can't see you anymore."

Taken off guard and clearly distressed, he questions, "Why?" and I feel his pain, as if I have just kicked him in the stomach. Serena sits a few feet away, observing indifferently, present to ensure that I won't back down. I feel awful. I can't possibly answer his question. How could I ever explain about George and The Energy? I choke and hesitate, praying that some miracle will occur in the next minute to save me, but instead Preston's anguish builds and he blurts out, "I swear to God on my children's graves, if you don't tell me why you can't see me anymore I will never speak to you again."

After a few moments, hearing only silence, he hangs up on me. . .

With Preston out of the way, Serena rededicates herself to flash card promotion. Her plan: win endorsements from influential people. Her first choice: Our President's wife, Barbara Bush. After all, Barbara supports education. So one day in her father's den, Serena, with a hint of merriment, suggests that I pick up the phone and call Washington. Taken aback, I balk, thinking, *Why would Barbara Bush endorse our product just so we can profit from her name?*

But my partner glares while I hesitate. Soon the rest get on my back too. "No" is not an option, so nervously, I call information. After being transferred a few times within the White House, I finally reach the first lady's secretary's secretary who tells me that they don't make appointments for this type of thing and besides, Barbara is not able to endorse *any* product. I sigh with relief, but only for a moment before Serena concludes that I simply wasn't confident enough. To prove me wrong, she calls and requests to speak to Barbara Bush herself. It seems rude to disturb people for our trivial (to everyone but us) project. Regardless, George beams with pride at his daughter's courage. "They are no better than us," he explains. "We turn them into parents to fear and worship. Politicians are really *our employees,* and it is our legal right to meet them and share our ideas whenever we want."

George makes some sense, but I'm still uncomfortable with pursuing Barbara Bush. Serena's call yields no better results. Still, a few days later she brings it up again, pushing the phone into my hand with a grin. My face turns waxen. This is the last thing in the world I want to do. I get through to the secretary. She remembers our previous call and seems annoyed. I don't know how I manage, but by babbling and forcing her to stay on the telephone I get an appointment. She probably says yes just to get rid of me. Barbara's personal secretary is willing to meet with us, although I am told flat out that they won't be able to help us with an endorsement.

The next week Serena and I are off to Washington, D.C. to bring The Energy to the White House. We do indeed meet with Barbara's secretary. Seated in cushioned chairs, we chatter about the future of the country and how our flash cards will help American students compete better with the Japanese. Although George has assured us that The Energy will attract Barbara, that she won't be able to stop herself from coming in to meet us, this does not occur. Later George explains that it doesn't matter because the secretary will transmit The Energy to Barbara, and the effect will be the same. I am beginning to understand that The Energy spreads like a virus.

We tour the White House and then head home on the train victorious. "Yes," we tell The Group, "The meeting was a big success. The Energy was so thick that it looked like the room was filled with fog. Now Barbara will carry it to President Bush!"

We are beside ourselves with excitement, and the following week, when a new piece of legislation passes the Senate, George explains that our trip to D.C. had something to do with it. . . .

After the Barbara Bush trip, Serena schedules many more. We visit several major book chains: WaldenBooks' Connecticut headquarters, Lauriat's Massachusetts offices, Encore Books in Pennsylvania, and Barnes & Noble in Downtown Manhattan.

Invariably, as each meeting concludes, an enthused buyer shakes each of our hands heartily, supplies us with forms to register Flash Enterprises in his company's database, and promises he'll consider it—seriously and soon . . . but we receive zero orders. I complain to George about the lack of sales. He seems to understand the problem fully and explains what I am doing wrong, "Elizabeth, the cards aren't selling because you send a message into the spiritual airwaves that you want to fail. Buyers in other states, even if they have never met you, pick it up, follow your instructions unconsciously, and ignore your product."

Then he adds gently, "Let's see if we can reverse the negative energy coming from you with the positive energy coming from me." With that, he volunteers to call a buyer himself. I bite my nails while he requests (not at all politely) that the secretary put the Barnes & Noble buyer on the phone right away because he has "something very important to tell him." George extols the virtues of our flash cards and throws in a little about The Energy too. I believe that George can do anything, but he doesn't get the sale either. However, he tells me it doesn't matter. The buyer felt The Energy and that will lead to bigger things later.

Meanwhile, Serena schedules meetings with two Canadian book chains, Cole's and W. H. Smith. In February we make an expensive and exhausting week-long trip to Toronto. Before boarding the plane home, Serena telephones her father—a twice daily ritual when we travel. On these calls, she generally prattles about the incredible impact The Energy had on the buyers. And she always asks him to shake his head over the phone, to seal our success with The Energy, and to protect us on the trip home. Afterwards, I *must* take my turn. I dread these conversations. George is always so warm and friendly to his daughter, but toward me, he is cold and stern. Clearly he favors Serena, even though I do everything in my power to please him. I must endure the headshaking as well, although I feel awkward and stupid about this ritual. I hear his body shaking at the other end of the line and the receiver banging against his cheek. Finally, after a few minutes he stops, and I must respond. A part of me feels like an imposter—that I don't mean what I say, I am only telling him what he wants to hear. "Yes, George, I feel waves of lightness; my whole body is alive. Thank you so much."

However, today when Serena calls, and I take my turn, George is in the midst of a rampage. After shaking for me, he switches gears and complains. "Everyone here is holding me back, and I'm sick of waiting for them to wake up. I'm seriously thinking of dropping the whole Group and moving ahead on my own. I can always open a hardware store or something to support myself."

An alarm goes off. How could I ever survive without George? I flounder to placate him, wholeheartedly committed to every word I am about to say, "George, whatever you do and wherever you go, I'll always find a way to be there with you, no matter what. *I love you.*"

"Well, I appreciate that," he mutters, confused.

In the spring, Christopher asks me to sign a petition from a local Teaneck group supporting Ross Perot. I have never heard of Mr. Perot, but soon after, I see him on TV. A straight talker, he informs citizens that they have the right to the *truth* about government spending. A national, political hopeful advertising truth? George is thrilled. Finally, a man who thinks the same—expose the authorities' secrets and empower the masses. George is all for disassembling the unjust system and finding a better way. Isn't that what we are working for in The Group?

George has often explained, "I could never appear on TV because my message is too powerful. Politicians don't want to give up their control. If they found out about The Energy, they would sense the threat and do to me what they did to Jesus Christ. We must build forces behind the scenes and then sneak in through the back door."

Ross Perot has appeared out of nowhere, and soon, George gets his revelation. "I know why Mr. Perot is here. He didn't decide to do this himself, The Energy chose him as our vehicle. Perot is my back door!"

A few months later Perot drops out of the election. Disappointed, about ten of us sit around the following Saturday morning calling him stupid, coward, and jerk. George headshakes for insight that soon comes. "Perot has done the spade work for us by waking up the people. Now it is time for us to step in and carry on. We will run for President!"

On that morning, the ticket of Pozer/Stavos (Carl and Max) is born, and we set about getting ourselves elected to the White House. Delirious ambition passes through like a tornado as we brainstorm. Pauline, currently dating Carl, will be the First Lady. Max, still intent on getting me back, points out that I "really blew it." I could have lived in the White House too, if I hadn't left him. We fax press releases to the Perot headquarters in every states. Serena, the BA in communications, is media crazy. Contacting and rubbing shoulders with celebrities and politicians is her favorite pastime. She adds several major newspapers, and TV and radio stations to our fax list. Our announcement reads, "Perot has withdrawn, but hope is not lost. We know what he was trying to achieve, and we can do it. The ticket of Pozer/Stavos is officially entering the race in his place. We will carry on Perot's mission!"

We fax all afternoon and by Monday receive a few responses. UPI contacts Max and interviews him on the phone. He chatters about truth, people's rights and how we have the answers. Wheels are turning and the train is moving. Necessary buttons and bumper stickers are produced within a week's time.

Max strolls his town's main street introducing himself.

"Hello, I'm Mr. Max Stavos. I'm going to be the next President."

And people respond, "Oh, that's wonderful, president of what?"

"Of the United States of America, of course!" he replies with a grin, reaching out to offer a hearty handshake.

Bewildered, they have no idea what to make of this glowing, confident young man with two shiny, campaign buttons pinned to his chest.

In order to be elected, we must get on the ballot, so Serena calls Trenton to investigate. One evening I return home to find her sitting on the office floor surrounded by xeroxes.

"What's going on?" I ask.

"I called about getting Carl and Max on the ballot. In New York State we need 20,000 signatures and in New Jersey, 5,000. We have a month to get them."

"Oh, Serena," I respond sympathetically, "that's so many; how can we do it?"

My business associate looks as if she would like to pick up a knife and stab me. "What's the matter with you?" she hisses, "Don't you believe in The Energy?"

I shut my mouth.

Meanwhile, Carl notices a black limo with heavily tinted glass parked near his house. The secret service is watching us; we must really be making an impression!

Every minute of free time we scurry to collect those 25,000 signatures. We canvass in malls, grocery stores, and office buildings. One Sunday I take my clipboard to the WillowBrook Mall, about 45 minutes from home. I force myself to approach people, and after two hours I have actually obtained twenty-three signatures. Responses are interesting: "Anyone is better than the man we've got now. I'll sign." and "I would even vote for Batman if he ran!"

Finally, a man asks me what our platform is. Unprepared, I stammer in confusion, "What's a platform?"

"You know, what they stand for. How do they stand on abortion?"

I babble something about changing the system and then flee feeling stupid. In this moment, I realize how ridiculous we are, exuberantly expending our time and energy to promote absolutely nothing.

A week later, the deadline for signatures passes and soon thereafter, Perot returns to the election ballot. Still, George assures us that our efforts were not in vain; they caused Perot's change of heart.

Although he can no longer offer her a bedroom in the White House, Carl has not given up on unifying with Pauline. One day I enter George's city office to discover the two "lovers" sitting on the floor, locked in an intense embrace. "We are going to have a wedding soon; this will be good experience for all," George declares.

I scrutinize their blissful faces and wonder how this is possible. Carl and Pauline never do anything but fight. However, I figure that George must know more than I do. Wedding plans take center stage for the next several weeks. In group sessions, Pauline's face is aglow—the anticipation of a blushing bride. She calls Virginia to inform her family, and wealthy Beatrice offers her Westchester home for the reception. Rings are inspected at local jewelry stores. George drops hints about an "Energy baby" that might result from the union.

When the engaged Pauline abandons their Queens apartment and moves in with Carl, there are changes for Lisa too. She decides to buy a house, something she has been wanting to do for awhile. Although most of her salary goes to George, money given to her by her father covers the down payment. But soon after moving, Lisa has trouble paying the mortgage. She fires up her calculator and concludes that she must cut back on George to make ends meet; there is no other way. George does not take this well and reprimands her. Her financial problems are brought on by defiance to The Energy. Lisa knows her calculator doesn't lie, but to George, calculators have no validity either. The demand to solve this impossible equation creates terrible conflict. At the same time, George offers Lisa a ride home, three times a week, from his Manhattan office. Each day, after they cross the George Washington Bridge and head North on the

Palisades Parkway, he suggests, ever so gently, that Lisa might enjoy giving him oral sex while he drives. After all, he really misses being with her. George has been so generous to honor her with these rides that Lisa feels she can't refuse. Besides, she soon notices that since she has been cooperative, she is no longer selected to be publicly criticized during Group meetings.

About two months after the wedding plans begin, Serena escorts Pauline, the bride to be, to the Paramus Park Mall for wedding gown selection. Caught between two difficult choices, the girls phone George for a consultation. But George, bowling them over, announces he has no more interest in the wedding. In one decisive moment, the dream marriage evaporates into a puff of smoke as George lectures later to Pauline's crestfallen face, "I did this so we could analyze another piece of The Program. You didn't think we were really going to go through with it, did you?"

Pauline struggles for a couple of days with disappointment, but then she lets go and forgets all about it.

Back at the office, I decide to expand from three science titles of flash cards to fifteen, covering most basic high school courses. I name the series *Exambusters Study Cards*, geared for standardized test preparation (SAT, GED, MCAT, etc.) The next several months are filled with activity. I author most of the science and math titles myself, often entering data into my laptop well beyond midnight. Other Group members volunteer for some of the remaining subjects: Carl writes English Vocabulary; Pauline, American History; Beatrice, World History; Lisa, French; and Christopher, both Algebra 2/Trig. and Physics. Serena is unable to write a title of her own; she was never a good enough student. I hire independent teachers for the remaining subjects of Japanese, Spanish, etc. The project's costs begin to mount rapidly, but caught up in the euphoria of my creation, I keep writing checks. Everything *feels* so right; I *know* it will all work out. New packaging is also under construction. George's son, Christopher, has just graduated from college with a computer graphics major. According to his father, Chris is the best artist in the county and the perfect, no, the only person to coordinate the package design project. It turns out that Christopher isn't as skilled as he claims, yet he bills me by the hour while he figures out his computer programs, on top of the work he is supposedly doing. His invoices begin reaching into the multi-thousands, and I feel I am being raped. However, I can't confront him; he always has an airtight alibi. Any mild complaints I do manage are met with vicious reproach.

Replacing him with a more competent outsider would be treason against what has become the entire Group's mission. His sister, Serena, is having an all-expense-paid adventure into the publishing world, but where are all of those sales she promised so confidently as her end of the bargain? They are "just around the corner" and according to her father, they would have happened sooner, if I hadn't been holding back the operation because I "wanted to fail." In addition, I still pay George more than $800 per week. Almost every day I find myself writing a check to another Sharkman: George, Serena, Christopher, Serena, George, Christopher, George, Serena . . . *Why must I give all my money to the Sharkmans?* a voice cries inside my head. It feels as if George and his two offspring have each inserted an intravenous tube into my veins and are slowly draining all of my blood. I hate this, but I honestly, for the life of me, haven't a clue as to how to extricate myself. Help me please; someone, help!

These days, Serena is in her element. She has just completed her first book, *The Chronicles in Shadow: Volume I*—a science fiction fantasy novel based on her experiences playing *Dungeons and Dragons* in college. The story is juvenile and poorly written, but she invests $3,000 to hire a local artist to create the book's cover. Her cover is superior to many in the Barnes & Noble science fiction section, and Serena pictures a bright future. With her creation, my flash cards, and books the other group members are working on, she envisions a prosperous publishing company about to be born. As protection from potential lawsuits, she reasons we should incorporate. "We'll do the same with both businesses," she decides. An appointment with Alan Brown, the Sharkman family lawyer, is set. I hesitate. I don't understand why this is necessary. However, Serena presses on with her father cheering behind.

"You have to step out and make a commitment," George explains.

The legal document signing day arrives, and before our scheduled meeting, I tremble on George's couch with severe anxiety. George, disgusted with me, reasserts, "You just want to fail like always." I am no match for him. Within the hour I obediently report to the lawyer's office with Serena at my side. We select the name Flash Blasters, Inc. for the publishing business. With products inspired by The Group, we are going to "blast through conventional lies and teach the world a new way to live."

Receding from internal conflict, my brain is sluggish, as if I have been drugged. Unable to think clearly, I must allow Serena to answer the lawyer's questions for me.

Mr. Brown asks, "Who will be the vice president?"

Serena replies, "I will."

"Who will be president?"

"Elizabeth will."

"How will the shares be divided?"

"Half for Elizabeth and half for me."

My muddled thoughts extend gratitude toward Serena for her generosity in awarding me the presidency instead of claiming it for herself. . . . As we exit lawyer Brown's office, my new, official partner's eyes sparkle as she declares, "Now that we legally own both businesses together, you don't have to pay me a salary. The profit will be split in half. We'll build up the photography business really big and then sell it. When we do, you'll get back the money (about $66,000) you paid to start it up."

My partner has promised me my fair share sometime in the future; I can't argue with her logic.

January to December 1993

Although he has lost the election, Perot's supporters have not given up, and United We Stand America—UWSA, forms chapters in each state. The grassroots citizens' group plans to work first at influencing local government, and then to reach toward state and federal officials. It is mid-December when Christopher receives a call from the Bergen County chapter. Anyone who is interested is welcome to attend an organizational meeting at the Bergenfield bowling alley, on the coming Friday night. George is excited and sends his daughter to check it out. A new mission in a larger playing field? Exactly what we've been waiting for!

Serena throws herself in aggressively, and she manages to grab the position of temporary Bergen County Coordinator. She organizes monthly meetings at the Riverside Square Mall in Hackensack. With Serena in charge, the rest of us rush to become members, and soon all of us attend every meeting. The first month is filled with activity. We form an active telephone tree; numerous committees are created, and Christopher databases the names of the few hundred county members. The Texas UWSA headquarters instructs us to conduct an official election for county officers. As luck would have it, no one runs against Serena, so she wins the official title of County Coordinator by default. We divide Bergen County into seven regions, each region containing ten towns. Directly under Serena, I volunteer as regional coordinator. Nora, Pauline, Carl, and Christopher serve under me as town coordinators. Beatrice, my mother, and Bess, New York residents, join the UWSA New York State chapter.

One Saturday, Lisa brings her visiting parents to The Group. For a few hours they sit at the back of George's den looking uncomfortable. Out to dinner that evening, Lisa's mother, with some measure of distress, speaks out, "I don't like what's going on in there, even though I don't fully understand it."

Her father rushes to his daughter's defense, "Come on, Lisa wouldn't do anything stupid."

Lisa stops dead, her fork, full of food, frozen in midair. She wonders, *Would I?*

In the past ten years with George, she has spent more than $100,000. *What have I gained from my investment?* she asks herself for the very first time.

The following Monday Lisa makes a life-changing decision. Instead of participating in The Group, she forces herself to observe. Always unhappy about the outrageous costs and the constant fighting, she begins to analyze what is really going on in this incestuous clique. Lisa decides to acknowledge the contradictions that she had previously dismissed: The day George criticized her for taking her cat to the vet, explaining that the cat needed only The Energy to protect him from disease. Then, as fate would have it, a few moments later Christopher had entered the den from the adjoining kitchen and asked where the cat carrier was; he was late for an appointment to take the Sharkman's cat, B.J., to the vet. Also, there is the health insurance George forbids us to purchase while his entire family is covered by Blue Cross.

Over the next several weeks, Lisa comes to realize how terrified she is of George, and she figures out that he has set this up on purpose to control her. She asks herself controversial questions such as, *What if The Energy doesn't really exist? Is there another explanation for the phenomena in this room, the auras we all see and the jolting bodies?* She observes him towering over me, Bess, or Laura, glaring and strong-arming. The failure of the Pozer/Stavos presidential election ticket, the lack of revenue from her New Life Design business, the misery she feels competing with Pauline and Bess to spend the most hours with George or to be the one he will choose to have sex with today. Lisa begins to realize her life is far from the paradise George promised.

As Lisa detaches, the big picture begins to emerge—a group of fifteen naive fools creating fantasies and then spending thousands of dollars to make those lies come true, and they never do. Now, she doesn't want to participate in the circus anymore, and silently, she begins withdrawing. Strangely, no one even notices that she has changed. Of everyone, I should be aware; during college we were inseparable. Yet dedication to The Group superseded our friendship years ago. Besides, I am knee deep in my own conflict.

Determined to escape the maze, it takes Lisa eight months to disconnect the ten years of wiring that bind her to her only semblance of family and her reason for getting up in the morning. When she finally feels ready, Lisa announces her departure. Like an unexpected death, I experience shock. She is one of us—a member of the team; how can she just walk out? We are in this for life; there is nowhere else to go. George is determined to change Lisa's mind and instructs us, her comrades, to knock on her door and wake her up. For the next two weeks, visitors arrive at her home each evening after work. Lisa doesn't like it, but she lets us in because she feels that if she truly believes in her newfound principles, she ought to stand up for them. We lecture passionately about her commitment to New Life Design and its potential profit. We refer to the French flash cards she had just written and the millions of copies that will soon sell worldwide.

At my assigned meeting, I sit stunned as Lisa patiently explains her position. As if she is speaking a foreign language, my brain cannot make sense of the sounds coming from her lips. I cry out to her, trying to bridge the impossible gap with fervent reminders of The Energy, but I am helpless to create a light powerful enough to find her in this thick fog—to lead her back where she belongs. Finally, she shares her hope that we can still be friends. But I counter, "No, that will be impossible if you leave The Group."

She looks genuinely disappointed; I don't know why I've cut her out, but it must be so.

Pauline and Bess, visiting together an evening later, remind her with intimate intensity, "You know you can't trust anyone out there. We are your only friends. Without us you will be alone forever."

They reference her years of investment to master an exclusive receptiveness to The Energy, and then she floors them, "I don't believe in The Energy anymore."

What? How could this be? She has become possessed by the dead world; she is beyond reach. We don't understand how this has happened, but we realize that we must let her go. We only know one thing for sure, her future is doomed. . . .

A week goes by and George, unable to accept defeat, invites her to his office one more time. Lisa agrees; she feels strong. After all, she has survived our tirades—threats of certain destruction from those she believed to be friends. She will find the strength to handle George. When Lisa arrives at his office, she observes that he has cleared everyone else out. This is not normal for a noon meeting when there are generally about five people. He greets her with a friendly, relaxed smile and asks how she is. She says, "Fine," and sits. Benignly, he attempts to coax an admission that she misses us and has made a mistake. Politely, Lisa affirms that her decision is final. His opening attempt frustrated, George climbs on his soap box to extol the virtues of The Energy. How could she be so stupid to throw it away? Still, Lisa maintains her position. Thwarted again, and accustomed to getting his way, George's eyes fill with demonic rage. "If you don't come back, your life will be worthless. You will fail at everything you attempt. Without The Energy, you will die impoverished, friendless, and soon."

Lisa is outraged. The veil has lifted from her eyes, and reality rushes in all too explicitly. George is banking on the fact that she still believes these outrageous fabrications and can terrify her into returning to the fold. Until today, she has lived in a world where lies prevail over logic, where free choice, critical thinking, and objective reasoning are consistently short-circuited by George's strategic phobia indoctrination. She loathes him for this cruel manipulation—exploitation of the fears he has methodically implanted and fertilized in her mind—his invisible weapons against her. Nonetheless, on the surface Lisa maintains her composure. She permits him to play out his routine and when the hour is complete, calmly hands him a final $40 check, shakes his hand and states that she still cares about everyone, but she isn't coming back. She exits the office where she has spent thousands of dollars for "therapy" and hundreds of hours competing with her "friends" for the honor of pleasing George. She reflects wistfully upon the years of precious time she has wasted ingesting George's fanatical warnings of certain doom, guaranteed for those who refuse to follow The Energy—lies she has only just erased from her mind after ten years of blind submission. She closes the door softly behind her and emerges, a free woman, into the spring sunlight of 71st Street between Park and Lexington Avenues.

A few weeks after Lisa's exit, Serena and I drive up to the WaldenBooks headquarters for a third time. We meet with yet another buyer who promises to place that opening order we seek so desperately. The scene following our "successful meetings" has always been the same. We return to George's den exuberant, reporting the buyer's enthusiasm over our *Exambusters Study Cards*, and the huge orders they have promised, which inevitably never arrive. On this day, as usual, we rush home quickly to replay this drama. However, when we enter, we discover George, Christopher, Beatrice, and Pauline drowning in a cloud of gloom. George tells us why, and there is fear in his eyes. "About an hour ago I went upstairs for a moment when I heard a cry and a thud. Ben fell; his back legs collapsed under him."

We notice the black Labrador lying on the floor, breathing heavily and in obvious distress. Serena and I shift from elation to soberness while George instructs us to gather around and lay our hands on the dog. We touch him gently while George holds Ben's head in his lap and begins headshaking. The thought that he is dying runs through our terrified minds, but George senses our thoughts and commands us to eliminate all negativity, to force ourselves into a positive place *immediately*. The gentle caress of our voices and hands over the next fifteen minutes does nothing to encourage Ben to stand up and walk. Aware that we are failing, George changes to a stern tone, commanding Ben to stop "playing bullshit games" and come back to life. Ben just groans. As other Group members visit that day, it is explained that Ben can't walk because he is holding back The Energy in his body. We must focus on him to release the blockage. After all, Ben is the most intelligent dog on the planet because he has been saturated with George's Energy for the last twelve years. He is a special part of our mission.

At the office later that afternoon, my mind returns to business concerns. *How can we get some real flash card orders?* The ringing phone interrupts my pondering. A man is calling from an independent publishers' group, and he invites us to participate in the June 1993, American Book Association trade show. It will take place in Miami, Florida. Desperate for exposure, I decide to take a booth, even though the $1,600 cost is unaffordable.

During that five-day trade show Serena debuts some innovative marketing, a sure-fire strategy to claw ourselves into significance. This consists of approaching celebrities (visiting authors signing their recently published books) and handing them a "gift"—a box of our flash cards. It happens that Oprah Winfrey is a guest, having just completed a book, and she is roaming the convention center floor, taking Polaroids with eager fans. Serena poses for a picture and then slips her a box of *Spanish in a Flash*; Oprah thanks her politely. Later that day, Serena accosts the body guard of Great Britain's former Prime Minister Margaret Thatcher while she is being escorted into an author signing for her recent book. The guard, slightly miffed, nevertheless receives a box of *Physics in a Flash*. That night on the phone, George praises his daughter's courage. When I take my turn with him I ask timidly, "George, I don't understand;

isn't it rude to push the product on these people? They don't seem to want it."

Ever patient, he explains, "No, we must do this. People are dead, and it is up to us to force The Energy down their throats like medicine. Otherwise, they will never have a chance of coming alive."

I still don't like it, but as usual, I remind myself that he must know something I don't. Feeling awkward and obnoxious, I am compelled to follow Serena's lead. The following day I join the line to receive an autographed copy of actor Leslie Nielsen's recently published book. When it is my turn, I present him with a box of *French in a Flash*. He looks bewildered but accepts it and thanks me. All told, the Miami trade show costs me over $4,000, but we only write about $300 in sales.

Impossibly dedicated to creating the future success of the flash cards, I am beginning to feel like a gerbil on a wheel. While Serena spends every Sunday shaking with her father, I usually collapse on the couch for most of the afternoon, exhausted from the workweek and breathing problems that keep me up most nights. Since I moved in with Serena, my symptoms have worsened dramatically. Brain fog surrounds me like a cloud, and I pass through each day as if walking in a dream. My period stops completely, and I have trouble eating. Although my stomach tightens with hunger, my thoughts deny that I need nourishment. *Food can come later; just keep working; you **must** make the flash cards succeed; they are the key to your future.* Instead, I drink another cup of coffee; I'm up to eight cups a day. George claims that we really shouldn't have to eat or sleep anyway. "The molecules in our bodies came from stars. We are made of stars, and stars are made of energy. Well, people, energy doesn't need to eat and sleep and neither should we. If we weren't so hooked to our crazy training, our bodies would make their own food, just like the sun. I hardly sleep at all anymore, maybe an hour a night. I can go without food for a long, long time without any problems. Once you break The Program, everything changes."

I eat one meal a day, usually late at night; I never seem to be able to find the time until then; working and attending George's groups are too much of a pressing priority. Between the cost of George's therapy and the never-ceasing expenses to get the flash cards off the ground, my inheritance is quickly dwindling. At this rate, I fear I will soon have nothing left to pay for food and shelter. I know I could not trust my mother to take me in if I became destitute, and anyway, that is the last place I want to be. The Group would blame *me* if I fell apart. After all, The Energy brings only good things to those who are faithful. I dread the thought of ever asking them for help, but in the other half of my mind, I cling to the sense of family brought about by our constant group activities. I am sure that somewhere deep down, they must care about and value me. After all, look at how much I have given them! Nevertheless, visions of pennilessness plague me. I cannot alter the negative direction my life has taken, no matter how hard I try, and I do try, but I don't know how much longer I can swim upstream. In a jungle where Sharkman is the lion king, every day, every hour, has become purely a matter of survival.

UWSA has become our total focus in The Group, and in June, Serena suggests that I join the "Say No to NAFTA" committee. A couple of times a month I drive down to the Edison, New Jersey UWSA headquarters to meet with other members of this statewide team. Our goal is to educate our New Jersey politicians about the bill. Once enlightened, we're sure they will vote against it.

I decide to organize a group meeting with our local representative, Marge Roukema, and on Friday evening, July 16, 1993, about fifty members attend at the Ridgefield Community Center. For over an hour, UWSA members passionately describe the potential evils of NAFTA. At the end of the meeting, as pictures are snapped with Marge and the meeting's coordinators, George approaches her. Gently placing his hand on her back, he bends down to softly whisper in her ear, "Don't forget that we depend on you to bring the truth to the rest of the government." As he speaks, he shakes his head ever so slightly to get The Energy into her.

The following day, Saturday, July 17, will prove even more exhilarating—a day of victory for George's group. Governor Jim Florio is coming up for reelection in November, and UWSA members appear to be a viable source of future votes. Therefore, Serena has been able to convince Florio's office to agree to a meeting with the Bergen County UWSA officers. In fact, the big event is scheduled to take place in George's dining room and adjoining living room at 1:00 P.M. today! We powwow early in the morning, in awe of what is about to happen, and George delivers the pep talk, "People, this is what we have been working toward, to capture the ear of a politician who can influence many people, to give him the experience, and maybe even an understanding of The Energy."

Between noon and 12:30, the rest of the UWSA members begin to arrive. I greet them, with my camera, in front of George's house. When most are safely inside, a white Mercedes appears at the end of the block. I recognize the driver, Judy Carlone, the Bergenfield town coordinator. I have spoken with her on the phone many times because, as regional coordinator in the UWSA hierarchy, she answers to me. Judy passes the house and parks. Locking her car, she strides toward me with a confident grin and greets me with a kiss on the cheek. I immediately wonder why she is acting so friendly, I barely know her, and then I figure it out. . . . *She's Italian; they are naturally warm!*

Secret service arrives next, and at 12:45, Florio's black limo finally appears. George's tiny living room is crowded with twenty eager UWSA members seated on folding chairs. They face the dining room where Serena, Christopher, George, and I have commandeered seats next to the governor's spot. Max Stavos is positioned on George's stairs at the back of the living room with a video camera, anxious to record this momentous event on film. Florio's primary agenda is to encourage us to vote for him. Therefore, his speech recounts many positive things he has done for New Jersey. He remains standing and delivers an energetic address, gripping the back of one of George's dining room chairs. Ten minutes into the meeting, George, seated directly in front of him, begins to shake his head slowly. Florio doesn't know what to make of this. He is clearly more than a little uncomfortable. Pretending to ignore George, who is now picking up speed, he continues his speech. Two secret service agents observe suspiciously, their hands unconsciously moving toward their concealed weapons. In contrast, to us this is all perfectly normal. Then Bess raises her hand and opens the door for George. Florio calls on her. She suggests gently, yet with subtle condescension, "Governor, you appear tense. We are all equals here. Why don't you sit down on the same level as the rest of us?"

George speaks up immediately, supporting Bess and edifying Jim Florio. "You see, Governor, the way society is set up, it enforces a program that demands politicians to stand above us like the authority, while the citizens view themselves as powerless children. Wouldn't it be better if we all cooperated instead?"

Florio appears flustered and I pity him. I sense that he is not accustomed to being challenged about his personal habits and private intentions. He yields, embarrassed under our pressure, seating himself hesitantly. The meeting lasts about half an hour. As the governor is leaving, we present him with a box of Group gifts. They include: copies of Serena's and George's books, a box of *Physics in a Flash*, Bess's demo cassette of her songs, and brochures advertising Christopher's computer design and Max's offset printing. Perhaps we can turn Governor Florio into a customer!

After the meeting, George reviews the day and Bess receives accolades for telling Florio *The Truth*. I envy her for that, and for another, more ancient issue—that she has managed to fill the role of George's mistress where I failed. Amidst the conflict-ridden relationship I have had with him an old familiar voice, dating back to our first meetings in Dr. Rogers' office, still emerges frequently, often when I am alone driving my car. It insists that George should really be mine. It is only a matter of time until I figure out how to get him; I simply haven't tried hard enough. Sometimes I argue that I despise George and how he treats me, but the voice's will is stubborn and won't release me from its so far impossible demands. Other times I brainstorm, trying to cook up a strategy to satisfy my unrequited longing. There is still a large part of me that is totally fascinated with our leader, a part that believes that I, above all others, deserve to win the most advanced man on the planet for my own. Shaking myself out of my introspection, I catch the tail end of George's speech as he proclaims, "Now Florio will win the election because he has listened to us and The Energy is inside him."

Governor Florio & Elizabeth

About ten days later, gubernatorial candidate Christie Whitman makes her own journey to George's home to introduce her platform to the same group of UWSA members. The meeting is quick and uneventful. Whitman stands off in a corner, speaks and departs. There is no interaction with her audience, and George does not shake his head.

In November, Florio loses the election to Christie Whitman.

In the months to come, the NAFTA committee meets with Rep. Robert Torricelli in his Hackensack office. Additionally, New Jersey Senators Bill Bradley and Frank Lautenberg receive our small but dedicated group in their respective Newark offices. At the conclusion of the latter visit, I offer to organize a statewide UWSA members' meeting featuring Lautenberg as guest speaker. The meeting is to be structured as a question and answer session with the senator, and a mediator is required to select questions and control the audience's behavior. The obvious choice, in my opinion, is George. However, during the next couple of weeks there is terrible unrest among the non-Group UWSA members. Apparently, they *absolutely* reject George as mediator and I can't understand why. They are hostile but won't give a specific reason. Serena attempts to make peace and it is finally revealed that after the headshaking at the Florio meeting, they fear a repeat performance in front of Senator Lautenberg. George takes their reaction as a high compliment, "This just proves how advanced we are; all of those people are afraid of The Energy."

Serena assures the members that her father will comply, so they give in. On November 4, 1993 about three hundred UWSA members from various parts of New Jersey fill the Ridgefield Community Center to capacity. George serves as mediator and keeps his head still.

My name is Judith Carlone. A native of Hoboken, New Jersey, I was raised in a middle class, Italian-American neighborhood. I am forty-four years old, married with no children, and loving of all animals. My indoctrination into Catholicism was the foundation of my spirituality. I discovered at a very young age that we have little control over navigating our lives, and that it is our personal relationship with God that lights our way, not the repetitive rituals of religion. I love the Church; its silent atmosphere always helped me to get in touch with myself. I can still remember the first time I felt the Holy Spirit. It happened one day after Sunday School when I was seven. I sat quietly in a back pew. To me, this was the best seat in the house, especially after mass. I watched the many rows of bright, red, flickering candles, eagerly delivering the prayers that brought them to life. The sun penetrated its rays through huge, stained glass windows, illuminating the altar with vibrant color, while faint clouds of frankincense hovered in the air. Enchanted by this visual feast, I asked God to help me remember the new prayers I had just learned in catechism class. The nuns were tough and demanding. They instilled fear in me that created performance anxiety, and I needed help.

As I gazed at the giant crucifix suspended above the altar, I suddenly felt an internal lift. Something invisible had entered my body and was pulling me upward, filling me with a sensation of love and peace. In that moment, I knew God truly existed. He let me know He was with me, and that with Him, I could do anything. The feeling was fragile and left quickly. He added something to me that day, something special. I'll always be thankful for that experience, and the memory of it.

I am involved in the real estate and insurance business and run a small agency in my town. Politics always seemed corrupt to me; I never had any interest and never voted. However, all of that changed in 1992 after seeing Ross Perot on TV. His approach to "exposing the truth" sparked my interest. He uncovered the buried love I had for my country and gave me hope that the United States could heal its immorality and become a better place to live. I was so impressed that I registered to vote and joined the local chapter of his grassroots movement, United We Stand America. This is where I first met Elizabeth.

The week following the Lautenberg meeting, Ross Perot debates Vice President Al Gore on The Larry King Show. Judy Carlone invites about ten of us to her house to watch on her big screen TV. I arrive earlier than the rest and she invites me to sit at her kitchen table while she prepares snacks. When she finishes, she seats herself opposite me. There is intensity in her eyes as she focuses on mine and commences to make some painfully direct observations about my personality and behavior.

I have always been perceptive about people. Even though I don't know Elizabeth very well, for some reason, I can't hold back sharing my opinions. I feel driven to break the ice and ask her permission to be frank.

"Would you mind if I tell you something personal?"

Elizabeth nods OK and I continue, "I think I know what your problem is; you are a little girl and not a woman; you are looking for a parent, someone to take care of you; you perform to get approval from others; you look to the outside for validation because you don't know who you are. No, I don't think you have an identity."

I don't know why, but although I hate what she's saying and don't want it to be true, I listen with an open mind. I do not defend or make excuses. Pausing for a moment, she catches herself, apologizing, "You know, I am getting very personal and I have only just met you. I hope I'm not offending you."

"No. If you are telling me the truth, then I want to hear it. So please continue."

Judy is direct. I am fascinated by this above all else. Because honesty seems to be her priority, not fashioning statements to avoid people disliking her, I trust her and value her opinions. For the remainder of the evening I am constantly aware of her presence. In fact, to me she is the only person in the room. However, soon after I leave her house, her comments slip from my mind. . . .

Late in November, our UWSA chapter stages a walk-a-thon to raise money. Serena, Nora, Pauline, Judy, and I organize the event, scheduled to take place at a local park. On the big day, about thirty members show up ready to walk for the cause, but I can only think of one thing, where is Judy? Finally she arrives. It's strange; I know so little about her, and yet, just the sight of her makes me feel warm and safe. So at the conclusion of the event, I linger behind. Hesitating like a school girl waiting for the right moment to approach an idolized teacher, I work my way over to her. I want something from her very badly but I don't know what, and I don't know why. . . . I invite her to lunch and she agrees. We jump into her car and head for Kenny Rogers Roasters in Englewood. At the table, over plates filled with chicken, mashed potatoes, and string beans, we happen to look up simultaneously. For a moment our gazes lock with intensity. It is as if she possesses some special knowledge that I must gain at all cost. A little while later, when she drops me off at my car, I don't want to break the connection between us.

I notice from the very beginning that there is something special about Elizabeth. She seems sweet and gentle and has a higher intelligence that attracts me. Although passionate about everything she does, sometimes I catch her wandering aimlessly, looking lost, lonely, and empty. In these moments, I experience an empathy so profound that tears fill my eyes, and my heart swells with sorrow. I see that she is full of conflict, and I also see the lighthearted, optimistic personality she has created to hide her pain. I wonder why I have these deep feelings and struggle for answers. At UWSA gatherings I find myself distracted by her. I admire her; she is smart and it shows. Her business partner, Serena, does not appear as well educated or refined. Her vocabulary is limited and she uses crude slang to express herself. As if we are internally connected, I know what Elizabeth feels and how she thinks. I am in awe of the magnetic force that seems to be pulling us together. Our involvement in the Perot group becomes the foundation for our friendship. With few answers, I am compelled to move forward.

We often have our core group meetings at Elizabeth's photography studio in Closter. As I get to know some of the other members, I notice that several have a personal connection to Elizabeth and Serena. A table in the studio is filled with business cards bearing their names. Their perception of politics and the world is unusual, and their opinions are identical. They appear normal, but when I talk with any of them, they gaze back blankly. It is an empty, penetrating focus that reminds me of the characters in the movie, Children of the Damned.

One day, Elizabeth mentions that she and Serena both attend a stress reduction group held at the home of Serena's father, George Sharkman. When I ask them to describe it, they say it's impossible. What happens in their meetings is unique—beyond words; I have to experience it myself to understand. With their vague answers, I sense they are hiding something as spooky as their glassy-eyed stares. I worry about what I might be getting into, and what Elizabeth is already a part of. Why are all of these people so weird? Why are they all together in this political group, and why do they all attend these stress sessions? I feel sandpaper and sense an unholy hidden agenda.

About ten days after the walk-a-thon, twenty of the county's core members gather in Serena's and my Closter den to watch the fast track vote for NAFTA on TV. We have gained publicity from our Lautenberg meeting, and Channel 7 visits to film our active citizens' group's reactions to what will take place tonight. Despite the application of our best efforts, NAFTA passes anyway. The following week it reaches Serena's ears that various members who had visited our den that night suspected we were devil worshipers. They sense something creepy and have become afraid of us. Serena laughs it off, blaming the Halloween decorations and trinkets she still has lying around the house from last month's holiday. . . .

Once a month we have county meetings in a large public facility in order to accommodate the hundred or so supporters of our cause. All of the members gather to hear the latest news and the town coordinators get their instructions. At one particular meeting I notice a man in the back of the room shaking his head back and forth continuously. Initially, I react in fear. When this passes, I conclude that he has some sort of medical condition, so I avoid looking at him altogether. Later I find out that this man is Serena's father, George Sharkman, the leader of the so often mentioned stress reduction group. This guy is weird. Why is he shaking his head? I begin to ask questions, but the only information I can gain is that his strange behavior has something to do with energy. I wonder, Is there really stress reduction going on or is this some kind of evil cult? The more I participate in UWSA, the more I try to figure out this other group. Serena appoints each of her zombie friends to various positions; they have become her administration. As the months pass, we try to get organized, but the core group begins to divide. There is an evil energy exuding from Serena's group, and the rest of us resent their controlling attitude and strange behavior. We sense their will to insert a hidden agenda, and this becomes the thorn in the side of the Bergen County chapter of UWSA. Elizabeth, however, is different. She follows but I sense she doesn't truly believe. I feel comfortable in her presence. So what is she doing with these dark people?

From observing Elizabeth's interactions with her friends, it doesn't take me long to conclude that many of the people in her circle have abused her. Serena and some of the others are bossy and parental. They belittle her frequently. I also begin to realize that Elizabeth is doing most of the work in their photography and publishing businesses, and yet, I discover, splitting the profits in half with Serena. What is wrong with this picture? An alarm goes off in my head. This woman works perpetually. She never takes a vacation and never has a boyfriend that will stay. She is chronically fatigued and dangerously asthmatic. She endures periods of depression where self-hatred makes it almost impossible for her to function. Underweight from poor eating habits and enduring incredible stress, I wonder how she finds the fuel to make it through each day. Yet at other times, she is more alive and loving than almost anyone I know. She is not like the rest; she does not belong there. I fear grave consequences unless she can reclaim herself soon. I decide to pay closer attention to Elizabeth's behavior, and I begin to connect the dots. At thirty-three, she is emotionally and socially undeveloped. Elizabeth tells me that she has been on a shrink's couch since the age of eight. She was raised to believe that she must consult an outside professional before making any personal decisions. Her mother gave her neither love nor affection; she was only nasty and critical. With no other family, Elizabeth was a lonely child, starving for human contact. I sense how incomplete she is. Sometimes she recedes, becomes childlike and stares at me like a little girl, desperate to be held—to be protected. As the weeks pass I feel her clinging to me emotionally, tighter and tighter, and I become aware of my own compelling desire to take care of her. Something incredibly powerful is pulling me to fill her needs, to support her, to be the family she never had, and to create a safe place for her. So I do, and soon discover that I have become her anchor, the doorway to her truth and the only opening she has to escape.

One winter evening, on her way into the Thursday night group, my mother slips on some ice in George's driveway. He hasn't put enough salt down, and in addition, the path is poorly lit. When she enters the room, Rachael tells George about the fall and suggests he add more salt right away—others are still arriving. He shoots her an annoyed look and I read his thoughts, *Don't blame me because you didn't pay attention to your feet. Thanks for criticizing me about how I keep my house. . . . I might get around to it later if I feel like it.* To her, he responds impatiently, "Go past it. You didn't really hurt yourself."

About ten minutes later, Rachael's face turns pale. Scared and small, she calls out weakly, "George I don't feel very well."

Then, her eyes roll back in their sockets, out of sight. As if jettisoned across the room, in an instant, George lands at her feet, grabs her arms and yells, "Rachael, don't leave us. Come back. Don't give in to the game."

A single phrase flashes through my mind. *She's dying.* My face turns ashen, and I cry out spontaneously, "No!"

In that moment, years of dissension fly out the window, and I realize that I have feelings for my mother. I am stricken with horror while the rest simply stare vacantly—like mannequins in a department store window. Tears form. But mercifully, in about a minute, Rachael comes back. The rest of The Group, including myself, praise George for "saving her life."

The following morning, George informs me that he did not approve of my emotional outburst last night, nor do the others in The Group. My heart twists from the blow, but my mind doubts, and attempts to go along with his thinking, *What did I do wrong? Did I let my weaker side take over instead of focusing on The Energy and trusting in George's abilities to save her?* Message delivered, George feels free to change the subject.

My mother soon complains of intense pain. "I'm afraid I've broken something in my arm," she tells George, seeking his advice.

"You're inventing a story, Rachael," he insists. "You didn't hurt yourself. Just leave it alone and stop using it as a distraction."

However, the pain persists, and three months later, my mother finally has an X-ray. The results show she has indeed broken her wrist. Furthermore, because she neglected it, her wrist has healed crooked and is now permanently deformed. The next day she informs George that he was wrong about her injury. "I did break my wrist that night, and you told me not to see a doctor. Now my bone has set in the wrong position."

"I was just giving you my opinion," he counters immediately, "You didn't have to listen to me. Your life is *your* responsibility. There will be no finger-pointing in this room. Just remember, every time you point a finger at me, there are *three* that point back at you!"

It seems unthinkable that I have reached the point where I don't rise up to defend my mother. The oppression has grown so overwhelming that I find myself trapped in a dark cave, incapable of feeling anything at all. My superficial personality is exuberant, nervous and giddy—a failed hype to force some kind of emotion. I wouldn't dare to even consider confronting George. Years of reconstructing our thinking and instilling fear have produced a protective shield around him, a thick wall of thorns that would shred me, should I ever attempt a challenge. Deep down I suffer from George's injustice to my mother, a person who followed his arbitrary instruction, advice that resulted in lasting damage to the only body God gave her. But my feelings are securely chained. George's bullying has rendered me an emotional rag doll.

In March, I attend a Long Island educational trade show on behalf of Flash Blasters Inc. After I have finished my business, I think of calling Judy G., my mother's old friend. I have not seen her in more than ten years, not since she and her two daughters, Karen and Jeannie, quit coming to The Group at our apartment in the mid-Eighties. While I was growing up, they had practically been members of the family, and I miss them. Judy answers the phone, and several minutes later, I arrive at her doorstep in Valley Stream. In the past several years, Karen, now twenty-five, has been married and separated. She has two children, Jack, age four, and Lulu, age three. Jeannie's daughter Crystal, an infant when I last saw her, is now in junior high school. Judy wants us to get together. We schedule a date for a Saturday the following month. I offer to make portraits of Karen and her children at my studio, so we decide to meet in New Jersey. I plan the day. Judy and her family will come to George's house in the morning. After that, we will go for lunch, and finally, to my studio. Judy finds this plan unusual. She wants to visit with me and my mother, not go to a therapy session with George. Unfortunately for her, I have taken control, and Judy is too polite to oppose me.

At noon on the scheduled day, her family of six arrives. With ten of the regular group members already crowded into George's den, many of us move onto the floor to open up seating for the guests. George is excited. Perhaps they will want to return to him. He fills them in on some of the important "new information" we are working on today. "You know, ladies, just this morning we were all brainstorming and came up with something incredible. You see a lot of hostility and fighting in this world. Well, *WE* just figured out why. Everybody's gonna die someday and they know it. Right? Well no matter who or where, *EVERYBODY* is *always* aware of this, and they are terrified. After all, what's the point of living, if it all ends up six feet under? People are angry because they can't do anything to change their impending demise, so they fill their lives with distractions to divert them from the terrible truth. Starting a fight is a great way to forget you're dying. Now if you want to change, you must realize there's a better way; we are discovering it here, in this room. Then you admit your hostility."

My mother cuts in, "George, I really have trouble with this one. I don't always feel hostile."

"Oh you better believe that you do!!! You're just insensitive to what's going on inside of you; but then again, what else is new!?" He sneers with authoritative sarcasm.

"Well, all right," she capitulates without hesitation, "on Monday at the office I'm certainly going to examine all of my conversations and look for that hostility. Actually, I know what you mean. People are all so phony and polite, but their friendliness is only social. If you don't give them what they want, you know, compliment them on their looks or praise their cooking, they'll turn on you in two seconds. All relationships are sort of . . . conditional."

In the next moment, Karen unexpectedly bursts into tears. "I am so sorry I ever left. I feel like I have finally come home," she sobs, apparently profoundly moved by what she is experiencing.

The rest of her family, however, do not share her feelings. Quite the opposite. Jeannie and her daughter, Crystal, find George to be nonsensical; they struggle to stifle impulses to laugh out loud. The three-year-old, Lulu, screams relentlessly in an agonized temper tantrum, as if the den's atmosphere is intolerable. Her brother, Jack, squirming perpetually, finally walks up to George and informs him, "I don't like you."

After that day, Karen rejoins The Group. She makes the hour and a half journey from Long Beach, Long Island, twice a week. She brings her children, who continue to despise sessions with George. As if no time has passed since her previous visits with him fifteen years ago, she automatically seems to catch on. George is thrilled and gives her special treatment. The model student, she is the example that we, his perpetually inadequate pupils, must follow. The others seem willing to accept that Karen is superior, that they are ungrateful under-performers in

George's squadron, barely worthy to even sit in his presence. But I can't. Sensing this, George becomes enraged, attempting, but not succeeding, to verbally beat me into submission. Lately, our relationship is becoming more and more estranged. . . .

When *The Celestine Prophecy* hits the bestseller list, George selects it as our new bible. Daily, we take turns reading aloud. All of us own a well-underlined copy and promote it energetically to anyone with whom we make contact. Encouraged by the success of this spiritual book, George decides to republish his own book, *Biofeedback and Beyond*, and with it, an audio tape entitled *Stress Release*. Publishing replaces shoplifting as The Group's favored activity, and Serena, the author, officially debuts her *Chronicles in Shadow: Volume One* in Fairlawn, at a weekend book signing in a tiny science fiction bookstore. Serena is not shy. She shoves a flyer at each person who enters the store. By the end of the day, she has sold 24 books. Heartened by her success, Serena seeks more opportunities to introduce the public to her precious volume. She approaches other stores and establishes a signing circuit.

A few months later, she attends the LUNACON Science Fiction Convention and participates in an author's panel. A Barnes & Noble science fiction buyer happens to be in the audience, and Serena attracts his attention. He finds her excellent cover artwork impressive and invites her to meet him at his downtown Fifth Avenue office. A few weeks later, 500 copies of Serena's volume are on their way to superstores nationwide. Through relentless persistence and an extraordinary stroke of luck, Serena has gained entry into Manhattan's exclusive publishing world. Now she has the perfect platform to do as many author signings as she wants. At this point, George jumps on board, and they both give free lectures, rotating between several local Barnes & Noble superstores in New Jersey. Serena also lands her first radio interview. She devotes herself almost exclusively, to seeking publicity for her and her father's books.

At his signings, George promotes his expertise in stress reduction. A blurb in a monthly Barnes & Noble newsletter reads, "George E. Sharkman, author of *Biofeedback and Beyond*, presents the first of four workshops in his 'Evening of Life' series. This evening he will introduce you to his unique methods of stress management."

George begins to draw peripheral followers, people who come to hear him speak each time he appears at their local store; people who are clearly interested in what he has to say; people who swear by his book filled with "revolutionary methods that achieve real results."

Along with book signings, our commitment to UWSA continues, and in March, we hold a second official election. Serena runs, intent on claiming another term. But this time there is competition. The group that opposed George as mediator for the Senator Lautenberg meeting grooms their own candidate, Mark West. They launch an aggressive campaign. Serena, the confident incumbent, doesn't bother with promotion; there is no need. Election day dawns, and eight members of George's group confidently enter the meeting hall to join 80 or so other members of UWSA. Of course Serena will emerge victorious. How could it be any other way?

Serena speaks first. She recites an impressive (to her) list of "valuable" contributions made during her six-month term. It all seems mere formality, until Mark takes the stage. All in one moment, the audience's energy consolidates—a direct line of focus from supporter to candidate. They are alive and rapt. I don't understand, but I do sense something real, an irrevocable changing of the guard. Foreboding increases as ballots are cast and counted. Twenty minutes later, the winner is announced—Mark West. Serena receives only eight votes—all from our group.

The unthinkable has happened and I must get answers fast. I stumble out into the gravel parking lot, trembling fingers clumsily poking cell phone buttons. "George, Serena just lost the election. What should we do?"

He seems shocked as well—temporarily at a loss for words. The man I believed *always* had answers, has none. Uncomfortable in the void, I stammer to fill in for him, "There must be a really good reason. A greater mission is coming."

This logic fits his philosophy, so he agrees.

Serena and the rest are irate over the election's outcome. They accuse Mark of unscrupulously influencing voters with campaign flyers and phone calls. Serena doesn't have a leg to stand on but losing the battle fuels her hostility. Hard willed, she demands respect . . . and another election. Her group's rage does not subside—evidence that their primary goal has been to control the UWSA Bergen County chapter, not to work toward the mission of government reform shared by the rest. No one escapes their wrath. They send letters and faxes to all the higher-ups: State and District Coordinators, and even Ross Perot himself. Relentless, they harass members by telephone, complaining of their mistreatment. And they create a petition to impeach Mark West. There is a power driving these people, some stubborn evil force that seems to have a life of its own. Fed up and exhausted, everyone wishes they would just go away.

Our meetings in George's den focus on Mark West's abuse of Serena. We must convince his entourage that the election was unjust. Judy Carlone, because of her friendship with me, is the only choice to bridge the gap. George suggests that I invite her to the den during an afternoon session for brainstorming. On the appointed day I contact a few additional UWSA members, but only Judy shows up.

I shiver at the thought of visiting Serena's father's house. This is where they hold their creepy stress reduction sessions. Elizabeth assures me that other UWSA members will be there, so I accept reluctantly. But when I arrive, I find only members of Serena's father's group. I quickly position myself in a folding chair next to the nearest exit. Several groupies are seated on couches and chairs, including Serena and Elizabeth. Instantly, I sense a strong energy field. Expressionless, they focus on me with staring, piercing eyes. I feel as if they want to insert something into my being. Petrified from the evil sensation, I silently pray to God and jingle my keys nervously, trying to hide my terror. I want to jump out a window, but I decide to force myself through my discomfort and try to calm down. This is my opportunity to find out more about what really goes on here. Serena's father, George, observes silently from an oak rocking chair in the back.

When Judy enters and scans the room, she appears severely agitated. Regardless, we dump our frustration on her immediately. "It's not fair how Serena lost the election. Can you convince them to listen to our side?" We implore her.

She eventually agrees to fax Mark a letter stating that she has heard our concerns, and that we have a right to objective consideration. Finally George speaks: Judy's support will accomplish positive things, even in her own life. Warm and encouraging, he stands and crosses the room to shake her hand and pat her on the back, just like he did with Representative Marge Roukema and the other politicians.

George and the others explain a little about the force that George produces. I have always been sensitive to energy fields, so why is this one so terribly frightening? Although I feel sandpaper, I try to listen politely. When I have endured more than enough I rise, excuse myself, and flee his den with relief. How could Elizabeth lure me into that awful group alone? I thought she was my friend. . . .

Serena contacts Mark West. He has received Judy's fax and agrees to host a meeting in his office after work that evening. Before leaving, our team of seven gathers in Coach George's den for a long pep talk. Psyched, we then drive off to certain victory.

In Mark's office we form a ring of seats. Each of the fifteen or so participants will have the floor for a few minutes. Mark's group makes their position clear—the election was conducted fairly. During their turns, Pauline and Nora are polite, asserting sweetly that Serena was a great leader, and they simply aren't being fair. In contrast, Carl and Christopher are aggressive. After all, George has assured us *we will win*, as long as we use our power to promote the truth. Imitating George's technique to break resistance, they yell, accuse and curse. As they rise up like angry bulls, a woman in the West group objects to their choice of four-letter words. Mark warns them politely—the obscenities must cease. But Carl boils over, "How dare you correct me!"

He continues his abrasive delivery. Mark loses it and escorts Carl to the door. The rest of us sit bewildered. This isn't working out according to plan. Helpless, we are at a loss to turn the situation around—a total contradiction to George's fervent promises of triumph this afternoon.

Meanwhile, I am more aware of Judy standing separate in the back of the room than of the noisy confrontation. It feels as if she is connected to me somehow, an ally. But George has taught us that outsiders are not to be trusted, so this feeling makes no sense. A little while later she slips away without saying goodbye.

The next day I am relieved not to be scheduled for George in the morning; I'm sure there will be hell to pay. . ., and I am right. At 3:00 P.M. I enter the den to find Pauline and Nora on the sofa sobbing. George has been raging all day, blaming us for failing to win back his daughter's position. Hoping not to draw his attention, I quietly find a seat and then hold myself stock still, barely breathing. I don't want to receive what George has just dished out to my tearful teammates. However, there is no escape and few minutes later, I fall under his glare. "How did you fuck up yesterday, Elizabeth? Why do you always want to fail?"

I truly have no answer. We did all we could, but Mark's people refused to give in. Barely audible, I squeak, "I didn't fail." Then, a little louder, "I am not a failure."

With all my strength I push against that invisible wall of resistance that barely moves a millimeter. But I'll do anything to avoid the agony of feeling worthless, no, worse, despicable, again. I abhor the prospect of joining the tearful Pauline, pale and twisted on the love seat across from me, receding like a child who has just been beaten for a bad report card. I grit my teeth and stand wobbly firm. Fortunately, most of George's wrath is exhausted from a full day of continuous explosions. My weak but determined opposition is sufficient. He gives up on me and starts shaking his head, dropping us all in disgust and reaching toward new growth for himself.

I avoid Elizabeth; it's been about three weeks now. I tell other UWSA members how she set me up to be trapped alone in a room with the members of Serena's father's group. Each time I relate the story, I heal a little more from the terrifying experience. Finally, I decide to call her. Despite that horrible afternoon, I have great affection for her. In fact, most of the UWSA members like Elizabeth. They find her a decent soul; it is only her involvement with Serena that turns them off. . . .

When the telephone rings I am relieved to finally hear Judy's voice. However, she angrily informs me in no uncertain terms that she never wanted to be in George's den with our Group, especially not by herself. She doesn't like what she feels in there. In fact, she declares adamantly, "God doesn't like it either."

I have no idea what she means, but my intuition tells me that someday I might understand.

Between work, George, and UWSA, life is so busy that I forget my income taxes until the first weekend in April. Sunday afternoon I spread my paperwork on the coffee table and throw myself in, adding columns of numbers. I avoid the two-inch thick stack of George's checks until the last possible moment; I always dread knowing the sum. My jaw tightens with each click of the calculator. After a few minutes, the green digits finally display a total—more than $42,000 for 1993. My eyes fill with tears. It's so unfair. I hate paying him; I hate having to go to The Group so much. I want to keep my money, not have it sucked away. I remind myself that there is nothing I can do about it. I simply must find a way to make more money. Next year, I reason, the flash cards will flourish, and George's cost will feel minimal. Still, my rage won't be calmed, and my chest hurts for the rest of that day . . . and the next.

The last week in April, Serena and I finally get a break. Cliff's Notes, one of the nation's largest educational publishers, accepts our product, *Exambusters Study Cards*, for distribution. Finally, after all of my struggles, the big things George and Serena have promised are about to begin. Only one more sacrifice is necessary; I must spend my remaining inheritance on producing inventory. But after that, everything will be OK, and I'll be able to pull myself out of the red.

In May, Mark West's administration hosts the UWSA monthly meeting. New committees are formed and I initiate the "Property Tax Reduction Committee." Several people sign up, including Elizabeth. I know she doesn't own any property to be taxed, so why did she join? This must be her way of staying in touch with me to continue our friendship. I call her a few days later and invite her to co-chair with me. She agrees. Our first meeting takes place at the Bergenfield Library. We enjoy a large attendance and make big plans. Are there any other kind? After the meeting, Elizabeth follows me to my car. Ready to go home, I get into the driver's seat and close the door. Elizabeth lingers outside gazing at me, so I roll down my window. She's not saying anything, but doesn't seem to want to leave. Finally, I break the silence and invite her for coffee. Relieved, she hops into the front seat and we drive five minutes to the local diner. Face to face, Elizabeth begins to talk about herself and her past, revealing many intimate details. She speaks quickly and nervously. Her sentences are disjointed. It is as if her thoughts come faster than she can speak them. We spend about two hours there, but for Elizabeth, this time seems not nearly enough.

The following day, a florist delivers a plant to my office. It is from Elizabeth with a card that reads, "I am glad we're friends. You are a miracle." It was sweet of her to send a gift, but I don't understand what she has written. How am I a miracle? I'm just a regular person like everybody else.

Elizabeth and I spend more and more time together. We see movies, go out to dinner, and wander through the aisles of Barnes & Noble sipping Starbucks coffee. She spends time at my house watching our big screen TV and chatting with my husband, Michael. She also continues trying to get me into her group. The more I resist, the harder she pushes. She admits she's been getting flack about her friendship with me from Serena, George, and the rest. It seems that none of the groupies have relationships with outsiders. This is not permitted. But why? When we are together, Elizabeth talks incessantly about The Group. She sings the praises of George's unique abilities. It is obvious that she worships him in every way, and I often wonder if they have sex.

Since Ben's fall last summer, George's primary focus has been on healing the dog so he can walk again. Yet Ben never does. He sleeps most of the time, and our group sessions usually include him lying on a mattress at one end of the den, or even in George's arms. Unconscious, his entire body jolts from The Energy, often quickly and violently. George claims that Ben has entered "the plane of total ecstasy. Now we must try to follow him there." In order to evacuate, Ben must be picked up and carried outside to the yard. George places the dog's front legs on the grass. Squatting on the ground, he then grasps a back leg in each hand and plants them firmly, holding the dog upright to do his business. George proudly states that he doesn't care if the dog pees or craps right on his hands, he loves him that much.

Even though Ben requires a "walking" every couple of hours, George doesn't seem to feel burdened being tied to the house every day, all day, to care for the dog. In fact, George states with confidence, "Ben is going to live forever, and I don't mind caring for him for that long. It is worth it."

I try to view it from his side, to justify the love and dedication, evidence of supreme selflessness that could only exist in a highly spiritual person. I cannot. Instead, the inordinate attention to the dog enrages me. However, I keep my mouth shut, because everyone else is following George's lead.

Ben soon develops an insatiable thirst. However, George limits his water to avoid more frequent trips outside. To me, this is blatant cruelty. I hate to see the dog's obvious suffering, so I timidly ask George if he might consult a vet to help Ben, but George will have none of it. "Vets don't know anything. We'll solve the problem with The Energy."

There is no swaying George's opinion. I wouldn't even dare to try. Soon, Ben begins to lose his hair. The inert, helpless animal with large, bare patches on his body, looks terribly decayed, as if he is already dead. Nevertheless, George proclaims he will reverse the process and restore Ben to the strong beautiful creature he was twelve years ago when Dr. Rogers found him during a mountain vacation in the Catskills. He holds Ben in his lap for hours, rubbing his body and insisting that the dog's hair is starting to grow back.

Saturday, August 27, 1994
And the weeks that follow

It is mid-afternoon when I enter the den. An oppressive gloom hangs in the air—Ben is not doing well. George clutches him with poignant sadness. The other ten or so faces reflect the same. Exceedingly uncomfortable, I don't know what I should say, so I sit in silent observation. Soon George announces that he is too involved; perhaps someone else should hold the dog. Painstakingly, he places Ben on Beatrice's lap. The minutes drag by in agonizing anticipation. We all feel impotent and yet responsible, as if there is something that we should be doing, that we are not doing. Finally it is 5:00 P.M. and time to leave. George and Christopher debate about taking the dog to the Oradell Animal Hospital nearby. On her way out, Bess assures George that things will turn around. He mustn't give up. "You have the right stuff to help him. Just believe in yourself." She smiles, reaching out to gently pat George's back.

I follow behind Bess, gazing at George feebly, asking if I can do anything. He waves me out, remaining frozen at the doorway while the rest parade past. Like a lost little boy, his eyes are round with helplessness and fear. I try to believe that George will foster some miracle this night, but in my heart I know Ben is dying. I sense an indomitable spiritual process taking place that none of us can influence, despite George's willful insistence that he and we, as a group, *must* alter Ben's destiny.

Later in the evening George telephones Serena at our house. He and Chris have admitted the dog to the animal hospital. The next morning, the phone rings at 8:00 A.M. It is George, and Ben is gone. Serena hangs up and sobs. Christopher, her brother, has lost his best friend, and today is his 24th birthday. Later that afternoon, Ben comes home in a white, cardboard box. Father and son bury him at the edge of the woods that encircle their back yard. Christopher carves an oak headstone. It reads, "Ben, a true friend." A paw print lies underneath. Crouching beside the grave, the two men talk to their dog, telling him how much they miss him. When they have said all they can, George rises to stand over the grave. Shaking his head furiously, he raises his arms toward the heavens in a desperate plea to make it not so.

Monday dawns and I dread going to George. I don't know what to expect, but I'm sure it won't be pleasant. I am correct. For the entire week, in Jewish tradition, George sits shiva in his den for the dog. He cries ceaselessly, tears streaming down his face in an endless river. His features are red and blotchy—a picture of perfect misery. Christopher howls and bawls frequently. George's wife, Doris, embarrassed by the drama she hears through the closed door, begs them to quiet down. But George only ridicules her for her insensitivity. We all attend our regular hours, sitting rigidly sober, competing to see who can mirror George's agony the most effectively. I try to keep my face blank and pray that George will not notice that I am less distraught than the rest. Although I try to force myself to empathize, I simply cannot.

On Tuesday, the second day of mourning, I arrive in the early afternoon. Spotting Beatrice and Pauline on the love seat, I read an identical expression on them both, "I deserve to be punished because I was very, very bad." There is trouble and I wish I could sink deep into the couch, out of sight. Soon George swings his attention to me, his reprimand accompanied by an intense glare, "TELL ME HOW YOU HELPED TO KILL BEN."

I stare in disbelief and try to reply truthfully, speaking in a monotone to avoid triggering him further. "I didn't kill him. I didn't even want him to die. I offered my help but there was nothing I could do."

My voice doesn't deliver any confidence; I am too afraid of him, but I try. It is obvious that the others (Laura, Nora, Beatrice, and Bess) have swallowed George's accusation that Ben's death was our fault, and that from this sin, there is no redemption. George rages at my blasphemous response. I recede, now groping desperately in my mental storehouse for some kind of double-talk that will satisfy him. I must neutralize him before my rapidly constricting veins cut off the blood supply to my brain, and I pass out from sheer terror. Finally, for the sake of survival, I resort to lying, which I abhor. Mumbling about concealed bad intentions, and that I am sorry and will try harder, I eventually manage to appease him. Laura, seated next to me, soon demands the floor, and George moves on. She has just received a spiritual message— inspired wisdom that if sufficiently explored might prevent this dreadful event from recurring. The rest of my comrades, with George at the helm, brainstorm about her ideas for the next hour. I stay out of it. Late in the afternoon George telephones the vet to ask why Ben couldn't have been saved. "Isn't there something we can still do? I just want him back, whatever it takes."

After that, George refers to the death as a mistake and a tragedy. "We will pay for this the rest of our lives," he assures us.

For several days, George, depressed and remote, barely speaks. He spends our sessions shaking his head and ignoring us. Without his leadership on the path toward ultimate truth, we collapse like deflated balloons. The oppressive stagnation is intolerable, and there is no hope in sight. I cannot imagine Hell to be any worse than this.

Thursday night group is somber while George directs us to continue trying to figure out where we went wrong, so we can learn from our mistakes. Beatrice concedes that when Ben was on her lap that fateful afternoon, she felt her negativity travel into the dog. Others speak out with similar admissions—our collective negative thinking killed the dog.

George praises our humility and then declares it is time to move on. He shakes solemnly, arms floating toward the ceiling. When his arms finally descend, George is overcome with sudden emotion. "I can feel Ben's body in my arms."

Choking back tears while his eyes light up with awe, he calls Christopher to kneel on the floor facing him. Then, George slowly transfers Ben's invisible body to his son's outstretched arms. Christopher sobs uncontrollably; he feels the dog too. George invites us, one by one, to experience the miracle. At my turn, I concentrate hard. Nodding with serious intensity I report, "I feel it a little."

Satisfied, he moves to the next person. I truly want to join this momentous experience, but I'm not sure I felt anything at all.

Later Serena interrupts our silent sobriety and the steady rhythm of her father's headshaking, "Dad. Dad. Look at the yard!" She is staring out the large picture window over the couch. "I see Ben floating. He is really with us!"

Tears run freely down George's cheeks as he too beholds Serena's vision. Bess and Pauline soon discern a faint outline of Ben's body suspended in the black night. Tonight's discovery has earned Serena her father's coveted accolades—praise the rest of us sorely need.

It is Wednesday, lunchtime, a couple of weeks after Ben's passage. Serena receives a call at the office from her father. After minimal conversation, she hangs up. Her face pales as she rushes out mumbling, "I've got to go."

Her behavior is more than strange, but I have learned not to ask questions. The Sharkmans reserve their secrets exclusively for those they deem worthy (usually never me). After that day, George seems happier. In fact, the following evening he is laughing and winking at Christopher. Very much his old self, he lectures, "We have arrived at a new level. Beyond the physical is the spiritual and the real truth. The world we see is only an illusion."

I notice a strange pungent smell, as if someone has used too much air spray, but I soon move on to ponder the mystery responsible for George's rebirth. Something is up that only the three Sharkmans know.

I'm not sure how, but a few nights later the answer comes into my mind. I catch George's eye and nod. Smiling in collusion, I am thrilled to be in the know. Now it is all so clear—the reason Serena turned ghostly pale before scurrying out of our office to carry out her father's command. George, spurred by momentous inspiration, had called his daughter from Manhattan and ordered her to meet Christopher at the family house immediately. There, they were both instructed to dig up the dog's carcass, to bring Ben home, into George's den. Now, too, I understand the reason for the apple-scented air spray on the coffee table!

The morning after my revelation, I report nervously for my 8:30 A.M., before-work session.

"Now it's time to take a look at him," I am informed.

I really don't want to. To postpone the inevitable, I slip into the bathroom. Meanwhile, George removes Ben from his hiding place behind the couch. A few pregnant minutes drag by. I can't remain in the bathroom forever, so I suck in my breath and muster my courage.

A slab of wood on the floor holds poor Ben's body. After a month of decay, the carcass is putrid. It has also bled, evidenced by matted fur and red stains in the wood. George instructs me to touch Ben. "Our disgust forms a barrier we must break in order to arrive at new discoveries."

Regardless of my revulsion, refusing to comply is not an option. After several minutes of hesitation, I finally sit down Indian-style on the floor next to Ben and gingerly place my fingertips on his back. I recoil and then try again. George is very proud, but for once I don't care. A few days later, for some unexplained reason, he decides to bury the body again. He and Christopher do this.

It's not over yet, and one week later, the next puzzle piece falls into place. George and his wife are spending Sunday at Doris's older sister's home on Long Island. During a solitary walk on the beach, at the water's edge, he is drawn to a palm-sized, white stone with a small hole in the middle. Grinning broadly, he slips it into his pocket; George has had an epiphany.

Monday morning the breaking news is broadcast. "Ben has come back to us," George declares. "His soul is in this rock. I have a job ahead—to transfer the soul back into the body. Then Ben will live again."

The white rock—the "Ben Rock," never leaves George. The moments he allows one of us to touch it are rare and sacred. God forbid it is dropped or violated in any way. Often, he places it in his mouth, sucking on it for hours while shaking his head. In awe of the "Ben Rock," we revere and cherish it.

George often brings us to the graveside during our sessions. One afternoon, after gently placing his rock on the headstone, he spots another white one on the ground nearby. It looks like a small potato. "Here," he says sweetly while handing it to me, "a gift."

Today we are alone, and I grasp it proudly, thinking, It's just like it was in the beginning. Whenever George starts something new, he shares it with me first, because I am the person most like him. During the next few days he gives rock "gifts" to the rest of The Group, and in the weeks that follow, we begin to offer rocks

Ben's grave covered with rocks

to outsiders, accompanied by our beneficent explanation, "The rocks will help you calm down when you are stressed out and speeding." Each day we sit with George holding rocks, feeling their energy, watching them change color and shape.

On a Saturday soon after, I arrive at George's around 2:00 P.M. as usual. When I make the left at the end of his driveway and approach the deck, I notice a small group standing solemnly by Ben's grave, across the yard. *Oh God.* I think, *Now what?* I really don't want to know. Regardless, I join them. Laura, Beatrice, Pauline, Bess . . . each is sober and serious with eyes downturned, while Christopher lifts the white box containing Ben's body from the grave. George is absent, but soon I spot him striding from the house toward us. My heart leaps expectantly; it always has at the sight of him, but as he approaches, I happen to look directly into his eyes. Like blinding headlights in a dark night, they seem to speed toward me. And in this moment there is something I have never seen before—blatant and consummate insanity. It terrifies me. George has gone over the edge. . . .

George is bursting, "This is the biggest thing we have ever done! You are all present at this birth, the beginning of Ben's new life!"

Laura states wondrously, "This is great. We are doing something truly important together as a team."

Pauline, doubly enthusiastic, adds, "Yes. We are finally cooperating instead of fighting!"

George, imbued with new purpose, reaches toward the sky and makes his declaration. "I am the Alpha and the Omega. I will know the beginning, and I will lead us all to the end. Everyone in the universe must come this way or perish. 'dog' is 'god' spelled backwards, and *Ben is god.* He has traveled to the other side. When I resurrect him, we will finally go home."

Soon our tiny parade escorts the carcass into the den. It, along with the white rock, is to become holy—an object of worship and the total focus of our existence.

When the afternoon session is finally over, I walk down George's driveway toward my car. It is here, on the concrete path I have crossed thousands of times, that in one decisive moment my head splits open and everything changes. *My God! Look at what we have become; we will do anything for George; he could even convince us to murder.* I slam to a full stop as my oppressed inner voice finally triumphs over rigid orthodox thinking and declares with undeniable commitment, *I hate the Black Dog Religion!* Our rocky, exhilarating, challenging, journey has culminated in this—the adoration of a black Labrador's carcass. Although I never would have believed this to be possible, George has broken through another new barrier, and I, for the very first time, cannot follow. *Where have I been all these years? How did I stray so far?* Now I see the role I have played with George—perpetual performance to gain his recognition, at any cost. My inner self proclaims distinctly, *This must stop now.* There is no negotiation. No more will I throw George flirtatious looks or flatter his supernatural powers. My unhooking has begun.

My sessions take a 180-degree turn. I enter the room as unassumingly as possible, hoping not to be noticed. A desire to play that familiar role of enthusiastic follower demands to be satisfied, but I resist. To pass the time, I discipline myself by focusing on the doorknob or a knot in George's diagonal oak paneling. Each day I work at breaking my connections to my family, my belief system—my life. As days turn to weeks, horrified at the person I've become, I begin to grasp the magnitude of my attachment. Like Gulliver tied down on the beach by Lilliputians, thousands of threads hold me captive. Each strand represents a thought, memory, or action. Taken alone, they seem innocuous, easily broken, but in their entirety they form a trap virtually impossible to escape. I realize that George has wielded weapons of intimidation and seduction to construct his masterpiece—an army of perfect soldiers existing solely to serve him—for the rest of his days. Marionettes he has painstakingly threaded, I watch him jerking our strings while we dance his dance.

Along with focusing on Ben's body to see it changing and growing, we now spend most of our time focusing with each other. The days of bonding through group activities (UWSA, business projects), personal issues (office, spouse, family), even discussing the books on our reading list, have ended abruptly. George is unreachable—a machine serving one sole purpose—resurrecting the dog. And he makes it clear that our only relevance to him is measured by our participation to further his cause. Stray conversation is now against the rules. "Come on everybody, it's time to work on Ben. Cut the distractions, people, and let's get going."

George selects a person with whom to focus. Afterwards, the rest pair up. Serena usually chooses Bess or Pauline. Gazing at Serena with the same worshipful eyes they often turn toward her father, the girls are honored to focus with the second in command. Personally, I hate to focus with Serena. Her eyes are creepy and cold, like marbles. No matter where we are, I routinely avoid her penetrating stare.

Bess often flatters George, "I have never met anyone with such determination. It's amazing, and that's why you get such incredible results!" And George bows his head in humble recognition of her compliment.

It is a fall Saturday afternoon, another bright and breezy day when I wish I could be outside enjoying the weather, not about to be trapped for hours in the dimly lit den, focusing on Ben. As I approach George's deck, where a flag with a black Labrador's image sways in the breeze, I realize—for the first time—that I am entering a church dedicated to the dog. There are several statues of similar black canines in varying sizes strewn across the coffee table and console. An afghan pinned to the wall, Serena's gift, presents several more Labradors. There are posters, mugs, T-shirts, light switch plates, and throw pillows, offerings to George from various Group members. As I enter, Bess, Pauline, and Beatrice are seated on the couch intensely absorbed in a conversation about the development of Ben's carcass. George turns to me excited, "Big news. Ben is creating worms! Brand-new life forms from The Energy I've been forcing into him."

I look down quickly to observe small, white specks all over Ben's legs. "Oh, I see," I reply, not knowing what to make of it. Not wanting to believe him, yet too afraid not to.

George continues, "Earlier today I saw one growing out of my arm too!"

Pauline giggles. "I certainly don't want to ask how that happened!"

George picks up a robin's egg that had been nestled next to Ben's leg. "I've been holding this egg for two days now. I can feel life beginning inside. Ben is helping it hatch!"

The dog's body is covered with assorted items, donations from Group members: a dollar bill, a business card, a broach, a feather. They are placed there to charge up with Energy, after which they will be taken home to end family conflict, or on the job to help get a raise, etc.

George cheerfully recounts how he and Christopher manage to hide the carcass from Doris. Three days a week, while George keeps hours in his city office, Christopher is responsible. Traveling to various appointments (in the tri-state area) with his graphic design customers, he carries his best friend in the trunk of his white Acura Integra under a blanket. At night they hide Ben in the garage and return him to the den only after Doris leaves for work in the morning.

Thoroughly repulsed by these people, I stare at the wall. Soon, without warning, I experience a strange sensation. It is as if a roulette ball, spinning around the wheel for a long, long time, has finally found its number. It seems that my friends have found theirs. Years of false accusations, character assassinations, and public humiliation have broken them in. Tamed like wild horses, I sense they have completely handed over their wills to George. They are docile and agreeable, willing to follow wherever he goes, never to question or oppose him again. An unholy peace hovers, and George appears relaxed, as if his mission is finally accomplished, and he can rest, confident that his devotees follow closely on his tail. *My God. That was supposed to be me too—a zombie, a fool reveling in insanity!* Although I have traveled the same path as the others, for some unknown reason I now understand that I have been spared their fate. Today I am watching them from the other side of the fence. I do not know how to thank God by name, but nonetheless, my heart extends its gratitude. Over the past several weeks, since the day I renounced the "Black Dog Religion," it feels as if I am a passenger on a train slowly carrying me away from them. I don't know where I am going, but I have no choice.

I had always displayed such enthusiasm, relentlessly demanding George's attention and monopolizing most conversations. I believed I was needed and significant. After all the experiences we shared together, and the enormous piece of myself I invested in my relationships with each individual, I can't believe that my profound detachment goes unnoticed. Yet as I slowly withdraw, I realize that losing me doesn't make any difference to them either.

These days Elizabeth and I struggle for hours: on the phone, driving in my car, or over cappuccino at a local café. Our bond is powerful. In fact, there is nothing that can pull us apart, not the others in our lives, not even our own minds that sometimes wrestle with our increasing involvement. Through our conversations, I discover that George has convinced Elizabeth to believe that she will die if she leaves him. But I see another part of her that nonetheless wants to be free. These opposing forces create terrible conflict. It is her soul that connects with me, not her mind, for that is owned by George, Serena, and her mother. Elizabeth admires me to the point of fascination. In fact, it seems as if I am the first person in her life who ever paid any attention to her. She absorbs every inch of me like a sponge and brings it all back to The Group.

Without UWSA to bring us together, Judy and I continue our relationship on the telephone—endless conversations that sometimes last long after midnight. One evening we drive to Hoboken, New Jersey, the ethnic neighborhood where she grew up. Judy points out landmarks from her childhood: the high school her father attended (with Frank Sinatra as his classmate), the apartment she shared with her family, the Catholic church where she was baptized and made her first communion. We come from such different worlds, she and I, and yet we feel as if we have known each other forever. Sometimes Judy lavishes me with compliments. She tells me that I am kind, generous, and fair, and she respects my intelligence and perceptiveness."

My response to her is always the same, "Huh? What do you mean? Really?" My thoughts focus solely on the role I play in George's universe. Otherwise I have no value.

Judy is passionate and direct—never afraid to speak her mind. Her honesty is refreshing and I can't help mentioning her to the others. At first I am tolerated; George is convinced that The Energy is attracting another follower. But my enthusiasm soon irritates them and the accusations start—I am childishly obsessed and have adopted Judy as my mommy. Bess lectures me with heartfelt sincerity. "Elizabeth, I know what it means to be seduced into thinking that one of the 'crazy people' has something going for them. I've come up against this mistake many times. But unless she joins us, the relationship is a dangerous distraction. You really should concentrate on getting her into The Group."

George chimes in warning, "Judy is a *powerful* person. You better watch out or she will control you and take you off track. If you lose focus, your business will be destroyed."

Serena nods in agreement.

"Ben was glowing all morning," George relates one Tuesday afternoon, "Beatrice couldn't help throwing her arms around him. Then she said, 'I love you Ben, you are the best,' and kissed him."

George seems prouder of Ben than he ever was of anyone else. In fact, he admits that he loves the decaying remains of his former canine companion more than his own children, principally because of Ben's divine status and the profound effect it will have on our spiritual future. As we sit, George holding the dog on his wooden slab, I concentrate on focusing into his eyes as I am required to do when we are alone. In a moment of weakness, I return to my old self, the faithful Group member, wanting desperately to satisfy George's heart's desire, to resurrect Ben. My solution is creative. I convince myself that I feel my ears growing longer, changing into a dog's ears. This is just the type of thing that will capture George's attention. I alert him, and he is instantly captivated, following my every word. Together we focus on completing the transformation, and soon a snout and tail appear. I experience an uncontrollable desire to bark and pant, and within about fifteen minutes I have become Ben for real. In fact, George can see his hovering soul surrounding me in a cloud of energy. Happy to be relieved of the conflict that has been building between us for a couple of years, I report with delight, "George, I feel Ben's personality in the room; in fact, I just heard him tell a joke!"

When our time is up, I rise and head toward the door, smiling and patting George's back in intimate comradeship. As I pass by, he rewards me, handing me a small piece of matted fur from Ben's decomposing belly. I slip this talisman into my wallet—evidence of my connection to George and the only life I know. These past few months of self-imposed separation have been more than difficult. Abandoning my resolve and backsliding, I have found a way to fill myself with George's approval, and I feel elated for the rest of the day.

When he is not applying himself to Ben's rebirth, George continues making his rounds—frequent book signings arranged by his manager, Serena. After several presentations in New Jersey, they decide to expand his radius, and George's first Manhattan lecture takes place one Tuesday evening at the Barnes & Noble near East 86th Street. My mother, Bess, Pauline, Laura, and Beatrice attend, seating themselves in the front row like a rock star's groupies. I arrive a little later than the rest, and when I scan the crowd, I spot them immediately. An aura of worship hovers—and I want no part of it. I settle into a chair in the back unobtrusively, nonetheless feeling a little guilty for not joining my friends.

George talks for a while and then declares that he has a little surprise for everybody. Laughing he warns, "I'm a weirdo, but don't be afraid." With that, he seats himself on a stool and begins to shake his head with slow determination. *Oh God*, I think, *Why is he embarrassing himself like this in public?* I look around, wondering how the audience, and a few managers standing on the side, are receiving his bizarre display. I grit my teeth in shame and pray for him to finish. Faster and faster he goes while the stool jerks from side to side, threatening to spill him onto the floor. His activity creates a loud, repetitive clatter as the metal seat slams against an adjacent bookcase. Not surprisingly, he draws a small, curious crowd. When George stops, he asks the audience if they feel some energy. A few people respond yes, but several others depart shaking their heads in disgust. George selects a woman in the second row with whom to focus. Under his intense gaze, she seems to slip into a trance like state immediately and soon claims that she feels calmer.

To end his presentation, George signs some books and hands out business cards. He invites people to his New Jersey group next Thursday night, "if they want to learn more." And a few purchase an autographed copy of *Biofeedback and Beyond*.

George's next lecture is held at the Barnes & Noble in Nanuet, N.Y. He begins by explaining that everything that happens to us in life is our own responsibility. If only we could accept this and stop blaming others for our misfortunes, we would be the architects of our destinies. A woman raises her hand to disagree, "How can everything be within your control?" she asks, "What about the victims of the Oklahoma City bombing? They didn't ask to die."

"Yes; even they were responsible," George replies, "Those people sent out a message in the spiritual airwaves that, 'It's OK to kill me.'"

Several members of the audience groan and exit quickly while George continues. "I know you don't want to believe it, but you are god. If only you had the self-confidence to accept it, what a wonderful life you would lead!"

An immediate rage twists the face of a sixty-something, Italian gentleman wearing a gold crucifix. He blurts out angrily, "You can't say that. It's blasphemy—against God." He turns and strides away, highly offended.

George makes an example of him, "See, my point is proven. That man reacts because his mind is too small to accept his own greatness, so instead, the coward runs away like a baby."

All of the local Barnes & Noble managers know George and Serena well. What they don't know is that the image of the sleeping dog on George's business card is Ben's carcass, hidden behind the den couch while his master is on the road. They have no idea that George believes that the heated, white rock he offers gingerly for them to hold for a moment—contains Ben's soul. They never notice that while he lectures, he is sucking on something small—a toenail from Ben's carcass. They have no idea that their customers might get into terrible trouble, should they accept George's offer to attend a Thursday night group.

I arrive one afternoon to find a buzz of activity. Small, black rocks are scattered everywhere, and George's coffee table is covered with black and grey, velvet pouches. Beatrice informs me with enthusiasm. "A new enterprise has been born. George is moving ahead and will soon be all over the globe."

George headshakes, sprawled in his overstuffed club chair with the "Ben Rock" in one hand and about fifty small, black "baby" rocks strewn all over his arms, legs, and torso. "Ben just gave birth to all of these;" he pauses for a moment and jokes, "take one."

George hands me a rock resting on his thigh. "Meet the *Enoch Touchstone*, the *Pet Rock* of the Nineties! Enoch is my middle name, you know."

The rocks are soon individually packed by an assembly line of Group members, each into its own velvet bag. Christopher prints tags that state, "The stone contained within will foster a connection between your spiritual self and the universal energy field. Hold it, and you will feel the vibrations of the cosmos moving through your body."

George explains, exhilarated, "All I have to do is shake to put in The Energy. The rocks will form a network, like telephone lines, and anyone who has one will be connected and receive new information as we discover it. This is how The Energy will start to take over mankind." Ben's initials, printed on the bag's tag, are declared The Group's official slogan: "**B**e **E**verywhere **N**ow." The rock retails for $10, and thanks to some marketing efforts on Serena's part, a few local New Age, gift shops have already agreed to stock a few. George explains that each rock has its own personality, and because a rock doesn't have a mind, it is more alive than people are. We must now model our lives after the simplicity of our rocks.

In addition, George's personal rules for living will accompany the rocks into the retail world, and George proudly hands me a small booklet entitled, *The Enoch Commandments:*

Discover the Splendor of Life. Inside are his eleven commandments—replacements for God's ten. They read:

1) You always feel good.
2) You succeed at everything you do.
3) You are never sick.
4) You respect all living things.
5) You are great.
6) **Be Everywhere Now.**
7) You know everything.
8) You keep everything simple.
9) You are forever.
10) You are relentless.
11) You already know.

George's craze with rocks increases, and he constructs a four-foot wall of loose rocks around his entire yard in order to connect Ben's now empty grave to his house. Completing an "electrical circuit," the energy will flow throughout his property. We collect rocks and bring them daily as offerings. We sit holding rocks in our laps, hands—and even in our mouths, as we focus with each other during group sessions. George shakes and holds a thirty-pound stone on top of his head, claiming he is changing its shape. As we spend our days focusing with those rocks, we begin to see the same auras around them that we have seen around each other, evidence that rocks are indeed alive. Ben's body is covered with rocks, and George reports that during the night, Ben vibrates with The Energy and the rocks are thrown off of his body, to be found in the morning, by his master, scattered on the floor.

Each Group member buys several *Enoch Touchstones* from George, at $10 each. Beatrice purchases a dozen—holiday gifts for her family. She returns with glowing reports of how calm and peaceful her children and grandchildren became once they held their stones—how grateful they were.

My mother distributes them at her office. She offers one to a bus driver, and when a bum on 86th and Broadway begs her for a quarter, she places a rock in his hand instead, telling him it is the key to a new life. Our French cousin, Michelle, recently diagnosed with cancer, receives an airmail package containing a precious black stone as a gift. My mother proudly reads Michelle's thank-you letter aloud to several heads nodding in agreement. They all know that, if her cousin uses the rock faithfully, her cancer will be cured. Pauline sends one to her mother in Williamsburg, Virginia. She is about to have an operation. When Pauline receives a telephone call a week later, the operation was a success—the rock gets the credit.

Nora makes good use of the rocks as well. After years of emptiness with his wife, it seems that her husband has found someone more compatible. One day Nora accidentally discovers them sharing an intimate lunch at a local restaurant. Her first response is jealous hurt, but George advises her to "sit on her reaction" until she can go beyond it. He also suggests she offer a rock to the woman to connect her to "something greater." Nora obeys, reporting how her spouse's paramour was profoundly affected by The Energy, and as a result, she and her rival have become fast friends.

In fact, every day there is another joyous report about amazing rock responses from outsiders: how family members, coworkers, and even total strangers become instantly alive, how these people all want to find out more. In the past I would have embraced any new project. In fact, I probably would have been the first horse out of the gate. However, now, while the rest dash about dispersing rocks like raindrops, I hesitate. But finally, with all of the peer pressure and praise everyone is earning for their rock successes, I give in and purchase three rocks. I select my one-time beau, Preston, to receive the first one. Several months after our breakup, we reconciled as friends. So one afternoon, I make the journey to his office in Hackensack. (He moved from my building in 1994.) Preston greets me warmly; we haven't seen each other for a long time. After a few minutes I hand him his gift, the rock in a bag, expectantly anticipating a dramatic response. Instead, he glances at it briefly, comments that it seems "very interesting," and shoves it into a desk drawer. Then he looks back at me and grins boyishly. "I want to hear all about you and what you've been up to."

I leave his office giddy. He couldn't have cared less about the rock! *I* was more important. After that day I don't give out any more rocks; I am pretty sure they aren't going to cure cancer either.

There is conflict at our office, much of it over Judy, and one afternoon while I'm on the phone with her, Serena bursts into the room, pierces me with her gaze, and motions for me to hang up—immediately. When I have obeyed, she lays down the law in no uncertain terms. "Judy can't call here. It's interfering with the business."

Her tone threatens that there will be hell to pay if I don't comply. Later, I tell Judy and ask her to page me instead. But when Serena hears my pager go off the following week, she instinctively knows it's Judy and turns from her paperwork to reprimand me. "I told you not to talk to her during the work day."

Quickly, I silence the beeping sound. A half hour later, while Serena telephones George, her daily ritual to report in to headquarters, I slip out to the diner across the street and call my friend.

Each day, Judy has made a habit of contacting me to check if I am OK, but today I tell her not to page me anymore either, that I will call her every afternoon instead. That night, at about 10:00 P.M., Serena returns home from spending the evening with her father and the rocks. I am on the phone with Judy. Serena glares instantly, forcing me to hang up. "You are obsessed with Judy. Our business is suffering, and that's why you have no money. You should stay away from her and spend more time with my father. Anyway, why do you defy him? He has warned you over and over of the danger. You have no respect for any of us anymore; all you care about is Judy. Besides, I don't want her calling the house in the evening; I could be on AOL and I'll be bumped off."

I wait, patient and silent, while she drains her stockpile of complaints and accusations, mechanically nodding my head. Like a henpecked husband, I have learned that there is only one way to handle Serena's unreasonable tantrums. Judy wants me to put her in her place, to tell her that she is not allowed to treat me this way. After all, I am a 35-year-old adult. Asserting myself to Serena seems simple to Judy, and she can't understand why I won't just do it. I try to explain that I am too fragile, but I can't make her feel what it is like to be inside my body, how Serena's anger causes me to collapse into impotent terror. These days, I am more aware than ever of my weaknesses and how very much I want to conquer them.

As the months roll by, Elizabeth and I cultivate a powerful bond. According to Serena, she has never seen anything like it. She warns Elizabeth that my presence in her life will surely bring about her total downfall if she does not wrench herself away. Soon, everyone connected to Elizabeth makes it clear that they despise me—her mother, Max Stavos, Serena, and especially, the head honcho himself, George. Policed by all of them 24 hours a day, she has no safe zone other than her car. My close connection to Elizabeth triggers their malevolence to surface. The people who are gaining the most try relentlessly to stop her. While we are working toward her freedom, they are instilling doubt in her about my intentions and reinforcing her insecurities. I have become George's competition. His ego is now threatened because his most passionate follower has met someone whom she admires more. This creates a battle for control that makes me an object of hatred and jealousy, and Elizabeth the pawn.

When I was growing up in the 1950's, Hoboken's population consisted mostly of blue-collar Europeans. A woman's responsibility was to raise the children, often four or five, while her husband worked long hours to support the family. Life was not easy. Who would willingly give up all of their time and energy for a paycheck that barely covered expenses? I lived in a cold water flat with my three siblings. Our only source of heat was generated from a kitchen stove that had to warm five large box-shaped rooms. At a young age, I understood my parents' sacrifice to raise us. Time off from work was often spent fighting and taking their frustrations out on the children and each other.

I never really knew my father, I mean, who he was inside. He had a violent temper that he directed at my mother and my siblings. I was the only one who figured out how to stay out of his way and avoid the beatings. The evidence of his rages covered the doors and walls of our apartment. There were dents in the sides of the refrigerator and cracks in the wooden door to the pantry. I spent my entire childhood in a state of fear and oppression, knowing that I lived with an enemy who could destroy me at any moment if I wasn't on guard duty all the time. While still a toddler, I learned to keep myself in an emotional straitjacket when he was around. Any outburst of laughing or sibling squabbling could drive him over the edge into an uncontrollable tantrum directed at any of us. To me, he appeared like a giant monster towering over us with abusive, verbal attacks, glaring eyes, and fists flying out of control.

We were basically good kids, and nothing we ever did could have warranted this degree of reprimand. I despised his behavior and lack of remorse for the damage he did to us. At the age of six, I remember a violent fight between my parents. An observer, I panicked that his rage might drive him to hurt my mother badly. Desperate to stop him before he went too far, I picked up the telephone to call the police, taking the chance that my father would turn on me for challenging him. Thank God he didn't. Instead, he simply removed the phone from my hand and everything suddenly ended.

My father was one way in the house and another in public. It was never spoken out loud, but my parents instilled in us the silent, indisputable message that we were forbidden to reveal what took place in our private home, even though we knew that the things that went on there were not right. Our house was not unique. At night you could hear cries coming from nearby homes; violence and abuse were a disease that had invaded our entire neighborhood.

Despite his temper, I respected my father's craving for knowledge and excellent discernment skills. He could sense an evil intention in a person like a rat smells cheese. These qualities I inherited from him.

It's funny how persecution holds no prejudice. It doesn't care who you are, what you are, or where you come from. George's kingdom was a familiar scene to me, a déjà vu. His personality reminded me of my father's: the unfounded rages, intention to oppress, need to control at any cost, glaring intimidation tactics, and the total disregard for the well-being of those in his camp. You never forget these crimes once you've seen them committed. If I had not been a spectator of my father's behavior, I would probably have never understood George's motivations, and the depth of Elizabeth's suffering, so profoundly. This, to me, was evidence of God's intervention.

Judy begins to question me about my business, asking me how Serena and I came to be partners, who paid the startup costs, and how we distribute the profit. Instinctively, I try to water down the truth. "Oh, Serena and I contribute equally," I answer, thinking about how she brings George's energy (which attracts customers and success), and that this is more than equivalent to my contributions of financing, time, and talent. However, I realize that I can never make a person who is not a member of our Group understand, so I try to push Judy off the subject, but she is persistent and pins me down for more specific details.

"Did you pay for the startup costs?"

"Yes, of course."

"What did Serena pay to become a 50% partner?"

"Nothing." (My thoughts remind me that The Energy is more valuable than my money. Otherwise, there would be no business no matter how much I invested.)

"Does Serena have any talent as a photographer?" she continues.

"Not really."

"Who spends more hours at the job? Did you ever think about it?"

I recall my late nights while Serena keeps regular hours and is always out the door when her time is up.

"I think I do. . . . But . . . you don't understand that Serena *has* to be here."

My unspoken thoughts fill in with George's voice—a speech he gave me just last week. "Serena can get money out of the customers, no matter what kinds of games they play. But you would give away the store, if she left it up to you. And another thing, while you are lazy about it, she is willing to spend more time with me. Last Sunday, I shook my head for twelve hours, from noon to midnight, and Serena and Christopher were here. Of course they wanted to run, but I forced them to stay. You are not my daughter; you can't help it that you are inferior to her. That is why you must let her lead the business. . . ."

Judy continues her query, ending my thoughts. "What exactly does Serena do?"

"She does the sales. I am too afraid."

"Who did the sales before she came into the business?"

"Well . . . I did."

"Then why can't you do them now? When did you lose the ability you had? Didn't you make a good profit all by yourself?"

I am in a corner. Her simple, clear logic reveals to me that there is something wrong with mine. I can't help admitting that she is right, but I don't know what to do with this information; it doesn't fit anywhere in my mind.

"Honey," Judy finishes ever so gently, "I think you're being exploited."

Exploited. What is that? I turn the word over in my head. Of course I know the dictionary definition; yet it is not in my working vocabulary.

It is in this considerate, yet unrelenting, manner that Judy begins to expose George's contradictions, hypocrisy, and lies to me, one at a time.

Elizabeth never gives up trying to get me into that group. One day, I finally agree to go. This time I am not upset. I know I must put myself into the war zone to get more information. Thursday night, when I enter the devil's den, I come to see the truth at a much deeper level.

The air seems thick, as if I've just walked into an opium den, and my senses lose their sharpness as a wave of sluggishness hits me. It feels as if my abilities to reason, analyze, and challenge are being drained, and I feel heavy and empty. George sits in a big armchair with a cane across his lap. I notice that his left leg is dramatically swollen, from the foot to the knee, and he quickly explains that a special energy has filled his foot, and he's been walking with a cane for about two weeks—inconvenient, but a necessary part of his body's spiritual transformation.

I notice that all of the groupies are women, with the exception of two seemingly weak-willed men. His devotees appear to share characteristics of low self-esteem and an inability to assert themselves. They gather around him seated on sofas and folding chairs, some even at his feet on the floor. They all stare at him vacantly as he shakes his head back and forth, slowly at first, then faster, for a couple of minutes. This is supposed to release the energy from his body, energy he believes can heal and protect—everything that God can do for us, only George seems convinced that he is the Almighty. In fact, he is sure that in the near future he will discover the key to life and death and achieve immortality for himself and those faithful to him.

I observe an outrageous ego that will accept no challenge and a status quo of hero-worship as his followers perpetually reinforce his position as omnipotent leader. Like a vampire, he feeds off his devotees' energy and requires their adoration to survive; without them, I believe he would be completely deflated. I am distressed and offended by the twisted lies that are being promoted in this room. I think of a treasured picture of George that Elizabeth carries in her wallet. This revolts me. The allegiance she and the rest have to George is incredible. My experience tonight confirms what I and some of the others in UWSA had suspected: that this is a cult, and George has set the whole thing up to benefit himself. In addition, what is this headshaking all about? Groping for answers, it finally dawns on me. I remember a day, after a particularly hard workout in my karate class, when I slipped into a state of deep calm from endorphin. I realize that George is high all day long, but instead of using drugs or alcohol, he has found another way to trigger his brain to release the chemicals that will separate him from reality!

I sit there for two long hours, focusing on the leaves of his Ficus tree and praying for protection. When we are finally released, I do not even pause to speak with Elizabeth. I feel so sick to my stomach that I rush home to vomit out of my system the appalling sights I have just witnessed.

The information I gather from my personal observations and from Elizabeth helps me to discern George's unique con. Elizabeth has told me about George's abusive mother. It is clear that he never resolved his hatred for her, so he created a dictatorship where he continually punishes his followers for his mother's crimes. He hates any kind of nurturing or feminine behavior and demands that the women eliminate all expressions of love and affection by convincing them that this is "mothering" and part of the destructive "Female Game" whose sole purpose is to manipulate men. He controls them by restricting their natural curiosity and by not permitting them to discover anything on their own, especially their personal feelings. He must conclude everything first, and if he doesn't agree then it isn't so. Anyone who tries to assert themselves is cut off with raging putdowns, glaring, hostile eyes and strong-arm threats. Domination is used to direct all of their thoughts back to The Group's doctrine and to block all possible exits. Along with all of that, their ability to distinguish right from wrong is repressed or beaten out of them.

In his den, I have observed all of this myself. During my visit, George even tested his approach on me, but gave up quickly, sensing that I was on the edge of throwing it back into his face. I am not afraid and would never allow him to make me recede. Unfortunately, he has found isolated, vulnerable women to victimize, and he is having a field day with them. . . .

And George has much to gain from his exploitation. He has convinced his followers that the more time they put in with him, the sooner they will reach their goal of immortality. In reward, their financial investment will be returned to them in some other way. Clearly this is George's reinterpretation of the spiritual Law of Reciprocity for his own benefit. When I discover that Elizabeth sees him more than twenty hours a week, I hit the roof.

"What? Are you crazy? You've been in there for more than fifteen years. What's he offering you for all of your time and money? A fair relationship is a two-way street. Unless there is an even exchange, one person is being taken advantage of. In addition, no man would ever want to stay with you if he has to compete with George. Do you want to wake up in twenty years and realize that you have wasted your whole life in his den?"

I hope the truth will find its way to Elizabeth. She looks bewildered, hesitantly agreeing that she wouldn't want that to happen. Perhaps there is hope for her. . . .

Elizabeth finally admits that George has had sex with most of the women, who now range from 32-72 years of age. He has directed them to fondle each other and to pleasure him (while they pay him for the honor!), but he never reciprocates. I can't believe this is going on a couple of minutes from my home. With all that I have discovered, I am beside myself with outrage, and I have to hold myself back from going right up to that son-of-a-bitch and poking both of his eyes out! I know I can't fight Elizabeth's battle for her; I must find patience and reinforce my trust in God, whose hand I see in both of our lives. . . .

A little bit at a time, Judy encourages me to acknowledge my accomplishments and talents. Her respect is refreshing salve on a burning wound. She points out that the people I choose to be in my life should lift me, not bring me down. What a revelation that an alternative exists to the interminable condemnation that has been my steady diet in The Group! I feel like a child just learning to walk, discovering that there is a whole world outside my crib. I watch Judy as she strokes the face of her little niece, calling her "sweet." Sweet? What is that? A person can take joy in another? In George's den everyone is inadequate, even despicable, barely worthy to be judged and hopefully corrected by his energy. I grasp each new concept that Judy presents, turning it over in my mind, commanding it to stay, even though it feels like a strange foreign object. Absorption is slow, but my eyes are opening, as if I have just remembered a movie I saw eons ago. Like Rip Van Winkle waking up after a twenty-year sleep, I can't believe all that I have missed.

The more of myself I reclaim, the more I understand what is going on in my circle. Like selling our souls to Satan, we have given our allegiance to George and he owns our lives. I can't figure out what valuable commodity we receive in return for the donation of our most precious possession. As I pass my sessions in observation, the mechanics of control and oppression for the personal gain of George and his children slowly expose themselves. I gather new information each day and compare notes with Judy each evening.

As I look at the world around me with new eyes, I realize how cut off I have been from others. I begin to notice the people I ignored before, having heartlessly judged them (with George's prejudices) as dead robots. Now, I see that their lives are like mine, with tragedy, joy, and the dream of a better tomorrow. I realize that I am part of humanity, not above and separate as George has taught. How extraordinary this seems!

One evening I view a football game on Judy's TV. I notice a light blue glow around one of the team's white helmets. *That's The Energy spreading out into the world*, I think. . . . Then, I suddenly wake up. Bolting out of the recliner, I rush into the kitchen, jumping up and down like a little kid, barely able to contain my exhilaration. "Jude," I declare, "before I would have believed that the glow around the helmets was from George's energy. This would have meant that the team was going to win. I just realized that the glow is only from the TV tube. There is a physical explanation. It's all about electrons and magnetic fields and has nothing to do with George and spiritual forces!"

These days I am losing weight, and my pallid face betrays utter exhaustion. George and Serena observe from their spiritual thrones, dispassionately contemplating my downfall. When the mood strikes them, they excoriate me for my poor health. I must be disobeying The Energy to look so terrible. Funny, every other person in that room, including them, looks just like me—twisted and empty.

George reminds us frequently that we shouldn't need to eat. "The Energy will fill our stomachs. The brain is miraculous and can take care of the body without food, if we would just let it do its thing."

Picking up a rock, he jokingly mimics taking a bite. "If we didn't have The Program, we would be able to nourish ourselves with these!"

Pauline, even more haggard than I, enthusiastically agrees, "Yes. I know. My stomach feels full and I haven't eaten for eighteen hours!"

Daily at my office, I drive myself relentlessly to perform, to fix the mistakes in my life. Sometimes I think of breaking for food, but a voice in my head commands, "Don't eat; you'll be OK without food. Do the more important stuff first."

Self-hatred, sometimes even a seemingly deliberate drive to starve myself to death, storms in my mind. It justifies itself by reminding me that I am a failure because I can't adequately support myself. Meanwhile, Judy struggles to get food into me. She cooks sumptuous Italian meals. Grinning with delight, she puts the fork-full of food into my mouth and watches to make sure I chew and swallow. Gently, she encourages me to finish what is on my plate and praises me when I do. Each day she asks what I have eaten and reminds me, "Your body can't run without fuel."

Judy is also concerned about my lack of exercise. "We don't need it," I answer automatically, based on George's assertions.

"Of course you do," she replies, "Your heart will grow weak without it. You spend too much time sitting in George's den. You know that swollen foot he had at the meeting I attended a couple of months ago? I figured it out; that was gout, probably because he spends all day in his armchair—not his 'special' energy as he explained to me."

Of course she is right. I am ashamed of myself. A college degree in science and I believed his ridiculous explanation! I learned about gout in high school science. How did I forget?

Later that week Judy escorts me to the Bally's health club in Englewood Cliffs. I haven't been to a gym since I was on the swim team in college, nearly twenty years ago. On the way in I observe several people on exercise bicycles. "They look ridiculous," I spit out judgmentally, à la Sharkman.

"That's what George taught you. It's not really true. Exercise is good for you," Judy explains patiently.

She puts me on a treadmill. As I try to keep up with the machine, asthma clamps my lungs. At thirty-five, I feel like I am ninety. I remember my dedication to physical fitness eighteen years ago: swimming, hiking, bicycling. *My God. What have I done to myself? How can I ever repair the damage?*

Karen brings her two children, now four and five, to The Group every week. They always protest, but their mother ignores them. I pity them as they sit together in a big, white chair, two beautiful, little dolls with jet black hair and creamy white skin, gazing into space, waiting impotently for their two hours to be up. George frequently asks them if they want to "sit on his lap and go for a ride." Once he tries to force Lulu, but she screams and pounds her fists on him until he lets her go. Instinctively, they want no part of him. Their mother knows all about the dead dog, but George never shows it to the kids, explaining that they are "too young to handle Ben's power," but he gives them each a rock gift, reminding them that it is precious and they should carry it in their pockets always; it will help them with their schoolwork and solve conflicts with their friends. When George focuses on Jack, he is man to man, "You know more than your friends because you come here; remember that *you* are their leader."

George makes an example of Lulu as The Female Program in training. "Look at her. Even though she is only four, she knows how to seduce and control men. She is already a little witch."

Lulu glares at him. Silently I cheer and pray for her to be strong. *Keep resisting until you get big enough to tell your mother you'll never come back*, I think.

One day in the car on the way to George's, the kids inform their mother, "George doesn't care about us, he only cares about his rocks."

Karen laughs as she recounts this to us. "My children are too young to understand that you care about them more than anyone else, but you do it without pretense and hypocrisy."

The following week, I decide to give in to Elizabeth's relentless insistence that I attend another one of George's meetings. I arrive an hour late and position myself on a folding chair at the back of the crowded room. Soon, I notice a foul smell that is quite revolting. There isn't another place to sit, so I try to tolerate it. However, when someone gets up to leave, I quickly jump into the vacant seat. Unfortunately, I still can't escape the odor. What is it? I wonder. Perhaps one of the women sitting near me needs a shower badly?

Apparently, The Group has just finished viewing a video movie portraying Jesus Christ as a modern day citizen. I notice that as George asks various members what they learned, he reprimands them when their interpretations are wrong, that is, not the same as his. While he puts them down, others rally to support him, hoping to score points. He particularly attacks Elizabeth's mother, Rachael, and I feel sorry for her. It seems unusually cruel, especially for a woman in her mid-seventies. Later that evening, George turns to focus on me. "You are quite new to our group. What do you think is going on here?"

Put on the spot, I try to respond as neutrally as possible. "Well, I really don't know much about your group, but I do know that I am very happy to have Elizabeth as a friend. She is a diamond." I notice Elizabeth looking down in shame, and I realize that what I've said is totally unacceptable.

Rachael intervenes to take the positive focus away from her daughter by interrogating me and trying to set me up as a fool. "How is your relationship with your husband?" she spits out, cold and nasty.

I try to tell the truth. "We have our ups and downs, but he is a good man and we love each other." I know this isn't acceptable, since they believe that married couples are co-dependent and have no genuine feelings for each other. My response

Michael, Elizabeth, & Judy

tonight will surely confirm in their minds that I am a bimbo, certain to pull Elizabeth the wrong way.

The following morning in the den an annoyed George demands, "Why did Judy lie last night about her husband? Married people are just children playing house. Underneath, they really hate each other. It is not possible to live together in harmony unless you have The Energy. You could be in real danger. One day her husband might wake up and realize you are taking away his mommy. If he loses control, he might very well take a gun and shoot you. . . ."

For the rest of the day, I wonder if what George said is possible. He has triggered my fear and that evening, I can't stop myself from spilling it out to Michael on the phone. But he simply laughs. "That's ridiculous. I would never hurt you. I understand that you need Judy. She cares about you too. The only one I might ever want to shoot is George!"

With my bank account rapidly approaching $0, I cash in my only remaining asset, a zero-coupon bond worth $5,000, deposited into an IRA fifteen years ago—an account to which I have never been able to contribute further. As I stare piteously at my Fidelity Brokerage statement that contained a balance of over $100,000 a few short years ago, I cry helplessly to no one listening. That bond was supposed to take care of me in the future; now what will I do? How much longer will this go on?

I cut back expenses everywhere I can, denying myself everything except essential groceries. After draining my father's inheritance, despite my better judgment, I turn to credit cards. How I will repay them, I do not know; I can only pray for a miracle. The mounting credit card debt (with 14% interest) quickly surpasses $30,000. Despairing, I wonder if I should stop buying Dunkin' Donuts coffee in the afternoon to save a few pennies. Perhaps I could put that $10 a week toward bills? While photographing weddings and Bar Mitzvahs I survey the dance floor for eligible men. Desperate thoughts come, *Perhaps I can find someone, anyone—even a person I don't like, to support me.*

Worrying about money is perpetual. More and more frequently I experience the horrifying vision of myself broke and on the street, worrying where my next meal will come from. Each day this nightmare looms closer, threatening to rip the veil between prophesy and reality and engulf me. Suffocated by this insurmountable issue, it takes all of my energy to coach myself through another hour, another day. During the night, I know Serena can hear my relentless asthmatic cough from her bedroom across the hall, but she never asks if I am OK. Sometimes I tiptoe downstairs to sit in my recliner, out of her earshot. I don't know why, but I feel guilty that the noise may be disturbing her sleep. In the morning I wake up exhausted. These days the asthma is continual, and I cannot mount a flight of stairs without pausing to catch my breath.

Like a slave, I force myself through photography assignments, pushing away the ever-looming truth—that all the money that I can barely find the energy to earn will go to George. During the day I constantly want to lie down and relieve myself from the interminable struggle to keep my body in motion. When occasionally I do, I am unconscious in less than a minute. I experience desperation I never could have imagined was possible. There is something wrong with my entire life—my body, my mind, my spirit, my soul. I think back to a riding camp I attended when I was eight, in Upstate New York's Adirondack Mountains. That summer, temperatures soared. About twenty horses walked a circuit with children on their backs, eight hours a day, in the brutal sunlight. There was no break as each group of campers was cycled through the activity. One day I noticed a horse in front of me sweating profusely. A little while later he collapsed. He just couldn't take another step. Now I feel like that horse. . . .

Every day, I struggle to pay George. What other choice do I have? I keep hoping that things will turn around, but they never do. Finally, one day, ashamed to admit that I need it, I ask for help. "George, I'm having problems with money; I don't know what to do."

My eyes turn toward him pathetically; I believe he *must* have the solution; I just need to show my willingness to yield.

George peers down, and his look tells me how he feels: responding to me isn't worth his breath. However, as if doing me a big favor, he offers a solution. . . . That morning, one of his more recent recruits (a rabbi who first met him at a book signing in the Nanuet, N.Y. Barnes & Noble) has offered to help him grow his flock. "The rabbi agreed to approach people at my next book signing. He will sell my rocks and encourage them to join The Group. Why don't you try the same thing and I will pay you a commission?"

This is his solution to my oppressive debt!? Where is his common sense? The man who claims to have all answers—wisdom beyond our capacity—can't even do basic math! I calculate quickly in my head. Even with a 20% commission, in order to pay off my credit card debt I would need to refer 100 people who would each see him once a week for two years. He currently has 20 paying clients. How could this ever happen?

With no solutions in sight, my shameful circumstances force me to cut back my George time to the bare minimum: five hours a week plus the Thursday night meeting ($900 a month). Beatrice, Bess, and Pauline still spend their twenty hours per week at George's side, and I feel left out, like a naughty child who must stay indoors during recess, pressing his nose against the classroom window, watching his little friends play. Although my withdrawal is so significant to me, my absence goes unnoticed by the rest. They just keep moving along, business as usual.

And rapidly, the most awful truth of all is bursting into my consciousness. Geysers of hurt erupt as the evidence points to one inescapable truth. . . . *My God, George will only allow me near him if I pay the admission price. Otherwise, I do not matter to him—and I never did.* I realize that now, when I really need a friend, the man to whom I have dedicated my life for two decades will never show up.

That night I have a dream. I am floundering in the icy water at the base of a large ocean liner. I look up to see George, my mother, and the rest standing on the deck looking down at me. George lectures to the others: my predicament is my fault. They nod in agreement, dispassionately watching me struggling to stay afloat. I beg them to throw me the life preserver resting only inches from their hands. But they ignore my plea and instead sing a chorus of "I told you so. You ignored our advice before, so now you will suffer your consequences."

Having gratified their need to bask in their self-importance, they disappear from view, moving on to new and pleasurable activities available elsewhere. I am erased from their minds and left to drown in the sea. . . .

For the first time, I understand betrayal and the terrible consequences of trusting someone blindly. Despite The Group's rhetoric, ("We are all here to help each other. . . . You just have to ask.") I am, and always have been, on my own.

So far, our Cliff's Notes sales have been disappointing and I have only succeeded in inflating my already outrageous loan to the corporation. Nevertheless, something won't let me give up—I still believe in *Exambusters Study Cards*. I keep the business alive on more than fifteen of my personal credit cards, rotating balances between them when I can't make minimum payments.

One Sunday, feeling I can no longer tolerate my unending failure, I decide to analyze the finances on paper. George, with his spiritual philosophies about running a business, would never support this, and thanks to his advice, I haven't kept records of loans, costs, or cash flow. Instead, for the past four years I have been basing my decisions on what "feels right." Serena has been just as careless, using The Energy to justify any expenditure. On the few occasions when I opposed one of her suggestions (usually some expensive advertising that later returned two cents on the dollar), she promptly reported to her father who reprimanded me until I gave in. As long as I have been able to write a check, this situation has perpetuated, but now the well has run dry.

I dig up tax documents from 1991-1995 and form piles of checks, categorizing travel, development, printing, etc. I calculate totals and list them on a spreadsheet. Five excruciating hours pass. A hundred times I want to throw everything in the garbage and return to George's convenient way of thinking. "Everything will work out OK if you just do what feels right." However, my personal drill sergeant holds a gun to my head, and I must finish, no matter what. Shame and rage mount as the horror of my massive mistake slowly reveals itself. I have spent more than $165,000, and after half a decade, succeeded only in creating additional, credit card debt, now $40,000. All of this money has been squandered by ignorance and self-aggrandizement. I would like to, but I cannot blame Serena and George completely. Yes, they certainly encouraged me, but I have been a victim of my own ego as well. Addicted to my fantasies of success, I have chased without seeking a reality check, and I have depleted my funds to pacify my needs.

Today, buried in the wreckage, I despise myself. And in this moment, drained of any remaining willpower or creative solutions, for the first time, I fall to my knees in humility. I have been following lies, and now, it is time to correct the mistake; I must stop listening to George and Serena once and for all.

My first thought is to declare bankruptcy in order to wipe out my credit card debt, money that has financed print runs of flash cards (merchandise now selling at a loss of fifty cents per box). The Jacoby and Meyers law firm in Passaic County offers a free consultation, and I visit them. The lawyer quickly examines my liabilities and reassures me, smiling. "You don't have to worry anymore; we'll take care of it. It's easy to declare bankruptcy. People do it every day. It's the legal way to make a fresh start. Just sign this paper, pay my $995 fee (on a credit card if you want), and in three weeks you'll be debt free."

A wave of excitement surges. What a joy to wipe away my years of debt in one sweep of the pen! I so very much want to take his advice. Yet, I hesitate. I desire relief more than anything, but having accepted my mistakes, I would prefer to repair them myself, not seek the wave of a magic wand. I also guess there are negative consequences to this course of action upon which he has not touched. With difficulty, I end our meeting. I need a second opinion.

Cliff's Notes notifies us that they have sold out most of our inventory—10,000 pieces in expensive packaging that lost money on every sale. They have established some new accounts, albeit slowly, and things seem to be headed in a positive direction at last. If our business is to continue, I must replenish their stock, but this time repackaged at a much lower cost. I open the *Business to Business Yellow Pages* and begin my search for a new manufacturer. After several days of research, I manage to redesign the product for less than half the former per unit price and select a new printer. For the first time, there should be profit from our sales.

Although I have worked alone, out of courtesy, I invite Serena to meet the printer. When I introduce them, he mentions that he didn't know I had a partner. Serena does not take this well. I sense an ugly rage erupting, even though she purposefully conceals it from this stranger. Doom impends as I recoil inside, praying that the inevitable will not come. The drive back to the office is made in pregnant silence, and when we arrive, my partner immediately closes and locks the door to our suite. My jaw tightens; I anticipate her reprimand. Finally protected by privacy, her face reddens, twisting into a vicious rage as she releases her venom. "I didn't exist to him! We are supposed to be partners, fifty-fifty, but you are pushing me out!" she states indignantly.

I don't know what to say. I try to explain that I have no bad intentions, that all I care about is putting the company in the black. I am willing to do the necessary work, as long as I get results. However, the engine fueling her crazed rage is boiling over, and nothing I can say will halt it. She accuses me of wanting to fail, defying The Energy, being impossibly self-destructive, scheming to hurt her, not valuing her contributions to the company—the same unfounded criticisms I have heard hundreds of times before. Winding herself up until she loses control, Serena lunges toward me and grabs me by the throat, pushing me onto the counter top. She shakes my head, screaming like a banshee and threatening to kill me. "You have contributed nothing to the company. I am the one who really cares. Without me it would have failed long ago."

Everything slows down in my mind as I silently ask myself, *Elizabeth, what do you want to do?* I realize that we are both about the same weight and height, and I think, *I learned a little Judo at camp, and I can still focus my fist. If I want to, I can punch her lights out. She's not really harming me right now, just scaring me and hurting my feelings. I don't want to be violent, so I won't do anything yet.*

I yield, neither defensive nor aggressive. I look beyond her wrath and wait. A little while later, for no apparent reason, her tantrum ends. She releases me from her grip and walks away without further comment.

Finally liberated, my delayed reaction bursts forth and I strike back, "What's the matter with you? I work hard, and you attack me like an animal for something I had nothing to do with."

Pain wells up, choking me. I can't tolerate another minute of Serena, and I run from the office, seeking the safety of our house. Inside myself I vow *again* that this injustice must end; I do not deserve to be treated like this. My surging adrenalin makes me feel that I could pick her up and throw her off the planet. Pacing my bedroom floor in frustration, I take deep breaths to prevent myself from hyperventilating.

The next day I am afraid to face George; I am sure that he knows all about the fight and will blame me. However, he surprises me, "Serena is a real witch," he states with a glint of pride in his eyes. Then adds reassuringly, "It's OK now."

Yet, I stay away from her. Not being able to face going to work, I return home. Sometime that afternoon, the phone rings. It is Serena. She sounds sweet. "I don't think all of this fighting is good, so I have scheduled a meeting with a business advisor. His name is Lou Gelbart, and he'll meet us tomorrow at 3:00 P.M."

She doesn't say she was wrong; there is no apology, but I realize that this is her attempt to remedy things. Relieved that the fight is over, I relax. "That sounds like a good idea, Serena, OK."

Actually, when Serena and I aren't fighting, I do have affection for her. We share bonds born from common experiences: the discoveries and activities in The Group, our struggles in both businesses, and membership in United We Stand America. Serena has even made me a character in her *Chronicles in Shadow* fantasy trilogy: Eliza, the buxom barmaid! We have passed many evenings relaxing on her bed, playfully throwing around plot ideas for her books, or watching TV like college roommates, in between the rest of everything.

The following afternoon, a new character enters the stage. Lou Gelbart, a "professional business consultant," is a strange bird. Neither lawyer nor accountant, he explains that he simply freelances: giving advice, writing contracts, and assisting with negotiations to obtain financing. He claims to be 58, but his weathered face tells me he has exaggerated by at least a decade. He is skinny, average height, and at the moment, single. Clothed in a tired leather jacket and black polyester pants, he slithers like a swinger on the make, while his body language delivers a failed attempt at seductiveness. Lou smokes thin, brown cigarettes and drives a beat up, turquoise Honda Civic. During that first meeting we find out that he has been married and divorced six times and has lived all over the globe, including Paris. Currently, he is seeking wife number seven. When Serena asks him why, since he has already failed several times, he pauses to ponder his motivations and then concludes, "I don't like to be alone . . . and it would be nice to have someone to do my laundry."

Lou also tells us that he has been indicted for insider trading and has recently served a short jail term after paying a $1,000,000 fine. If that's true, then he has only just recently begun rebuilding his life, and he must be hungry for cash. How has this unconventional creature entered our lives? Serena had called several listings in the *Yellow Pages* and he was the only one to answer his telephone!

After protecting the secret for as long as I can bear, I finally find the courage to tell Judy about Ben. She listens without comment as I recount the grotesque details. In fact, she seems to accept it. Judy is the first outsider to find out. When I describe the "worms" Ben was creating, and George's explanation, Judy disagrees. "That's crazy, Elizabeth. I'm sure they were maggots feeding on rotting flesh."

I could kick myself! I have seen as many horror films as the next person. This is basic Biology 101 information. How did I come to throw away my 16 years of school?

The next day (I don't know why), I inform George that Judy knows about the dog. He does not take it well. "Why did you go and do a stupid thing like that? She might want to hurt him." Then he becomes pensive. "No, she can't hurt me or Ben because The Energy protects us, but she can hurt you."

Why would she want to? I wonder.

When Elizabeth tells me of George's plans to bring back the dog, it confirms what I have suspected all along, his goal to become a Messiah endowed with powers of miracles, healing, and the ultimate—resurrection. This also explains the source of that awful smell permeating his den the last time I attended his group. According to her, the carcass was laid out on a board on the floor, hidden under a towel, only two feet away from me! It seems that George hides Ben from anyone who is not an inner circle member. George must know that what he is doing is wrong; otherwise, why would he need to conceal it! This man is not only devious and manipulative, he is also deranged and potentially dangerous to himself and those who have put their trust in him. With what I have just learned, I am more afraid than ever for Elizabeth.

During our first meeting, Lou Gelbart agreed (for a fee of $500 each) to put together partnership agreements for Flash Blasters, Inc. and Expressions Photography, Inc. The contract signing was scheduled for the afternoon of September 15.

The signing day arrives, and in the morning, it occurs to me that perhaps Lou might be able to help us find financing for the flash cards. We have been looking for an investor, co-publisher, loan, anything—for a long time. At the office, I make the suggestion to Serena. Serena's favorite activity is attending meetings, and she especially enjoys preparing proposals. However, today her reaction is abnormal and strange. She shoots me an ugly look. "That is a bad idea. I don't want to do it. And don't talk to him *behind my back*. Mr. Gelbart shouldn't get any more involved than he already is."

"Why? I don't understand. Give me a good reason." I protest.

She offers nothing further, but her glare injects fear into my heart of dreadful consequences should I defy her. Then she changes the subject. *We have hired a professional advisor and she doesn't even want to talk to him about our immediate needs. Why?*

Lou arrives on time, and we sign and notarize the agreements. They contain details regarding the disposition of partners' shares upon breakup or death. Stated therein, we each own 50% of both businesses, with Expressions currently valued at $80,000. After we have finished, Serena, true to her daily habit, rushes out. She can't wait to go and sit with her father and the carcass. As she exits, she glances back at me to make it clear that I had better keep my mouth shut. . . .

But I won't. I must keep *Exambusters Study Cards* going, and I must repair my finances. Although I fear her, the instructions she planted won't paralyze me. I lead Lou into the other room to show him product samples. For the next hour I passionately, almost hysterically, recount my entire, eight-year journey of creation, hope, frustration, and defeat. I describe how the idea came to me (from my teaching and tutoring), the endless meetings with book chain buyers, the potential I see, and my frustration at our lack of momentum. *Help me. Please*, my expression pleads. Lou is riveted to every detail of my saga. His eyes widen as he, through my narrative, experiences the roller coaster I have ridden. He is impressed with my persistence and ambition. Most important, he genuinely understands why I believe in the flash cards. And after that day, Lou comes to believe in them too. A connection has been forged between us. Where it will lead, I do not know. . . .

Meetings follow where Lou asks the questions that Serena's lawyer should have asked, but never did, on the day he made us legal partners. He wants to know how Serena has paid for her half of the business to equal my contribution of money, talent, and time. The excuse that Serena's contribution of $0.00 is offset by The Energy only works in her father's den, and she seems to know this. Therefore, whenever Lou challenges her, she answers a different question, referring to her exceptional sales and brainstorming skills.

Lou telephones me regularly, calls that don't include Serena. He continually challenges the details of our partnership, exclaiming with resonant fervor, "You can't *gift* shares of a corporation. They must be bought or exchanged for something tangible such as labor, accounts, or contacts . . . something."

It sounds logical, and yet, as if my mind were an empty blackboard with one sole phrase scrawled authoritatively across, I respond in monotone, programmed determination, "Serena must be my partner. I can't make you understand, but it *has to be*."

But Lou is a relentless drill. He possesses a drive to convince me, to split my head open with the facts he knows to be true. Thus, he confronts the brick wall of my thinking again and again. He will not stop blasting me. In my head, even as I drive to work or sit home alone at night, his strident, demanding voice rants.

"You can't just give away shares of a corporation. *How did she earn them?*"

Nevertheless, the Flash Blasters, Inc. agreement has already been signed. What can I do? Hire a lawyer and take her to court? I could never afford that, and I am too afraid of her father. The dots simply aren't connecting.

Early in the month, we all hear that our fellow comrade Caroline's 91-year-old mother is going down. Cancer has overtaken her body, and she is in intensive care at a nearby hospital.

George lectures Caroline, "There is still time to save her, but you must let me lead."

That evening, he visits the hospital. For over an hour he shakes his head at her mother's bedside. The next day, we hear about his success. "Although she was only half conscious, when I placed my hand on her forehead, she understood that I was there to save her."

George makes several more uninvited trips (at no charge) to the hospital during the next two weeks, shaking his head vigorously to turn her disease around. The mother's condition stabilizes for a few days and then continues its descent. Meanwhile, back at the den, Caroline schedules extra therapy sessions to help her get through. The entire Group focuses on helping her.

Bess donates her insight. "Caroline, you must have some secret hostility toward your mother that you are not facing. This is interfering with George's attempts to heal her."

The rest chime in, encouraging her to confess her destructive intentions. She must be humble if her mother is to ever have a chance. Caroline, dazed and confused, protests continually. She can't understand where to locate these unpardonable thoughts inside her mind.

Within a few weeks, her mother passes away. Due to the funeral, Caroline misses a few of her regular weekly sessions, but finally returns to George's den one Saturday morning to try to strengthen herself with his "stress reduction therapy." A group of eight or so is present, and they barely give her time to seat herself before proceeding to shoot incisive "truths" her way.

It is Bess who leads the herd. "Caroline, you had your chance to save your mother by helping George, but instead, you chose to hold on to your negativity."

The exhausted, grieving Caroline, like a rabbit (with nowhere to run) attacked by crows, is helpless against this onslaught.

And now that the core truth is revealed, the rest follow Bess's logic, throwing stones. Tears of disbelief and injustice well in Caroline's eyes. She wonders how she will ever make it through the remaining half hour of her session. Finally, the clock moves enough to free her. But even as she is halfway to the exit, Serena delivers the *coup de grâce*, "Why won't you just admit that you killed her? You have betrayed us, your true friends. We have spent weeks trying to help you see the truth, and you just spit on us by ignoring us. You especially owe my father an apology."

Caroline barely makes it to her car, parked in front of George's house. That evening George receives a telephone call from Caroline. She has invested more than a decade of her life, but after today, she won't be coming back. She excuses herself politely by explaining that she just doesn't feel there is anything more for her to learn in The Group.

The following week, Nora, Bess, and Pauline each telephone Caroline on separate evenings to convince her to come back. "You don't realize how bad your life will become without The Energy."

And after several days, George calls himself, flourishing the disciplinary, sarcastic tone that has always gotten him his way, "Well Caroline, are you through with your little vacation? Ready to come back?"

Caroline is shaky, sad and confused, but she knows one thing for sure, she wants no part of us. Hesitantly, but with inner resolve, she replies, "No George, I don't think I'll be able to."

George's face, instantaneously three shades brighter, roars, "You have used The Energy for 15 years now; without it, you will never survive, Caroline. Your health will decline quickly and you will be dead soon."

The next day he fills us in. "Caroline is just another stupid fool who has walked away from The Energy. It was nice knowing her, but now it's time to move on. We have more important things to do. Next."

With that, he shakes his head and eliminates her from his mind forever.

Another Thursday night, and Ben is resting in his favorite spot: George's lap on his wooden board-bed. The dog expired more than a year ago, and his carcass has passed through several stages: bleeding, flesh rotting, and additional hair growth. Now the skull is partially exposed near the snout, and the bone inside the eye sockets is clearly visible. Dry, leathery skin clings to the ribs, and small patches of hair remain here and there. One of the legs has broken off, but those bone fragments have been painstakingly positioned in their former location, awaiting the day when Ben will need them to walk again. George compliments us on our patience and persistence regarding Ben's resurrection. "Each of you has become conditioned from many hours of focusing. You know, if I showed this to an inexperienced person they would freak out from the enormous power of what is happening here. People can't just walk in and look at Ben, they have to be prepared; they need to train with The Energy first. This is not a stupid baby game; this is really going to happen! Now everybody focus on this."

George picks up a light bulb and begins to shake vigorously. "Just give me a little time and I will make it light."

Soon, an amazed Bess declares, "The light bulb is getting longer!"

Within minutes several others observe it changing shape or glowing slightly. George continues shaking. I concentrate too. The bulb appears slightly longer . . . until something I had forgotten a century ago surfaces of its own accord: "the power of suggestion." Perhaps the more intelligent part of me has had enough crap because finally, after believing lies so many times,

I see the truth. Nothing is happening, not now, not ever, to the light bulb, to the rocks, or to Ben! Our group has merely perfected the art of creating and inhabiting an alternate reality. There, what our minds have imagined, we believe to be real, and conversely, what is real holds no value: Black is white, and white is black. . . .

It is 8:30 A.M. the next day. Focusing with George as I usually do during these morning sessions, I slip into a familiar state of foggy, relaxed oblivion. Unexpectedly, George breaks the silence . . . and his words stun me. "Doris left. She moved out in August. Don't tell anyone. No one else knows except Serena and Christopher."

"What? How?" I stammer.

"I was taking a nap in the morning one Monday. For some reason, I was really tired. When I woke up a little after noon, all of her stuff was gone. Her sister Susan, from Long Island, snuck into the house and helped her. They must have been planning this for awhile. Lucky for her I was asleep. If I had been awake, she never would have gotten past the front door!"

During the next few days, George informs the rest of The Group of Doris's departure. No one had suspected a thing, and their response to this monumental event is . . . absolute indifference. They fail to notice the contradiction because somehow George's former assertions have been magically erased from their minds: "No matter what, Doris will *never* leave me, The Energy won't allow it."

The unexpected loss of his wife of thirty years doesn't seem to fluster George in the least, and his mission continues as usual.

"Hey Elizabeth, I have a new gig," he informs me one morning soon thereafter. "Every Wednesday I meet with a group of about twenty inmates at Sing Sing Prison in Ossining, N.Y. They all read my book and are really starting to feel The Energy. I have your mother to thank; it was her idea and she wrote me the letter of recommendation."

My stomach tightens at this news, another group of people who have let him into their lives, who take him at face value, only listening to his words and never knowing the man behind them. I wish they could see him as I do.

These days, I keep my asthma inhaler within reach 24/7. While I sleep, my fingers clench it in my palm. And thank God, because in the middle of one night I wake up suffocating. It feels as if someone is squeezing the breath out of my lungs with a powerful grip. Desperately, I reach for the rescue inhaler. About to faint, I place it in my mouth and squeeze. Instantly my lungs relax, and I have oxygen once more. *My God*, I realize, tears of relief flowing down my cheeks, *I wouldn't have even been able to pick up the phone to call 911.* I think of how George forbids us to visit doctors. . . .

Life and death, I have gazed over the precipice, even if only for a brief moment. What would George have said if I had died? I realize that he wouldn't have cared at all.

The next day Judy begs, "Honey, I think you should go to a doctor for your asthma."

She has been trying to convince me for several months now, and I have always resisted her, using George's excuses that I must find the way myself to push past my physical symptoms. Besides, I have no money for doctor's bills, and I have no medical insurance. But after last night's episode, I finally give in. She makes an appointment at her own doctor's office for the next day.

The doctor finds my lungs to be severely swollen. After an X-ray, he informs me that there are spots on my lungs from tissue damage. In addition, after years of struggling to breathe, my lungs are 20% larger than they should be. The acute asthma I am experiencing requires immediate and daily attention. He prescribes three different inhalers to control my condition. After a trip to the CVS pharmacy, I return home, take the medicines, and fall into a deep sleep. A huge burden lifts from my back; I know I have done the right thing.

The following day, Thursday, November 17, I enter George's den at 2:00 P.M. for my regular two-hour session. He is sitting with Pauline, chatting. They face each other from opposite ends of the couch with their feet up. It is the kind of comfort two people settle into after they've just had sex, and I wonder if they have. When George sees me, he stops his conversation abruptly to address me, "How are you doing?"

"Fine. Nothing's new," I return, my voice flat.

He seems to want to probe me about something, but I don't know why. Finally he comes out with it, "I heard you went to a doctor."

I haven't mentioned this appointment to anyone. However, I do write things on my desk calendar and Serena, the snoop, must have reported to her father. "Yes, for my asthma," I respond.

Sensing that his territory (my mind) has been invaded behind his back, the demon that possesses George growls and dons his battle armor. A violated dragon, he stokes the flames in his belly, ready to spit fire, intent on repossessing his stolen property.

"You know that doctors are all liars and we don't need anyone in our group going to one," he shouts wrathfully.

I don't argue with him. I simply say nothing. However, he continues voicing his displeasure until he has worked himself into a frenzy, finally sputtering out, "Admit that you and Judy are playing a game."

I can't agree; his accusation is simply not true. My lack of cooperation fuels him, and he stands up almost touching my body, violating my personal space. He glares down at me while I stammer an impotent defense. "No, Judy and I just like each other; it's not a game."

Pauline sucks in her breath at this blasphemy. I don't understand what is happening. I have done nothing to provoke George, yet now he towers above, focusing his overpowering will upon me. He commands me to admit that he is right, that I am playing a game with Judy—a game with one sole purpose, to provoke him to react. But I cannot lie, even though in this moment my survival seems to depend on it. Fortitude and determination I never knew I had rise to oppose George's force-feeding, and in this moment revelation comes: *Oh my God! All* *along he has been shoving **his will** down my throat to control me.*

In the next moment, he shoves me onto the love seat. Leaning over me still, he commands, "Admit you are playing a game; admit it!"

I am frozen and can make no move to defend myself against this powerful man twice my weight, and a former Karate Black Belt. Now, in addition, I am mute from terror. Pauline sits in silence, emotionless, but I read her silent message and discern her betrayal. She believes I deserve this treatment for insubordination.

"Admit you are playing a game," George repeats again.

His hand lifts and strikes me in the face. He has lost it but I still can't move, neither for fight nor flight, and I can't force the lying words out of my mouth that will subdue him. George loses control, slapping me again and then again. I am so numb from shock that the blows don't even hurt. . . . Then, all of a sudden, in the midst of his tirade, George stops dead. As if yanked by some invisible string attached to the middle of his spine, he staggers backwards several feet and falls into his white rattan swivel chair. He appears dazed, as if someone has just struck him, and mumbles in confusion, "I can't do this anymore."

I have no idea what has just stopped him from outright killing me in his violent fury; it seems like a miracle. Hurt feelings flood my chest. *What makes him think he has the right to treat me like this?*

Ten minutes later my pager beeps. It is Judy. I can tell that George knows who it is and is jealous, but he doesn't say anything. At 4:00 P.M., when my scheduled time is up, I rise and leave, handing him his $80 fee on the way out. The concept of going to the police does not even enter my thoughts—a mind where George is permitted to make his own laws, and *his* rights come before mine. The things that happen in his den occur for a higher reason. The way it is, is the way it must be.

I call Judy from my office. She sounds concerned and asks if I'm all right. I hide the truth, telling her I'm OK and trying to change the subject. I am too weak from shock to deal with her inevitable outrage. I know she will want to rip his head off. . . .

I realize that my process of separation has its own road map, and I must yield to the course. Whether I understand or not, each event is necessary to move toward the goal. There will be no maneuvering here, no premature actions taken from thought or reaction, neither mine nor hers. This procedure is as delicate as brain surgery, and my emotional well-being is at stake.

Two days later, when I finally do tell Judy, my distress has mostly passed, and she is able to accept that as much as she would like to, she cannot retaliate for me.

That Thursday evening, only three hours after the incident, I return to George's den for The Group. I don't know how I even get my feet through the door, my hurt is so huge. I am still hoping that after these extreme events he will finally reveal what I still believe *must* be buried somewhere inside—that he cares about my feelings, about the trauma he unfairly inflicted on me. However, there is nothing like that.

Instead, he informs us scientifically, "The Energy sent me a message today while Elizabeth and I were together. This will benefit us all. We can't fight anymore. We must do things a different way."

I sit in silence, containing my raging feelings. There is no hope of explaining my side. I will never convince him of my rights. It is all beyond that now anyway. I finally face the facts; George has been tested enough; he truly has no conscience. . . .

A few days after the attack, in the middle of a conversation, I sense a motor kick into gear inside of him that like a recurring nightmare, I know will drive him to attack like before. This time, I figure out the necessary dialogue to pacify and distract him until he calms down. I have changed; I will never let him touch me again.

It is Tuesday afternoon, about a week after my visit to the doctor. Serena leaves at 2:00 P.M. as she usually does to head over to her father's den. However, at 3:00 P.M. she returns unexpectedly, informing me that she wants to talk. She commands me to drop what I'm doing immediately, and my stomach sinks from anticipation. I sense in her tone that what I am about to hear will not be pleasant.

"Elizabeth, I have just rented an apartment. I am moving on the first of December."

I stare at her blankly, completely taken off guard. I had no idea she was even looking, and I can't handle the sudden upheaval of all that is familiar. "Serena, how long have you been planning this?"

Her reply is whimsical and disconcerting, "I just got the feeling to look in the paper last Sunday. One listing sounded interesting, so I went to see it. It felt right when I walked in so I decided to go for it."

Reality sinks in. I have only two weeks to find my own place. The last time I tried to rent a decent affordable apartment in Bergen County it took several months. On top of that, the winter holidays is the busiest season of the year (family portraits, holiday cards, etc.). Most important, I am worse than broke. Moving is costly. Nevertheless, Serena is set; in fact she has already signed a lease.

An hour later I enter her father's den. Ignoring my inevitable turmoil over his daughter's decision, George says nothing to me. But of course he knows all about it; he and Serena are thick as thieves. Finally I whine and whimper, "Why did she do it?"

His voice is cold and adamant. "Because this is good for *her growth*."

"But how will I find a place in two weeks? I can't afford to stay in that house by myself."

George doesn't respond, but my emotions are running out of control, and I throw a fit. "It's not fair. I hate her. Why? Why? Why? What will I do?" I work myself into a frenzy.

Expressionless, he observes me and finally responds, irritated at my scene, "You'd better calm down. You're raising your blood pressure, and your veins are popping out of your forehead. You'll give yourself a stroke." Enough said. He starts shaking his head.

That night I call Judy in tears.

"What's the matter, Honey?" she asks, and I recount the day's events. Softly she reassures me that maybe it's for the best. "You can stay with us if you can't find a place."

"Really?" I can't believe it. The idea of someone offering help when I am in distress is unknown to me. . . .

The next day I cannot suppress my intense feelings of hurt from Serena's dispassionate abandonment, and I throw them in her face, "I hate you, you stupid, cold, insensitive bitch. How could you just get up one day and leave without telling me?"

I fling four letter words at her, making my throat hoarse from screaming out of control, but she is unresponsive and instead stares blankly at me in the same manner as her father had the day before. I want to go for her throat, to hurt her back for the pain she is causing me, so I grab my pager and throw it at her chair, wishing I had more courage to aim higher and smash her skull. It breaks, costing me $89 to replace it. Serena maintains her silence. I am so frustrated by her indifference that I turn spiteful, throwing out the most hurtful secret I have, a terrible reality from which, up until today, I have spared her, "You used me and then dumped me just like your father. That son-of-a-bitch seduced me, my mother, and every other woman in there. He assembled his own personal harem behind your mother's back. Every day, for ten years, there was an orgy, *established for his pleasure alone*, and he laughed all the way to the bank!"

The arrow hits the bull's-eye. This new information about her precious father drives her into a state of shock and high anxiety.

Suddenly, I feel ashamed at my childish retaliation. Guilty, I flee the studio to escape further confrontation.

The phone on my desk rings and I glance at the caller-ID. "Expressions Photography" flashes, and I pick up eagerly. "Hi, Liz."

"Hi, Judy. It's Serena."

I am surprised and instantly suspicious. "What's up?"

"I need to talk. Elizabeth and I just had a fight."

She sounds upset and humble. Sympathetic, I ask what happened. After she offers some details, I wonder whether her distress might create an opening to finally reach her about her father's corruption. "I know that what Elizabeth told you was hard to hear, but you are an adult now, and maybe it's time for you to understand your father's true nature. He has taken advantage of many people for his own selfish purposes."

"No, you don't understand my father; he means well," she answers automatically.

My voice is wise, gentle, and caressing, an honest attempt to deliver the truth for her own good. "You look up to your father, but he is a human being and humans don't always do things for the right reasons. If you could only look beyond your image of him, you would see him for the person he truly is."

"I do see him for who he is," she states matter-of-factly. "He's just trying to help people with what he knows."

"I know that's what he wants you to believe but, as they say, 'You can't judge a book by its cover,' and actually your father has hurt many people very badly, and Elizabeth in one of them."

"No; he hasn't. People just don't understand him, so they make up stories to put him down."

Serena's stubborn intention to defend her father cuts off my optimism with the speed of a falling ax. I realize it's hopeless, so I quickly end the conversation.

Over the next week, with the help of Christopher and her father, little by little Serena moves out. First, her collection of numerous posters that graced almost every wall in the house, then some small pieces of furniture, next a few dishes. As each item disappears, my sense of abandonment intensifies. As if Band-aids are stuck all over my body, this exodus rips them off painfully, one by one. I keep praying this isn't happening until one day a week later, her bed is gone.

Reality finally sinks in, and I open the newspaper, circling a couple of listings close to my office. After viewing a few insultingly rundown, overpriced flats I find one I can tolerate and sign a lease (400 square feet of personal sanctuary). I move some clothing in my car, and a local man with a van does the rest.

After all of her things have been transferred from the Closter house, I visit Elizabeth's new place for the first time. Although the premises are modest at best, there is a different feeling in the air. "You know Liz, it is very strange but in Closter I felt turmoil, and here I feel peace."

"You know, you are right."

Sitting down on the floor among brown cartons containing her meager possessions, Elizabeth's tears begin. "Judy, what have I done to myself? In four years I'll be 40. I wasted all of that time when I could have been saving for my future. I have no family; I'm all alone. I've missed the chance to make friends, date, marry, and have children. I've allowed myself to be abused; the scars are all over me, and I don't know how I'll ever heal. I want my twenty years back. I want them back. I want them back."

I bend down to give her a hug, and she throws her arms around my neck, pulling me closer, clinging to me like a lost child. I realize that right now I am the only person she has in the world. I hold her, reassuring, "At least you are waking up now. What about those poor women, Nora, Bess, and Laura, who are ten years older than you? Think about their torment if someday they realize they've given away their entire adult lives. You have time left to start fresh, and I know there will be new and good things."

"What's a good thing?" Liz sighs sadly, and I realize she really doesn't know.

"It's OK to grieve for your loss. But don't ever forget that your trials have made you strong and courageous. Your character has been baptized by fire."

She looks up into my face, pensive for a moment. "Of all the eyes I have ever seen, yours are the most beautiful."

"Really? Why do you say that?"

"Because you came out of the darkness when I had no hope. You reached out and pulled me to safety. You showed me that God exists. I will never stop being grateful. In a way, you saved my life."

In this moment of both victory and vulnerability, I know more struggles lie ahead. So, when my hand brushes against the crucifix around my neck I spontaneously unclasp the chain and place it on Elizabeth. "Here's a piece of me to protect you when I'm not by your side."

Elizabeth strokes the ruby-inlaid, gold cross and smiles. Then she hugs me even more tightly, sobbing into my chest for a long, long time.

One Thursday night instead of gathering in George's den, we take a field trip, joining a group that meets at the New Age Center in Nyack, New York. It is led by the center's director, Dr. Pollinger, Ph.D. We form a circle of seats, about 16 total. The other group describes experiments with various New Age techniques such as Yoga, Reiki, and crystals. Then George shakes his head and talks about The Energy. Noticeably skeptical, Dr. Pollinger asks us why we are so dedicated to George and his philosophies. My mother speaks first, then Jan, Pauline, Beatrice, and Max. A year ago, my friends' testimonies would have been terribly significant to me. I would have nodded my head in silent agreement, so grateful to be blessed with my precious membership in our exclusive circle. But tonight it all sounds like empty double talk and generalizations. I feel alien—an imposter in my own family. When George shakes his head again, the director asks me what I am feeling, and with difficulty I squeeze out a few words. "I feel powerful surges of energy in my entire body. The intensity makes me shake."

The words have barely left my lips when unannounced, my next revelation appears in my mind: The sensation of "Energy" is not mystical; it is nothing more than adrenalin triggered by my fear of George!

The director comments after I do. "I see something that distresses me; I see immense dependency in this room."

I know the man is right, and by defining the problem this outsider has just handed me another piece to my puzzle; I grab it eagerly. But George is nervous. These circumstances are something that he would do anything to avoid: intelligent criticism from a confident, grounded outsider who refuses to let George lead him. Like a child making excuses after being caught cheating, George begins to babble. His speech accelerates, distracting the listeners with theories, logic, and reasoning, until they have completely forgotten what was said before. When

George senses that he has pushed himself beyond possible exposure, he ceases.

After the meeting, we return to Teaneck in silence. Sandwiched between Max and Pauline in the back seat of Beatrice's car, I am a stranger in familiar surroundings. When we all return to George's block, he waves everyone inside for a powwow. My comrades file into the house obediently. But not me. Instead, I find my car and drive home quickly. Exuberant in my independence, I know my absence will not go unnoticed by George. . . .

The following evening Bess has an engagement with her bluegrass band at a Long Island café. I drive out to see her on that chilly Friday night, offering a ride to Nora and Pauline. Bess and Pauline (who sometimes accompanies her) spend the evening singing, leaving Nora and me at the table. In that dark club, away from watchful eyes we chat spontaneously for the first time, and it seems I have made the acquaintance of a warm and decent human being.

While entering George's den the next morning, I spot Nora. Quickly, I look into her eyes and smile. But already mesmerized and under George's aura, Nora returns my gaze blankly—her lamp extinguished. Where is the Nora of last night? She has fallen back into the ranks, an obedient soulless soldier. As I watch her holding rocks and staring at Ben, I realize she has no idea that two completely contradictory souls inhabit her body.

Still considering bankruptcy, I contact a second lawyer. As opposed to the advice of the previous lawyer, this one points out that as president of two small corporations, a bankruptcy would most assuredly come back to bite me. The credit card companies don't simply forgive the loan and go away. They will find the means to seize assets and a portion of my salary. To generalize, my life will become miserable in ways I cannot even imagine.

His comments verify my fears. I must solve my financial problems another way. Now there is only one option, something I dread more than anything, something I will postpone as long as I possibly can: I will have to cut back even further on my hours with George.

It is becoming clear that Lou Gelbart has chosen to commit himself to Flash Blasters Inc. and *Exambusters Study Cards*. Despite the lack of a signed retainer, Lou throws himself in with intensity, requesting historical details—especially sales figures. Within days, he creates a marketing plan and outlines startup costs. Then he schedules a meeting. We reach a preliminary agreement regarding his fee going forward, and as the meeting ends Lou requests his deposit.

"Of course Serena and I will split the cost," I state with momentary, newfound confidence. For the first time, I have betrayed my original agreement with Serena—the one where I foot all the bills. What I have said is unpardonable. My partner turns to shoot me a poisonous look, and I tremble. Then, as she rotates her head back toward Lou, she erases that look instantaneously. When their eyes finally meet, all evidence of rage is gone, and she smiles sweetly. He, noticing only a pause in conversation queries, "Serena, why wouldn't you want to invest? It is half your company, and this new course of action will turn it around. You have told me many times how much you believe in your products."

Serena is cornered in front of an unbrainwashed third party, and my emotions throw celebratory streams of confetti. Yes! Victory! I have exposed her injustice in front of a non-Group person where she can't get away with the bullying she does behind closed doors in Daddy's den.

After Lou leaves, I anticipate a physical attack. I brace myself, but none comes. She simply walks to her desk and begins shuffling some papers. Then, about ten minutes later, she approaches me. Her eyes seem soft, and her face, saccharine.

"Elizabeth, I was going to offer to pay for half anyway. You didn't have to say that in front of him and embarrass me."

I am amazed (and impressed) by her chameleon-like skill of attitude shifting. Nevertheless, I know she is lying.

In keeping with my 18-year program, I buy George a holiday gift: a CD of *Beethoven's First Symphony*. I know that sometimes George likes to shake his head to classical music. On the day I choose to give it to him, when I enter the den, I find I almost can't bring myself to present it. I have no steam left to interact. I manage nonetheless, and nodding his head perfunctorily, no thank you forthcoming, George returns immediately to focusing with Christopher. These days, he rarely speaks to me. When I show up he glances briefly, throws out a mechanical "What's doing?" and then turns to someone else, anyone else, before I even have a chance to respond. Sometimes he seems upset, on the verge of exploding. What is driving him so crazy? For my part, it is increasingly difficult to remain in the room; George's presence repels me. Today, as usual, I force myself to focus on a spot on the wall until my time is up.

February 1996

Although I have never learned to pray to God by name, my heart cries out fiercely and plaintively to some higher power for assistance. The injustices born from Serena's presence in my life are becoming an insupportable burden. But in my mind she is a permanent fixture, an institution from which I would never even consider parting. . . .

My days are filled with a whirl of activity as Lou and I brainstorm about moving the company forward. Serena offers very little input except to frequently ask how much it will cost. It is clear that several thousand dollars will be necessary, including Lou's consultation fees. Each day the figures change. Today the projected costs are $3,000; tomorrow, $5,000. Although she hides it, I sense that Serena is squirming.

Lou and I also put together a proposal that will compensate both Serena and I justly for our respective contributions, both past and future. These earnings will be far from equal. Going forward, Serena's salary will be entirely based on real performance.

In Serena's presence, Lou has never appeared to take sides. Therefore, she views him as an unbiased problem solver and phones him frequently with questions. Unbeknownst to her, behind the scenes Lou continues to insist that Serena has "got to go." He stresses that she contributes practically nothing and has no legal right to her shares of either corporation. Through the fog of my habitual thinking, I still only half understand what he means.

Soon, Lou schedules another meeting to go over the final figures, and Serena is presented with a $6,000 estimate. We have no time to spare either. Serena nods as if to cooperate, but I don't see how she possibly will.

The next day Serena arrives late at the office. Barely removing her coat she states firmly, "I need to talk with you about something. Now."

An impulse of fear shoots through me. I have no idea what she wants. Funny thing, after all the time we've spent together, today Serena looks like a stranger.

"I am leaving Flash Blasters," my partner informs me bluntly.

Never in a million years would I have imagined this coming. After all of her injustice, my initial reaction surprises me; I am extremely agitated and in truth don't want her to go.

"Serena, why can't we work things out? With Lou we are about to turn the company around. Why would you want to leave now anyway?"

"I just feel it's time to move on. My books are demanding more of my attention and I want to focus on them and the photography business."

While I am sincerely protesting her decision to exit, the sensation of a thousand pounds of bricks being lifted off of my back, literally, comes all in one moment; I almost cry out from relief.

Our discussion ended, she calls Lou and asks him to draw up corporate dissolution papers, and one week later, February 13, they are signed. With the company in debt, there is nothing to split, and Serena walks away empty-handed.

It is Friday evening, just a few days after Serena's departure. Still unsettled about the event, there is another, more pressing matter I can put off no longer. I drive aimlessly on Route 4 in Paramus, seeking to distract myself from the inevitable: I must tell George that I am cutting back on my hours, that I can't afford his fees; I must do it tomorrow.

I feel like a Swiss cheese. There are holes inside all over, as if a vacuum cleaner is sucking out all that is familiar, only to propel me into outer space where it seems I'll drift forever, disconnected from anything I have ever called home. That night

I dream restlessly, and the next morning, rise late. I am filled with anxiety, not wanting to leave the security of my bed.

I arrive at the office at 2:00 P.M. to find that Serena has already left to go sit with her father. As if lost in thick fog, my emotions smother me. I only know one thing, I must go through with the plan. Sitting at my desk, I stare at the wall, unable to work. Everything seems pointless. Pushing against my resistance, I pull out an index card and write down my new schedule: two hours a week and the Thursday night group. This still amounts to an unaffordable $5,200 a year, but it is the least amount of time I feel I can commit to and still remain connected. . . and sane. Fears seize me. Deprived of the frequent contact with George on which I depend, *what if I crack up?*

I procrastinate as long as possible until time runs out. Leaving the office, I make the five-minute commute to George's house. As my feet direct my body down the driveway, terror escalates. *No, I don't want to. I can't. A tantrum rages. Why me? I did everything I could to stop the avalanche of impending poverty, and it happened anyway. Why? Why? Why?* More than anything in the world I want to turn and run. But I cannot. An invisible hand pushes me firmly and steadily onward, despite my conflict. It doesn't matter what I feel, think, or want. Something bigger is calling the shots and I have no say in the matter.

February 24, 4:00 P.M.

I enter the room, just as I have nearly 3,000 times before over the past two decades. George is sitting in his chair as usual with the dog. They are all engaged in focusing, serious and pious. The regulars, Max, Laura, Nora, Serena, Christopher, Pauline, Bess, and my mother, are all present. The rocking chair facing George's chair is free, and I sink into it. George looks asinine to me, a grown man worshiping a disgusting, rotting, 18-month-old dog's carcass, like a child clinging to his blankie and talking to an imaginary friend. The others appear ridiculous too. Mature, college-educated women emptying their bank accounts to participate in this stupid charade. I know that many of them have been sitting in the den since 9:00 A.M. They have spent all of these hours imagining the dog's hair growing, his skin glowing, his spine changing, and his body transforming into a god. They have fed him bagels at lunchtime, morsels that have disappeared mysteriously because the dead dog "ate" them (when for a moment they were out of the room). I am sick of the whole thing. I want to blow up a bomb in the middle of the den and wake them up. It feels like revisiting my third grade classroom and trying to sit at my old desk. I no longer feel at home here. Participation in this absurd drama has been impossible for quite some time, no matter how hard I have tried.

After a moment, George pauses his spiritual interaction with the carcass and looks toward me. Nodding to acknowledge my presence, he throws out his trademark phrase. "What's doing?"

It seems he would prefer to ignore me. Perhaps he even wishes I wasn't there at all . . . I look up soberly, my conflict written all over my face and body posture, and I stammer out, "Nnnothing really."

"OK." He returns his focus to Ben. I sit immersed in my private feelings, focusing alternately on a knot in his paneling and the corner of a picture frame. None of my comrades, or my mother, so absorbed in their focus on the mission, sense my distress. As I hold the tightly folded index card in my sweating palm, I think of how much I want to be able to confront George like an adult would, someone with the right to make choices in their own best interest. I want to be able to deal with his displeasure face to face, and stand my ground. I pray that magically this strength will emerge, sometime before the end of the session. As the clock approaches 5:00 P.M., I sense impending doom and begin to recede even more than I could have ever imagined was possible. Finally, it is quitting time. George exits his trance, consults his watch and coos softly, comfortingly, familiarly, "OK, everybody. It's time to go."

I sit frozen in my chair, watching the rest file out slowly. Some throw him a warm smile, rub his back with affection, slip him a check, or wish him a nice weekend. He returns these pleasantries to his students with the gaze of the kind and knowing professor of successful living that he knows himself to be. Finally, they are all gone except my mother, who is using the bathroom. George and Serena remain in the room. During this ten-minute exodus of followers, I have not moved an inch. George glances over my way, picking up my hesitation, but pretends to ignore me. I can hear his thoughts. *Whatever's wrong with her is not my problem.* Finally, I can hold back no longer. I rise slowly and approach the door. By this point, what little resolve I had before has drained completely. My face is white, my mouth dry, and my body shakes uncontrollably. The 12-foot trip across his carpet feels like a mile. Near the door, I intersect with George and turn toward him. This is it, my decisive moment, and there's no backing out now. Hanging my head in shame, I extend my hand and offer the index card. "Here."

"What's this?" he questions.

"That's my new schedule." I don't look at him, but race toward the door, knowing I can't handle his response. I exit quickly, right after my mother who has just emerged from the bathroom. Just before I close the den door and step down to the deck, I glance over my shoulder to see him opening the card and staring at it in confusion. My step is lighter as I stride rapidly down the driveway, toward the welcome sanctuary of my car, grateful that it is finally over. I catch up with Rachael and invite her to dinner. My mother never turns down an invitation for food, so the date is set. We settle into my car, parked right in front of George's house, and I take a few deep breaths. A few moments later, I sense something and look up. George is positioned just inside his front entrance. A menacing, shadowy figure, he glowers at me, his face portraying a combination of hurt and anger. "Elizabeth," he roars, "just don't bother coming back at all."

I would have never expected this in my wildest dreams! I look back at him expressionless, simply nodding in acknowledgment. I have received his dictum, and I will comply.

George disappears inside while I remain motionless in my seat, not quite knowing what to do. My mother finally asks me why I am not moving the car. Steeped in her characteristic oblivion, she has no clue as to what has just transpired. Staring at the steering wheel, I reply, "George just threw me out."

"Well, that won't affect my relationship with you." Her response is cut and dried.

"I'm really glad to hear that," I return, having feared I would lose her too. "Let's go eat."

As I drive down his block and turn onto the main road, the implications of this turn of events begin to sink in. Two decades a prisoner, I have just been freed. I am too shocked to throw up my arms and scream "Yeah!" But I do feel a deep sense of relief. I know instinctively that today's outcome is right and healthy, and I will be able to deal with the consequences. Experiencing profound gratitude, I would drop to my knees to thank God, right now in the car, if I could.

My mother and I grab a bite at a local diner. When I have positioned us at the table and placed our order, I excuse myself and head for the pay phone to call Judy. The sound of her familiar voice on the other end of the line brings welcome comfort. "Jude, guess what? He threw me out of The Group!" I tell her with a decent measure of awe.

"How do you feel?" she inquires.

"Great! I mean, OK." I tell her how it all happened. "My only regret is that I wasn't able to speak to him directly about reducing my hours of therapy. The index card was cowardly."

"That was the only way you could tell him," she reassures me. "The important thing is that you accomplished what you set out to do. Your method doesn't matter."

I hadn't thought of that, and she relieves my burden. "What do you think about it, Jude?"

"I think it's good. This is what we've been working toward for more than two years. It's graduation day!"

Working toward? Graduation? Maybe Judy knew all along that I was moving toward today, but I certainly never had a clue! The option of leaving The Group permanently never even entered my mind; George brainwashed me well.

Judy and I chat awhile longer, and then I return to the table. Dinner is uneventful. Rachael, totally focused on sampling the array of foods set before her, is completely disconnected from me. It feels as if I am taking a preschooler out for ice cream. In this restaurant, I experience my mother's nature at a deeper level. Despite our biological tie, Rachael is no different than the rest of The Group; she is no friend of mine. For her, the most significant issue during our meal is whether or not she will have enough room to order the chocolate cake for dessert. I realize that I will never make my mother understand, so after our meal, I drive Rachael into the city. Kissing her on the cheek, I wave as I watch her enter her apartment building, the place where George's cursed groups began so many years ago. With my mother safely inside the lobby, I dial Judy from my car phone and recount every minute detail of the day's events while I drive north, up the Henry Hudson Parkway and over the George Washington Bridge toward home. By the minute, reality sinks in ever more deeply. Handing that index card to George today was the hardest thing I have ever made myself do. Now it is over, and I am still here.

Monday morning, I force myself out of bed, into the car and up the stairs toward my office door. I will have to face Serena, a prospect that terrifies me. I have committed an unpardonable sin. George has thrown me out, and I have allowed it rather than begging him to let me back in. No one has ever done this before. Although I have lost George, I am still stuck with Serena and her inevitable punishment for my treason.

Serena is already there. I want to avoid her, but that's impossible. I anticipate an attack, but to my relief, she seems harmless: weak, pale (whiter than her usual white), and confused. We avoid each other until quitting time, and after that day agree to split the office hours between us. On rare occasions when we find ourselves together constricted words are exchanged, and only about business.

After a week of silence, Serena's facade finally dissolves. "Why did you make him throw you out?" she inquires, seemingly distressed over last week's events.

I truly have no answer for her. If she is still on her father's side, blind to the injustice I have suffered at his hands, then just like Rachael I will never make her understand.

I reply simply, "I had no choice," and return to my work.

At night, I pace the floor of my apartment's tiny living room. Every other person who left The Group has been chased to come back. I wonder what my friends are thinking, especially Pauline, Nora, and Bess to whom I have felt closest. I wait for the phone to ring and yet, at the same time, I know in my heart that it never will. How can they all walk out on me like this? Even though I would normally pass George's street on my way to work, I can't bring myself to look at it. I couldn't bear the sight of all of their cars lined up in front of his house, knowing they are all moving along just fine without me. So, instead, I take the long way around.

I can't believe that the people Elizabeth has known for all these years would let her disappear without calling to find out what happened to her. Even her mother doesn't check up on her.

I try to make excuses for their unforgivable behavior. Maybe they are all afraid because George would perceive this as a betrayal and punish them. I know their addiction is even worse than Elizabeth's, but in my heart I still can't justify their indifference. How devastating for Elizabeth to realize that those she considered family never really cared!! Holding Elizabeth's hand through these terrible days, I suffer almost as much as she does.

The second week passes—no calls from anyone. It feels as if my entire life has fallen over a cliff into the abyss. Fury against those who have abandoned me storms, as if the blood in my veins has turned to acid. I have violent, vengeful thoughts, and I want to act on them. *I could expose them all!* I would start with Nora, the middle school teacher. I'm sure Northwestern Bergen County's elite wouldn't want their children being taught by a woman who hands out "energy" rocks (accompanied by a tag stating George's web address underneath Chris's drawing of Ben's carcass). I imagine her being fired. Beatrice might lose her husband (and with that, her cushy lifestyle among Westchester's upper crust) if I addressed a revealing letter to Mr. Beatrice's Manhattan office—filled with explicit, ugly details that I am sure, he already suspects. George and Serena would be evicted from their precious Barnes & Noble lecture circuits if I were to open my mouth and notify the chain's central office on 17th and Broadway.

No one has ever wanted to get back at George like this, and I am sure he must know. Leaving my office at night, paranoia takes over. Images of Christopher hiding in the shadows loom. I picture him choking me in the dark parking lot behind my building, just to make sure that I will keep quiet.

I caution her to consider her actions carefully. "Elizabeth, when you interfere with a person's selfishness, their natural reaction will often be to retaliate. After all we've been through, I don't want to see you hurt. As unfair as it is, for now, you must try to move on with your life. You are not the one to discipline George and the others for their wrongdoing. Don't worry. God doesn't like what's going on in that den. In time, George will get his."

At the office, I gain the courage to ask Serena a question—risky, because I might not want to hear the answer. But regardless, I *must know*. "Serena, what did your father tell the rest of The Group about me?"

"That he threw you out; he'd had enough of your interfering."

"Did he tell them I was having money problems?"

"No. He said you were a wreck because instead of respecting The Energy, you blamed your misery on him. You wouldn't admit you were making a mistake with Judy and let him help you let her go. But you're no loss and already forgotten; everybody's just moving forward to better things."

George has been tested (by my absence) and by his actions has revealed his true feelings: After all these years, I never meant anything to him. I'm just a cigarette butt in the gutter— used and discarded.

Since the day George evicted me, I have been wondering how things will be different. Now I sense a tiny light inside, as if my spirit is emerging from hiding. As time passes, this light brightens. I know George is responsible for its absence during my lost years. How did he accomplish this?

At times I experience something strange. Pressure begins deep inside and rises, finally releasing itself from my body as if a resident ghost has just vacated, carrying an oppressive attitude that crushed me for so long that I had forgotten it could ever be any other way. This occurs spontaneously, on and off, for a few weeks. I am an observer, watching my rebirth.

It feels strange to rejoin the rest of humanity. No longer part of George's coterie—spiritual Navy Seals on whose backs rests the fate of humanity—I am now unexceptional. My mind doesn't know how to think like a regular person, and my thoughts drift back to the security of former membership: the comfort zone of daily reporting for duty and receiving instructions (instead of being responsible for making my own decisions); the part I played in The Group, so long and so masterfully—my identity; a sense that my life was complete and on track. I begin to compare myself to other women in my stage of life instead of to my former "siblings." No longer imbued with the mission, I feel filled with holes. Others have spouses, homes, children, hobbies, vacations, memories, and social circles; they are many things to many people (and to themselves), roles they've developed over a lifetime while I was shut in George's den. I want some of these things for myself; I don't want to be a loner and a weirdo. How will I ever join the mainstream and get a life for myself without the luxury of the time they've had to evolve naturally? How will I ever be happy?

Big questions come: Who am I? Does my life have a special purpose? For each question, where once a ready answer was supplied by the bible of The Energy, there now exists a paralyzing vacuum.

And I feel the loss of my friends' energy. . . . I miss them all; I cannot help it.

Thursday nights are the hardest. I had always looked forward to the group meeting more than any other. To distract myself on those evenings, I attend free Barnes & Noble lectures. One in particular is about soul mates. The speaker describes reincarnation, explaining that sometimes you travel with the same souls during different lifetimes. I don't know if I believe in that, but after the lecture, I approach and ask her a question, "What if you really love someone, but everything you try (to get them to return your feelings) doesn't work?"

Her response is immediate: "That may be a signal for you to let go; perhaps your business on this earth is not with them."

I turn over her words in my mind. She must be right. It all happened the way it did, and now it's over. My job is to build a new life. . . . But how do you do that? With my newfound freedom, I should be excited—filled with anticipation, but instead I find myself fighting bouts of depression. I try to shift myself out of these moods by counting my blessings: my businesses are solid; I have two cats to keep me company; my friends (Judy and Michael) are there for me; I am a good person with ambition and goals. . . . I learn to coach myself, *You may feel bad now, but everything will get better bit by bit. Just have patience.* These comforting thoughts help a little. And every night before going to bed, I pray. Holding on to the ruby-inlaid, gold cross that I wear around my neck always (a gift from Judy), I speak to God. I will never let myself forget what He has done for me. "Dear God, thank you for protecting me. Please help me heal. Please lead me where I need to go, and please, I would never ask you for anything, but I lost my father and Joe, so please don't take my Judy from me."

And I awake each morning in safety. No one will hurt me anymore. I experience peace I have never known.

Soon, I give myself an important assignment—to reestablish contact with other people—"the outsiders." I don't want to keep viewing them, à la George, as "worthless fools" and "enemies doomed to destruction." These days I purposely push against The Group's protective membrane that I respected for so long. I must violate the secrecy and expose the truth to those who know both Serena and me. I feel guilty talking behind her back, usually on our office phone after she has left for the day. I am paranoid that the Sharkmans have bugged it, and an image of Christopher in his father's basement, listening to me as I reveal ugly details of financial rape, group sex, battering, and dog carcasses, haunts me. Business associates, Pennsylvania cousins, special customers . . . over the next few weeks, many hear my story.

When I speak, I tighten, sure that something inexplicably horrible will occur because I have revealed what The Group has worked so hard to conceal. Yet I push at the membrane of fear, because I sense that one day, it will break and fly away. Amazing to me, many respond in the same manner. They never liked Serena. They sensed I was in trouble and wanted to help, but they didn't understand what was wrong and were too polite to ask questions. As I portray some of the more extreme details, outrage rises naturally in many. They throw out solutions in a vain attempt to help me obtain retribution. "Can't you take the son-of-a-bitch to court and sue him? Tell me where he lives, and I'll go over to his house right now and punch him in the nose; Sharkman should receive what he has dished out."

Preston reassures me, "Gee, I wish I had an Uncle Guido. I'd send him over to pick up George and deposit him in the dumpster behind the Closter K-Mart!"

Their empathy comforts me. From now on, I believe I will always have allies.

An old memory returns: a Thursday-night Group visitor (from Brooklyn) rushing from George's den into the strange, black, Teaneck night, looking to hail a cab home. My mother had invited a coworker, promising the man a cure for chronic back pain, but after ten minutes of George's shaking, he had exited abruptly without looking back.

Other images return: Pauline's mother, visiting from Williamsburg, Virginia, could only stand 30 minutes in the den. She spent the remainder of the four-hour, Saturday afternoon session on George's deck, defiantly reading a novel, waiting for her daughter to emerge and drive her away. . . . Bess once brought her niece, age ten, to participate. After several minutes the child bolted from her chair toward the exit. Despite Bess's persuasion, the little girl refused to return, and instead chose to remain in her aunt's car for the better of two hours with nothing to do. Another time Bess brought in an office associate who seemed like a possible recruit. But the following day, Bess was lectured about "bad energy" and George's "evil." We all had a good laugh when Bess told us about those crazy misinterpretations. . . . But now I know her coworker was right. The "outsiders" were on to George all along. Why wasn't I?

On a mid-March Sunday, I call my mother and invite myself over. I have neither seen nor spoken to her since last month—my last day with George. I ring the bell, and when she answers the door I feel that familiar pain from her betrayal. I wish I had never decided to visit. She offers me a seat in the living room and a cup of tea. Facing Rachael today, I am confused and distraught. I try to make small talk for a bit, but I can't maintain it. "Why did George get rid of me?" I cry out instead.

Mom's callous response is automatic. "Because you were rude and selfish. You should have had the courtesy to discuss reducing your hours with him and ask his opinion. He decided he'd had enough of your disrespect."

"Why doesn't he care about me and my side?"

"George is special. We need him to show us the way. *He doesn't need us, and he doesn't have to care about anyone.* His only responsibility is to his mission."

"What about his children? He must care about them."

"No. Christopher and Serena are like us. They are responsible for their own lives and must get their guidance from him. Right now, his only concern is learning from Ben, because he believes that Ben is god and will help us to be god too."

"What is wrong with you?" My eyes bug out threateningly. I want to choke her for her stupidity. "Why doesn't that bother you? He doesn't give a damn about you either!"

"That's OK; I don't care about him either. All my life I have been looking for a man like George, and all I want is his Energy so I can grow. Anyway, all the people in that room are only out for themselves. That makes them no different from the rest of the population. *All people* are basically phony; they just act nice so you'll give them what they want. But they'll turn against you the moment you inconvenience them. Bess and Pauline are like that, just ass-kissers competing to please him. They make me sick!"

As my mother grimaces, repulsed by the image of her two female competitors for George's approval, a picture pops into my head. I imagine all of George's women sitting in adult-sized highchairs. They beat their spoons on the tray screaming, "Daddy, pay attention to me." I realize that behind the spiritual dialogue, that's what's really going on.

"But Mom, he took all my father's inheritance from me. Why aren't you angry at him? I'm your flesh and blood." I soon lose control, screaming how George victimized me. My mother observes impassively, cautioning blandly that I'd better calm down.

"This anger is not good for you. In fact, in general, you don't look healthy at all. I think you were better off when you were in The Group."

I continue screaming, demanding that she validate my assertions until I exasperate her. Retaliating for my annoying tantrum, her lips form into a snarl as she defends her position, "Look, I did my job raising you. You never respected me but defied me instead. Now you are over 21—*you are on your own, kid.* I wish you well, but it is not my problem what happens to you. I am only responsible for myself. Remember what George says, we can't waste our time playing Mother Theresa with each other."

"But Mom, people are human and they need each other—to love and share life; *I* need love!"

"Then you're *stupid*. Just shut up the Valentine's Day crap! Love is a big excuse for not growing up. All you need is yourself. That's what George is helping me with—to become myself. You are just stubborn and stupid. You defy George's wisdom, even though you know he has the *only* answers. That is why you think you need other people—like that Judy person," she hisses.

My mother is hostile and prejudiced, and I despise her for her allegiance to George—and not to me. It's not fair; she's *my* mother, not his. A mother is supposed to love you. That connection doesn't end when you reach 21.

"Mom, what about the money? Don't you hate that you give him more than $20,000 a year?"

"Sure. I don't want to pay him, but George is the best bargain in town—only $40 an hour. A psychiatrist in the city charges over $100, and they don't know what they're talking about. Because George cares that we come along with him, he has remained reasonably priced."

"But Mom, he knows you and many of the others have a hard time paying your bills because of your involvement."

She snaps at me. "He has a right to make a living! Do you want him to give away his genius for free?"

"What living? Don't any of those stupid people know how to use a calculator? What do you think he makes with those big groups? It's got to be at least $1.5 million over the past three years!"

"That's none of my business. All I care about is that I'm making progress."

This conversation isn't going the way I had planned. I thought I had some serious ammunition to wake Mom up with all I have figured out about George, but the person in this living room is a stranger. I'll just have to try harder. . . . "You view him as a professional!? What about all the sex he had with his so-called patients? When I was living here after college, he had you every Saturday and Sunday morning while I was in my bedroom. Do you have any idea how awful that was?"

"I never had sex when you were in the apartment," my mother declares, righteously indignant.

"Yes you did, but you don't remember. I will never forget it. Why did you do it anyway?"

To my surprise, my mother becomes candid. "Well he needed someone to experiment with, and I wanted to help. One time I even went down to a sex shop in the village and bought one of those things on a strap."

"A dildo?!" I gag as the word rolls off my tongue.

"He wanted to know what it would be like to have sex with a man, but he didn't know anyone to try it with. It didn't work out though. The thing kept slipping off me."

The image of them is too sickening, and I push it out, changing the subject quickly. "Well, if George is the genius you say, why does he need to attack everybody with his temper? He went after me several times. You obviously don't care that he strong-armed me, and that really hurts."

Referring to these painful moments brings back profound hatred. My head feels as if it's about to burst from the frustration of watching my mother consistently choose my tormentor's side instead of mine. To my surprise, she hesitates for a moment and then murmurs, "Well . . . I wasn't in the room during the occasions you are referring to, so I'll have to take your word for it, but I don't really feel very comfortable, in fact it's kind of scary, when he threatens Laura or Bess. . . . I really don't think it's a good idea for him to do that."

Hope rushes through me. Maybe I've finally found a hook, my mother's sense of right and wrong. . . . Maybe now her conscience will take the reins. This could be the beginning! But in the next moment my illusion is smashed as she tosses the revealed truth into the trash and returns to her former position, "George is not yet perfect, although he is really close. He says that there's still five percent he needs to work on. That temper is part of his five percent."

She really pisses me off. My mother is willing to accept what she acknowledges is injustice until George is ready to change, even if that day never comes. "Mom, he's a hypocrite too. He tells us not to go to a doctor, and then he sends Christopher to the eye doctor. He tells us not to buy health insurance because The Energy will take care of us, but *he* buys it. What about that?"

"That is part of his five percent."

I guess that excuse will cover him forever, even if he murders somebody. . . . "If his energy is so great then why are all the women, like Bess, Pauline, and Laura, broke? Why doesn't The Energy make them rich? George failed with them."

"Their failure is their own fault. They are stupid and don't listen to him, so they lag behind."

I should have known she would blame it on the girls. George is so great and can perform miracles, but when things don't go well, it's always the other person's fault, never his. How convenient for him! My mother is so hostile to them too, as if they are garbage. I don't feel that way about Pauline, Bess, and the rest. I considered them friends and cared about them. We have shared a lot together, and it breaks my heart to see them oppressed under George's whip. Now that I have figured everything out, I wish I could help them get free. I would do anything for them, if they would let me. "But Mom, when is the graduation? When does everyone grow up enough not to need George?"

"Why would you ever want to be anywhere else when he is always changing and growing? He gets new information first; we can never catch up to him."

"Right, so I guess you'll be with him for the rest of your life. Nice setup for him—lifetime annuity," I spit sarcastically and then, ashamed of my ugly attitude, immediately switch to a gentler tone. "Mom, I don't want you to keep hurting yourself. I need you to understand why George is evil. This can't go on.

He must be stopped. Don't I have any validity as your daughter? Won't you even consider my information?"

My mother turns her head away stubbornly, and I realize I may never reach her. Most people dislike being lied to or stolen from, but Rachael doesn't seem to care. She is trapped in the same brainwashing as I was, but for her it is different. She seems to want to live in George's fantasy world. All through our conversation, she has purposely blocked any information that will expose his hypocrisy. I don't understand how she can devalue herself and worship another person. Where is her self-esteem?

That afternoon, our confrontation lasts for more than four hours, until I am spent. In one way, I feel relieved. My failure to reach my mother has hurt terribly, but now that I know her better, I feel a little freer. I hate her for abandoning me. Except for the biology—that she gave birth to me one December day at the end of the 1950's—I have no mother. Right now, too exhausted to maintain my rage, an aching sadness fills me. Today for the first time, I recognize something important: I have spent my life trying to make my mother love me like I need to be loved, and she has always refused.

Freshly out of The Group, I fear running into any of my former comrades. Even so, while Judy and I share coffee in the Dunkin' Donuts around the corner from her house one spring evening, Max Stavos enters, forcing me to confront painful feelings. Waving us an enthusiastic hello, he soon seats himself next to me at our table in the back.

"How have you been?" I ask tentatively, at a loss for words.

"Oh great, I've been going with George to visit Sing Sing Prison, and the inmates are really getting The Energy; it's fantastic!"

Max puffs his chest like a proud peacock and continues. "You know," he leans in closer, confidentially, "there were about five suicides at the prison last year; they've never had that many all at once. Of course they kept it hushed up, but Governor Pataki was looking into it. Now you people *know* why that happened—some of the guys couldn't handle George's Energy, and they had to kill themselves to run away from it. That's how powerful he's getting!!"

Max, who has nothing else to talk about, continues by authoritatively spouting George's philosophy. "Have you noticed that there are disasters happening all over the world: wars, floods, earthquakes, shootings in schools and post-offices? Did you ever think that in this area nothing bad is happening? Well, where do you think our protection is coming from? George's Energy, that's where!"

We sigh as the lecture goes on.

"You know that the planets are held together with resistance."

"You mean gravity?" I query.

"Whatever. . . . Anyway, there's going to be a change very soon. The resistance will break all at once. All of our thoughts and programming will be removed in one instant, and the planets will fly away."

"Then what will happen to us?" I interview, curious where his ridiculous logic is leading.

"There will be a giant void that no one will be equipped to handle. Unless you are prepared, you will be toast."

"How do you prepare?"

"I'm doing what I need to do. What about you?" He shoots me a disapproving look. "Boy, you're down the toilet now. You treated George like shit. He had no other choice but to let you go. I feel sorry for you."

Judy responds, "Well, that's George's side of it, but what about Elizabeth? She has a story to tell too. You haven't heard her side."

"Elizabeth has no side," Max retorts defiantly, then continues pontificating about The Energy and god. Repeating one of George's favorite phrases, "We are all god," he points to each of us in turn. "Elizabeth is god. Judy is god."

"If Elizabeth is god, then why does she need George?" Judy asks.

Max's face turns beet red at this unexpected challenge for which he has no comeback. His body shakes as he rises quickly, mumbling, "I have to go." With that, he races toward the Dunkin' Donuts exit leaving his coffee on the table, barely touched.

It sounds like George is predicting the Apocalypse, prophesied in the Bible with the second coming of Christ. However, instead of the survivors being filled with God's love, they must seek to be filled with George's Energy. Max and the others seem to be in a desperate race to accumulate this Energy, like squirrels storing nuts for the winter, to protect themselves from being destroyed. As ridiculous as their behavior may seem to us, George's predictions are in line with many spiritual groups who anticipate the year 2000 and the cataclysmic spiritual changes it may bring.

"Elizabeth, I know you think I spend so much time with my father because he is my parent." Serena's statement comes from nowhere during a slow afternoon at the office. "I know you think he forced me to be involved, but it's not true. I am an adult, and I make my own choice. I *want* to be there, and I always have. I believe that somehow, before we were born, we chose our parents, and I chose my father on purpose."

My eyes widen at her confidence. I have always felt sorry for Serena, assuming she had been brainwashed when she was too small to know any better. But now, after all that has passed, I am not so sure. Regarding her father, unlike myself, her allegiance has always seemed absolute. I know that without conflict, there is no hope for change. Since she has opened up the topic, there is something I've been wanting to ask her for awhile. "Serena, do you remember the light bulb getting longer in The Group last year?"

"Yes."

"How do you know that it was really getting longer?"

"Because I saw it."

"But what if your eyes were playing tricks on you?"

"No, it was real. I felt it."

"That doesn't prove anything; feelings can be wrong."

"No; they weren't."

"If you're so sure you're right, then prove it to me."

"I don't have to; as long as I know, that's what's important. If you don't agree with me, that's your problem."

"Aren't you interested in finding the truth?"

"I *do* know the truth because I feel it."

"But there are facts that are indisputable. Two plus two always equals four; that is not an opinion. The sciences of physics and mathematics are built on a foundation of universal laws."

"Come on, scientists think small; they are insecure and cling to their theories like babies clinging to a teddy bear. You know the scientists never gave up The Program. They are still controlled by their mothers and wives. How can they discover anything real when their own lives are a wreck?" Her eyes bug out self-righteously, as if to say, "What are you? A total, stupid idiot?"

I believe in the scientific method, so I continue to challenge her. "What if I measured the light bulb with a ruler before and after your father held it? What if the measurement didn't change? That would prove your father did nothing, and you were imagining because you wanted it to be so."

Serena doesn't hesitate for a moment, and her retort is absolute. "No; I wouldn't admit that, because the ruler could change length too."

Son of a bitch, I think, *Where did this young woman (age 28) learn to slip out so skillfully?* Her denial of reality is more than frustrating, it is terrifying. "Do you mean that there is no frame of reference for anything?"

"No, because everything is constantly changing. What's good for me today may be bad tomorrow because there is new information."

"Do you have any permanent rules about the right way to treat other people?"

"No, because I am always changing."

"Then how do you stop yourself from hurting people?"

"When you make the intention to move ahead, you can treat them however you need to. Any decision will be correct, as long as you keep yourself on track."

This is her father speaking, but obviously it is her too. "Don't you believe in evil?"

"No; evil is just an illusion."

"What about murder? That's evil!"

"No, because the person who is killed asked for it in some way at some time."

She is so stubborn and insane, but one more thing pops into my head that I can use to trap her. "Yeah, and what about the fact that your father told Lisa, Caroline, and me that we would die if we left? We are all still very much alive."

"My father didn't mean physically; he meant spiritually dead, and you all are without The Energy."

I am awed by her thinking process, so irrational, so self-serving, defying rules of logic, common sense, and human conscience. It all feels so impossibly wrong. How did I ever survive with them for so long?

Troubled emotions surge for several hours after we have parted, my distressed right brain moaning, *I wish I wasn't stuck with her as my business partner.*

What are the other options? My left brain counters.

None; I guess. And for the moment, that is that.

The phone rings in my kitchen. It's about 7:00 P.M. on a balmy July evening. The woman's voice is familiar; it's Pauline. This is not a casual social call because she misses me; I am sure of that. My frequent complaints to Serena at the office—that none of my "friends" have called me—probably spurred her, a change in behavior to conceal their hypocrisy. Subjected to her lame superficial chatter, my hurt feelings rise, and I express them. "Why haven't you called me? We were college roommates for three years! Weren't you concerned with how I was doing?"

Pauline is nervous immediately and quickly changes the subject, recounting George's wisdom on which I am missing out. Her robotic recitation annoys me, but I am coming to understand more. I see her as a gerbil on a wheel, investing her energy in this empty distraction until her time expires. Pauline has traded her most precious possession—her free spirit, for a ticket to George's amusement park. In these moments I understand what it is to sell your soul to Satan.

The call ends quickly; there is no common ground between us anymore. Hanging up sadly, I remember Pauline once telling me that her stomach twists when she walks up George's driveway—that she often hates being there. I wonder if these feelings are the seeds of a future attempt to escape. I worry about Pauline and the others who still remain; I am so sorry I encouraged her to join. Now I would do anything to change the past. . . .

The other day I passed Pauline on my way to work; she was riding home on a bicycle after another all day session at George's. My first thought was that she enjoyed cycling, but after questioning Serena at the office, I uncovered the lousy truth. In the past few months, her car has deteriorated and is marginally serviceable—available only for emergency. And I know only too well, where the funds that should be invested in a new vehicle are being channeled. Rapidly approaching her fortieth birthday, does she ever think of her future? Thirty-five years from now, I imagine a gaunt septuagenarian, alone and penniless, trying to stretch a can of tuna across three meals. I know she has no rich uncle who will leave her money. Her active years will have been squandered in George's den; whatever resources this world might have had to offer will never have been cultivated. George will be in his mid-nineties, his precious carcass abandoned for a walker or a cane, if he is living at all. He certainly won't be doing too much headshaking! Dreams of an exclusive nirvana will be long forgotten—the magic carpet on which he chauffeured us will be moth-eaten and grounded. These things are inevitable, despite the fact that George has a way of making us feel that youth and vitality are guaranteed forever. Often I pray to God to save their souls, especially my mother.

There is more bad news for Pauline, and the following week, Serena informs me that Pauline has declared bankruptcy. "My father said it's a good move. She can make a fresh start."

"Are you kidding? Pauline went broke because your father manipulated her with his greed. I know your father has more than a million dollars."

"No, he doesn't."

"Serena, I can do simple arithmetic. I bet he has much more—which you and Christopher will inherit someday."

"No, he lost a lot of his money."

"Don't lie to me. I know he never buys anything, not even his groceries. How could he have lost it?"

"Well, that's none of your business."

Nothing but lies and evasion. It is so sickening. Once again, I wish that I didn't have to spend every workday with this woman.

Before Lisa and Pauline parted, they had purchased their Queens co-op apartment together. So, that night I call Lisa with Pauline's news, but she already knows. This bankruptcy releases Pauline from paying her half of the mortgage, leaving Lisa stuck for the entire sum. In addition, she tells me that Pauline ran up

$50,000 on credit cards. This information was included in the lawyer's report. Now Pauline has no assets to her name, and bad credit to boot. Then I remember, "At least Pauline has that pension set aside from her old job in Bess's office."

"No; she doesn't. When she left a few years ago, she liquidated it to pay a debt she owed to George."

Each day, *I want to make the bastard pay*, fights against, *I should let it go and move on.* There must be a way to have George arrested or get part of my money back, so I decide to visit the Bergen County Prosecutor's office.

The officer who interviews me focuses on the details of the sexual encounters, planting seeds of hope, "Perhaps we can go after Mr. Sharkman as a sex offender. Leave your information here, and give me a call in four weeks."

I leave the building shaky, fearing that George is omnipresent and must already know what I have done. Right now he is planning my punishment. On the other hand, perhaps something good will come of this because I was willing to step forward.

One month later, I dutifully call the Prosecutor's office for a followup. The man to whom I had spoken neither remembers me (until I make him look up my paperwork) nor has time to talk. As if doing me a favor, he explains that I wasn't a minor, and George didn't employ physical force. Superficially, it appears that I complied under my own volition, so there was no legal offense committed. I learn that the law can handle overt crimes that leave manifest damage. George's crime was invisibly performed using mind control, which is not against the law . George has been careful to stay legal. In the moment, my hope is dashed, but not my desire for restitution; I will have to try something else. . . .

Maybe I'll try Preston. He's a social butterfly and knows a lot of people. And indeed, he does have someone in his Rolodex for me—a former judge with an office in Englewood. Preston is optimistic. "Perhaps he will feel passionate about the crimes George committed and want to help."

On the phone, his friend sounds excited and encourages me to move quickly. "I think you have something here. I'd like to meet."

A few days later, Judy and I visit him. I am nervous but hopeful. He extends a warm welcome and invites us in. On the way to my seat, I plop a Baggie on his desk. It contains $192,450 in canceled checks with George's handwritten signature on the back of each one. He winces for a moment and then reassures me in an official manner, "You definitely have a case."

"What do I need to do now?"

"Just give me a $3,000 retainer and I'll start today," he states definitively, as if writing this check would be a mere formality.

But I hesitate, "How much do you estimate it will cost in total?"

He pauses, not seeming to want to answer. I continue to focus on him, silent, waiting for a response.

Finally he volunteers, "Well I can't be sure. Could be about $50,000."

I tighten at the figure. "And how long will it take?"

"The details are complicated, so perhaps three to five years."

Judy intervenes, "And on what grounds will you bring him down?"

The lawyer began to babble. He tries to present a strategy that sounds legal, but it doesn't appeal to our common sense. It is obvious my case would be far from clear cut.

Finally, I interject. "I told you I was broke. Where do I find $50,000 for your fee? I would never hire you knowing I couldn't pay!"

I refuse to watch yet another person trying to exploit my friend, and rules of social decorum can't hold back my feelings. "What's wrong with you? It is clear there's no hard evidence against Mr.

Sharkman; you would have to prove wrong intention and that is hard to do. Elizabeth is just a dollar sign to you. Where is your sense of decency? You would only be leading her on a wild goose chase, putting her even further into debt and cultivating false hope. I can't stand being in this office another moment. You are nothing but a dead end. Elizabeth, Let's leave."

And we do.

A new coffeehouse and club, the Coffee Dog Café, opens for business in Harrington Park about five minutes from my office. On a brisk, clear fall afternoon, I stop by to sample their brew. While waiting for my change, as serendipity would have it, a flyer next to the register attracts my attention. Bess and her country-western group, *Shaking Stone* (named after George's rocks no doubt), will be performing this Saturday night. Most of The Group will surely show up. Curious or masochistic, I'm not sure which, I make my plan to stop by (bringing Michael and Judy with me for support, of course). Serena and I speak at the office every day, but she never mentions the event. A year ago, I would have been energetically involved—distributing flyers and serving as official photographer on the big night. Now I am shunned.

Saturday evening the tiny café is crammed. Almost the entire Group, with the exception of my mother, is present. Beatrice, punitive, glares at me from across the room. I can read her thoughts, *You were a very naughty child to leave The Group.* Pauline avoids looking my way altogether. In fact the entire atmosphere is heavy with opposition—Hatfield vs. McCoy. I sense George's irritation over our invasion. However, pretending to be cool, he strides over, extending his hand like a politician. "How are you doing Elizabeth?"

A phony smile covers rage and hurt. Without giving me a chance to respond, he retreats as quickly as he has approached. From the other side of the fence, I view The Group through new eyes. George's army keeps close rank, always focused on their general, ready to ask "How high?" whenever he says, "Jump." Their world appears small and ludicrous.

Bess begins her performance, and soon George is shaking his head purposefully to help Bess's inner talent emerge. His routine is so familiar, and he looks ridiculous. As usual, the café's non-Group customers seem uncomfortable. Yet, for my part, I am having great difficulty preventing myself from laughing out loud at his inane display. I want to laugh too, from relief—aware that I am free from the cage, and because his world doesn't make sense to me anymore. Soon, I notice he has stopped. Why? Then I figure it out. This is the first time there have been people present who are on to his game. Judy, Michael, and I know what he is doing and why, and we wouldn't be shy about revealing George's unscrupulous motives to whoever might inquire.

I notice that after George shakes his head, unexpectedly, I feel drowsy and confused, as if someone has just slipped me a mickey. I struggle to fight this feeling and to find clarity. I don't understand how, but I think that when George does this, there is some type of mesmerizing energy shift. Last year, I attended a stage hypnotism show at a local club. During the evening, a couple of people in the audience fell under, even though they hadn't been directly hypnotized by the performer. I observed the mysterious, but real, power the hypnotist had over certain individuals when, at his suggestion, they performed ridiculous humiliating tasks on stage. I remember Elizabeth telling me that George learned hypnosis as a college freshman. From what I have experienced tonight, I presume that George uses some form of this skill to control his ignorant victims. I believe that Sharkman has power, and that he is dangerous.

After the concert, I intersect with George, seated in the middle of the room. I reach and grab his hand. Hanging on, I look straight at him—the source of my pain. His eyes are vacant black marbles. Catatonic, as if under some supernatural spell, his hand is lifeless. He doesn't seem to realize that I am there touching him. George's absence catalyzes my epiphany: all along, my terrible need for a loving father convinced me that George needed me too; but I was wrong. George is silent and makes no motion to acknowledge me. There is nothing left to say and I choke on goodbye. Releasing his limp hand, an explosion ignites in my solar plexus. Like hundreds of people rushing pell-mell to escape a burning building, legions of lies slam against each other—illusions, convictions, hopeless dreams . . . They fly upward, desperate to vacate my being. And so, I bid farewell to the person I was—immersed in George's aura.

It is Christmas day and I make the twenty-minute drive from my apartment to Manhattan's Upper West Side. My mother meets me in her lobby. As we ride up in the elevator, she refers to *Conversations with God*, their current bible. "That book has so many wonderful things. I realize more and more each day that I am god, but I just don't want to accept it."

A question pops into my head. "Mom, I don't understand something. If you believe that you are god and God is all-powerful, then did you create the universe?"

"No."

"Well, then who did?"

Quickly, nervously, she mutters, "I don't know." and changes the subject. Her instant wall lets me know there will be no further discussion.

Once inside her apartment, I notice that she is wearing a T-shirt covered with images of rocks, advertising *The Enoch Touchstone.* Across her belly The Group's slogans are blazoned: "One God Fits All" and "**Be Everywhere Now**"—dead dog Ben's initials. Her apartment is a monument to George, with propaganda strewn everywhere. Books are stacked on her marble, kidney bean-shaped coffee table in piles threatening to topple—the same table where cocktails once rested on expensive coasters as my parents' well-heeled guests, the cream of the 1950's Upper East Side intelligentsia,

My mother in the 50's

exchanged views on psychology and politics.

I recognize several items from The Group's reading list: George's book, *Biofeedback and Beyond*; Serena's *Chronicles in Shadow* trilogy; *The Celestine Prophecy*; *Way of the Peaceful Warrior*; *Ageless Body, Timeless Mind*; and many more. These books contain metaphysical concepts, something they can chew on during their meetings, and reading them also fosters a sense of connection when they are away from their guru. Black, velvet pouches filled with George's energy rocks are scattered across the furniture and floor. Of course, my mother has purchased this paraphernalia from George. *More to line his pocket with*, I think angrily, *as if he hasn't already stolen enough from us already.* Rachael informs me that George is selling the rocks on his own website. "He's gaining worldwide exposure now," she chirps, then continues, "George has made a new discovery: Our programming taught us to hold back our feelings. We must give our feelings validity even as our minds insist on dismissing them."

"Mom, he said that exact thing ten years ago," I reply with disgust, "I can hear it in my head as if it was yesterday."

"Oh yes, it may sound the same, but now we are at a higher level and the meaning is different," she retorts confidently.

They always have a comeback to avoid the truth. . . .

An outright non sequitur, she inquires if I still feel The Energy.

"No. I don't believe in The Energy any more. I'm sure that what I thought was Energy was actually an adrenalin rush, triggered from fear of George."

Her candid response surprises me, "Yes, I know what you mean; I am afraid of him too."

"Why? I had something to be afraid of. He never hit you."

"Oh yes he did."

I am horrified and my instinctual protectiveness responds. "What! Why? When?" I exclaim outraged, ready to call the Teaneck police and a lawyer.

"Awhile ago. He didn't strike me, but he did grab my collar and shake me forcefully. It was very scary. He saw that I wasn't committed enough, and this was the only way to get me out of my fog. The first time it actually worked. I understand why they give shock therapy to mental patients. The second time. . . ."

"The second time! You mean he did it again!"

"Yes and it was different; I didn't like it one bit. It was one Saturday afternoon in his den. Everyone was there. George got mad at me for not being focused enough and jumped out of his chair. He rushed at me and put his hands around my throat. He started moving them this way and that. I felt like he was deciding whether or not he might kill me. I realized that with a room full of people who were on his side, and the woods behind the back of his house, they would help him bury me, and no one would say anything. Eventually he decided to let go of me. The next day I told him in no uncertain terms to never do it again."

She imitates her stance during the encounter, a mother correcting a naughty child.

"And he listened?" I inquire.

"Yes. But after that, I stopped attending Saturday groups in the den, just in case."

"Well, it upsets me even more that he touched you than me. You are 76! How the hell does he believe he has the right to do that? To someone who is paying him no less!!"

My mother switches to defense, "Don't worry. I can take care of myself."

"Did he admit he was wrong after you told him to stop, or just obeyed you?"

"George didn't think he was wrong, he never does. He still felt free to assault the others. One time he got mad at Laura. I think he was going to drag her by her hair across the floor and throw her out the door. Serena walked into the den doorway and yelled, "Dad." He ignored her at first, and then she yelled louder, "Dad," and he stopped. It's not that Serena felt sorry for Laura, it's just that she wanted to protect her father from getting into trouble with the law."

All of a sudden she stops. Looking at me intensely she demands, "You're not going to tell Judy about this are you?"

"Why not? Are you ashamed?"

Provoked, she lashes out, "It's none of her business; that's all. Keep your big trap shut about my private affairs."

Now mentally kicking herself she sputters, "You'll tell her. I know. You tell your mommy everything. I wish I never told you. That all happened over a year ago anyway."

A pregnant silence ensues and then my mother switches her attitude. "Elizabeth, I know he has problems, but won't you admit that he has valuable information?"

I sigh deeply, "Yes, he mixes some truth with his lies, and I have learned from him at times. But I can find that information in any pop-psychology book, and I don't have to drain my bank account or get beat up to obtain it."

Rachael ignores my statement and continues trying to reason with me. "All those years you were with him, he was dominated by his personality and his bad temper. I think that's the reason you had such an unfortunate experience. But since he dedicated himself to Ben and the rocks, he has changed. Mostly, he is much more placid. Now it's like teamwork. He is working on his project and when you come in, you are working on your own growth. There is simply an exchange of information. Kind of like an art class with each person at his own individual easel."

I don't believe he has changed, but I keep my opinion to myself. "You know, Mom, after Serena and I rented the house together, she set it up so that we would drive in her car to her father's office in Manhattan, and I ended up spending eight hours there because she did. It got to the point where I was giving him a check for over $2,000 every couple of weeks."

Rachael grimaces noticeably and volunteers candidly, "Yes I know what you mean. He is very motivated by money, and he has his methods of getting more out of you. On a particular day he might tell you that you're doing really well and then add, 'You should stay an extra hour so we can keep going.' The following week it's expected that you'll continue this new schedule. Then if you try to reduce your hours, he accuses you of losing interest in The Energy. He lets you know that if you step back at all, then he'll lose interest in you. He threatens to withdraw the attention he would normally give you as a punishment."

I realize that my mother is remarkably aware of the reprehensible aspects of George's M.O., particulars that took my naive mind years to figure out. Still, she welcomes the opportunity to continue swimming in poisonous waters. Why?

Without explanation, she pops a small, black rock into her mouth. I withhold comment until she queries slyly, "I bet you're wondering why I'm sucking on the rock!"

"Why?" (I really don't want to know)

"A month ago I went to the dentist. He said I would need a root canal for my two front teeth; the enamel is literally peeling away."

She pulls her bottom lip forward to reveal a horrible gap between the two rotting teeth. I wince at the sight. Then she continues, "I told George about it and he advised me to suck on a rock to help my teeth. I do it as much as I can: at work, at home watching TV . . . and I know you won't believe this, but the enamel is actually growing back!"

I feel as if I am viewing Rachael from high on a mountain top. Her world is ridiculous and fruitless, but this is the life she has chosen. She appears to thrive on the lies George concocts and to reject the truth with equal commitment. There is nothing I can do about this, and it dawns on me that my mother lacks the character traits of a righteous person: compassion, respect for the truth, common sense, and a need to love others. It is as if our souls were created from opposite seeds, and I think to myself, *Mom, you gave birth to the wrong child.* I remember something: the sad irony of Rachael's testimony to George, included in the back of his book, *Biofeedback and Beyond*, written many years ago, when we all first met. She had ended her endorsement with this—"Thanks to Mr. Sharkman's enlightenment, my daughter and I are friends."

When I am about to leave, Rachael presents me with a wrapped Christmas gift. It contains six pairs of cheap acrylic slouch socks in tasteless colors. She probably bought them at a bargain store on Canal Street. I smile weakly in an effort to thank her, quelling my hurt—she really doesn't know any better. I recognize the accompanying card. It is one of several free samples she acquired from a stationery store thirty years ago. The card is yellow with age, and after the corny, canned verse, my mother has written—in true George fashion, "December 1996, To Liz, Wishing you growth that grows and grows!"

As the days pass, Serena and I fight again and again over nothing in particular. The tide of unrest rises, tossing us helplessly in turbulence until we are exhausted. It falls, allowing only a short recovery before rising once more. One day, in the heat of an unusually severe altercation, Serena runs out in tears.

That night, she tells her father of our conflict—impossible to resolve. His solution—she should invite me to his book signing at the West Paterson Barnes & Noble the following evening. George explains that I have been away from The Energy too long, that the exposure to his power will calm me down and resolve our rift. When Serena proposes his plan, I accept. I want to know what they are up to.

I arrive after George has started. He is in the middle of explaining to the audience that they think small and this keeps them from achieving their true potential. "You people only use 3 percent of half your brains."

How many hundreds of times have I heard that before! He continues with his analogy that the world is a "personal mail-order catalog, if only we could find the courage to claim our merchandise. For most of you, this is too big, too scary. . ., but the truth is, you are god; I am god; everything around us is god; even this rock is god." George reaches into his pants pocket and withdraws the familiar, white Ben-rock, holding it aloft for all to see. "Each person has only one responsibility—to give himself a wonderful life."

Serena, who still serves as her father's manager, nods hello as I seat myself next to her at the back of the audience. I try to focus on his speech, and for the first time, I discover that I can anticipate much of what he is going to say. Even though his lectures are off the cuff, I know him like a book. Where before I was convinced that he was constantly changing—he was so fascinating to me, now I find him equally boring. When a "truth" pops out of his mouth, I can easily identify the volume from which, in his vast library, he has plucked it. I watch him babble meaninglessly and yet, observe how skilled he is at making his explanations appear terribly important and significant indeed.

In a moment, I flash back to my former self, reentering the body of that hopeful, trusting little girl, completely entranced by a confident, charismatic man. I realize I couldn't have done any different—that if somehow I went back in a time machine, instead of being able to correct the past, I would only make the same mistakes all over again. My life flashes before me: painful lessons learned over ravaged years. I watch myself evolve toward today. No, I do not worship this man anymore. Thank God.

For an hour, George does card tricks with faulty logic, confusing some and rousing others. In fact, the spectators appear to be divided into two camps, a sort of bifurcation. Several are unimpressed, even disturbed; the concept of becoming a god doesn't seem to interest them. But others have clearly attended his lectures before. (They have copies of his book in their laps.) Rapt and fascinated, they drink in George's promises of self-aggrandizement and the permission he has granted to be totally self-focused—even selfish. Having been on both sides of the fence, I would never again choose George's. The basic tenets comprising his philosophy feel wrong to me: to pursue self-serving ambitions at any cost, rather than considering the needs and rights of others; to deny that love and doing the right thing sometimes require self-sacrifice; to develop and revere the mind over the heart. I would rather try to be a better human being than to pursue godhood (and I believe that these two are mutually exclusive). Yet, I do realize that as George goes out into the world, he will find his kindred spirits.

After the lecture he approaches and sits down to face me. "How are you doing?" he demands with authority, preparing to intimidate me into believing that I am not doing well without him.

"You know." I respond. I refuse to fall into his trap by offering anything specific that he can turn against me.

"I want to hear it from you," he commands.

"I'm fine, but I wanted to hear what you thought."

"There's nothing in my head; I do not have thoughts," he informs me as if I am stupid not to realize the obvious.

George has always made this claim, to prove that he is spiritually above the rest of us poor slobs in The Program. But he is lying.

He looks into my eyes—to focus his Energy on me—and I return his stare. George hands me Ben's rock. He wants me to feel how powerful he and the rock have become, to understand from its vibrations how imminent Ben's resurrection is. The rock is hot and charged from George's body energy. I do not imagine the stinging sensations I feel in the palm of my hand as I grasp it. George's ability to electrify an inanimate object is powerful and scary. Locked in his gaze, I ask him about evil, which know he embodies.

"It's a lie; an illusion created by the mind," he responds with authority and certainty—the foundation of New Age reasoning. I think of something I once heard from a preacher on the radio, "Satan's greatest con is to convince people that he doesn't exist." That idea seems to fit this moment.

George's powerful will reaches out, groping and shoving, trying to uproot me and suck me into his energy field. Inside I am anchored with a strength I never knew I possessed. "Is love an emotion?" I continue.

"No; love is everything. Love is god. You are as big as god but you need me to get you there. Someday all people will discover this and come to me, because of The Energy. They *must*. I am the way and the truth. If you don't work with The Energy every day, you won't be prepared when the big change comes."

This is his "threat of Armageddon" speech. But George can't make me feel like I need him to survive. He isn't my savior anymore. In his face I see infinite, cold, profound nothingness. I see the span of his life, eternity without love or God. I experience an eerie suction, as if a giant vacuum exists behind those eyes, endless outer space with no hope of life, ever. So that's what Hell is. I want no part of it. To quote Judy, "You cannot truly know God without knowing his enemy." Today I understand who George Enoch Sharkman is.

We focus in silence for a time, but soon George abruptly breaks the connection. In a heartbeat he is on his feet. I watch him turn and stride away quickly. He doesn't say goodbye.

Friday morning, January 17

It's been a week since I attended George's lecture. Serena and I have been fighting nonstop. I want to close the bank account, change the locks, grab Serena and physically evict her from the premises. I'm holding myself back. But I don't know how much longer I can stand her. . .

At 1:00 P.M. Serena leaves for the day but returns unexpectedly, an hour later. That's when she breaks the news. "Elizabeth, I've decided to leave Expressions. We can't get along and I don't want to be here anymore. I'll sell my half of the business for $40,000. That's what Lou Gelbart put in our partnership agreement."

I stare at her with dumb relief, murmuring weakly, "OK, if that's what you want to do." I add that I don't know how to handle it legally, but I will consult a lawyer. Serena agrees, and exits adding, "Our relationship has been the deepest rivalry I have ever known."

Saturday morning, January 18

I arrive at the office. The wall above Serena's desk is bare. Only yesterday it was filled with black and white photographs of herself and her two cats. I think back wistfully to the laughs we shared on the day I took those pictures, when her white cat shed all over her black outfit. My separation pain commences.

Tuesday noon, January 21

I meet with a lawyer. Initially, he assumes I need a standard partnership dissolution, but then I can't help pouring out all the ugly facts. I recount the story of how we came to sign the fifty-fifty corporate agreement at the offices of the Sharkman's family lawyer, and he explains that I signed under duress, at psychological gunpoint. According to him a combination of fraud, extortion, and conspiracy have been involved. As he outlines a plan, I know I have found the right person to help me.

"This is what will happen next. I am scheduling a meeting to be held at my offices. Ms. Sharkman will bring her own lawyer. A court stenographer will be present to take down all conversation. In front of this group, she will not be able to twist the facts."

The meeting is scheduled for the following Friday, January 31. This is it, the beginning of the end.

Wednesday, January 22

Serena is insisting on her right to sell her shares of Expressions Photography to a third party—shares she stole from Elizabeth. It is getting ugly. Something must be done, but I'm not quite sure what. On my way to visit Elizabeth at her studio, at an intersection just minutes from my destination, I find myself taking an unexpected detour. Immediately, I instinctively know where I am going. But, as if invisible hands have just grabbed the wheel, this navigation is not coming from any plan I've made. I feel upset and frightened about what I realize I am going to do.

A few minutes later I pull up in front of Serena's mother's gift shop and shut the engine. I sit behind the wheel, my mouth dry from anxiety. Pacing in front of the building, I hesitate before gaining the courage to open the door and enter. I remember seeing Doris at George's house three years ago when Christie Whitman visited the UWSA core group members there, but I know she will not recognize me. I browse through the gifts aimlessly as my mind races, searching desperately for an opening statement. Finally, I decide to purchase a small stuffed bear. I approach the counter to pay for it, and as she removes the price tag from the item, I know it's now or never, so I take the bold step. "Hi, are you Doris?"

"Do I know you?" she inquires hesitantly.

"I don't think you would remember me. My name is Judy. I was at your house when Governor Whitman visited and I remembered you as Serena and Christopher's mother."

She smiles and looks pleased as I comment on how handsome and charming her son, Christopher, is. I add, "I'm good friends with Elizabeth and I know Serena very well from United We Stand America."

Then, I take a deep breath and plunge into unknown territory. "You know Elizabeth doesn't see George anymore."

Doris doesn't seem upset at the mention of her estranged husband, and I am relieved. "Yes, and neither do I," she responds.

We both smile and I know she can feel my sincerity. I exit the store, confident that an opening has been created to connect with her in the future if I want to. As I drive away, I realize why I have visited her so spontaneously. Now, I head for Elizabeth's office to give her the stuffed bear I purchased from Doris. We intentionally position the bag, labeled prominently with her mother's store name, where Serena can see it. I want her to know that I have seen her mother and leave her wondering what was discussed. I know she will be terrified at the possibility that I might reveal her father's secret infidelities. When Serena arrives and spots the bag I notice her tighten, although she clearly tries to hide her reaction.

Saturday, January 25

Serena confronts me. "I know all about how Judy visited my mother," she spits out, trying to intimidate me. However, her facade is transparent and underneath, her tension is apparent.

"Oh yeah? So what's the big deal? She went to look for a gift for her niece," I retort, making light of it.

"She was asking her personal questions," Serena accuses.

"No, she wasn't. She was just talking about Christie Whitman's visit to your father's house." However, my eyes are daggers, piercing her. Disgusted with the entire charade, they tell another story, *If you don't get your ass out of here, your mother and her divorce attorney will know all about your father's adultery and the dead dog he brainwashed his children to worship. Don't think I wouldn't step onto a witness stand and declare these things under oath if I had to!*

Sunday, January 26

I write an outline of George's behavior to help my lawyer better understand my circumstances. This is the first time anyone has officially, for the purpose of exposure to outsiders, documented George's temper, bullying, and assertions that The Energy is solely responsible for any success. Judy and Lisa sign the document as witnesses who would be willing, if necessary, to testify in court.

George Sharkman's techniques
of humiliation and isolation

1. Glare at you with rage
2. Threaten to throw you out, claiming that if you push him to that point, you will die in a year, friendless, and poverty- stricken.
3. Yell the same phrase repeatedly to drown out anything you are trying to say.
4. Ignore any opinion that contradicts his belief system.
5. Grab you and throw you out of the door, or slam you against the wall for disagreeing with him.
6. Randomly select a daily scapegoat and engage the rest of The Group to verbally attack and humiliate them.
7. Tell you repeatedly that you are a valueless failure without his Energy.
8. Tell you repeatedly that non-group members are dead robots who will eventually be destroyed by their own stupidity.
9. Organize social activities solely with other group members, and forbid outside relationships.
10. Praise members who spend the most hours (and money) with him. Threaten and humiliate anyone who tries to cut back on their hours.

Tuesday, January 28

My lawyer calls Serena's lawyer and informs her that Serena must leave the corporation with no compensation due. Her lawyer doesn't understand why I am so unreasonable, so my lawyer faxes over my synopsis of The Group's history. She calls him back and declares that Serena has given her no retainer, and she doesn't want to get involved.

The following morning Serena informs me that her lawyer has withdrawn from the case, without telling her why. "Anyway," she adds whimsically, "I have good news for you, we can do this without lawyers! You can cancel that meeting in your lawyer's office that you scheduled for this Friday. I called Lou Gelbart, and he says we can just make up a new document, and then I can sell my shares of the corporation privately."

I bite my lip. She seems to possess some type of ESP that warns her when she is on the brink of being unmasked. I know that I will never, ever allow her to sell her shares.

Wednesday, January 29

Judy accompanies me to the office to protect me. Serena wouldn't dare start up with Judy there. For some strange reason, Serena likes Judy, and she always has. So today, Serena seems pleased to see her. Our work schedule is light, so the three of us chat, reminiscing about our history together: UWSA, flash cards, people we all know from The Group. Curious how Serena will respond, I ask her a question. "Your father is not like anyone else we know. What drives him to do such strange and antisocial things?"

"I don't know. He just feels like it I guess."

"But why? Many of his experiments fail. What is he trying to prove?"

"Nothing to anyone else. He just has to find the answers to free us. He is driven."

"Driven by what, or whom?"

Serena has no answer and soon announces she must leave. As if she already knows what I will soon discover—that this moment is goodbye, she requests a hug from each of us. She approaches me first, but I am uncomfortable and pull away. However, Judy throws herself in, projecting her natural personality into her arms as she envelops Serena with genuine warmth. Serena has no warmth to return. She remains pale and stiff—like a corpse.

"Come on Serena," Judy requests, "Give me something real. Are you a robot? Are you dead? I would get more feeling out of hugging my ironing board!"

Serena doesn't appear to understand, and a few minutes later she exits politely. And that is the last time I ever see her.

Thursday, January 30

Lou Gelbart calls me at my apartment around 10:00 A.M.

"Serena wants a settlement for her five years of input into Expressions Photography."

"Then she can take me to court."

Lou pauses and sighs. He knows I am right. "OK; I'll tell her."

I arrive at my office at 2:00 P.M. for the afternoon shift. An eerie emptiness strikes me. I look around, but nothing is amiss. I sit down at my desk and begin some paperwork. About ten minutes later, the phone rings. It is Lou. "The keys are there on your desk. Didn't you see them?"

I glance down and sure enough, they are there, a few inches from my arm; I hadn't even noticed! The bully has finally run away from me. And she has left with nothing.

I look around the office—my office now. They are gone, truly—all of them! In awe, humbled beyond words, tears fill my eyes and I thank God.

I call Judy with the news and she comes right over. I throw my arms around her, thanking her for supporting me selflessly for so long. We page Michael at work, texting, "The demon is out!" Engrossed in a staff meeting, Michael glances down at the small plastic box vibrating on his belt.

"Yes!" he blurts out, unconsciously raising a clenched fist.

His boss looks curious. "What's up?"

"Long story. Another time I'll *try* to explain."

It's been over a month since Serena's exit, and on a Saturday, I telephone my mother. We haven't spoken since the big breakup, and I am curious about the Sharkman's take on it, which my mother will be sure to channel. After a few moments of empty small talk, I get to the point. "Did you hear that Serena left my business?"

"Yes, and she has decided to reach higher. She is running for state assembly on the Independent ticket; Max Stavos is running also, for state senator. There is even talk of billboards to promote Serena!" she adds with bona fide enthusiasm.

"What will Serena do now that she doesn't have a free ride in my business? She will never make that kind of salary again."

"Serena is going to make it," my mother states resolutely. "But how are you doing?"

I know she doesn't believe in me, but I answer honestly anyway. "I am shaky, but OK. It is strange running the two businesses all by myself; it is a lot of work!!"

My mother has her own advice for me, "You really want to come back to The Group. I know you do; you're just in denial."

I do not respond; how can I? We continue to chat about this and that, but ten minutes later, a non sequitur, she repeats her previous assertion. Before we hang up, she has stated it for a third time. It doesn't matter to me if Rachael repeats it a thousand times. From the first instant that George banished me, I have known one thing for certain. I will never, ever go back.

I telephone Judy G., Karen's mother. I haven't seen her since that fateful day, three years ago, when, because of my stupid planning, her daughter and two grandchildren joined George's group. Now that I have left, I feel guilty and responsible. I hope that if I can get Judy on my side, together we may be able to pull Karen and the kids out. Judy G. hints that she is afraid her daughter is in a cult, and she has a bad feeling about George. I fill her in on some of the details, but I do not want to go too far and shock her. Instead, Judy (Carlone) and I plan a visit to her home in Valley Stream, on Long Island. I know I must reveal the truth, but I haven't figured out how to begin. Judy G. is distressed over how much money Karen is spending on George. She knows that as a single parent, her daughter can't afford it. She also senses her daughter's powerful allegiance to George, and it scares her.

Judy and I drive out on a Sunday afternoon. Judy G. welcomes us warmly. (She once told me that growing up, I was always one of her favorites.) We all decide to go out for an early dinner at the local diner. What I need to reveal will be upsetting to Judy G., and I'm not sure how to begin. So at the table, munching on bread sticks and sipping iced tea, to break the ice, I decide to talk about my own experience. I take her back to Dr. Rogers' office, to the day when George first asked me to take off my shirt. Judy G.'s eyes pop. In one dramatic moment she gets the message and instantly reacts. I assure her that Karen is not involved sexually with George, but that there are many other equally unwholesome goings on in his den.

"We must get Karen away from George. I am sure she will want to leave when she hears what you have told me," Judy G. states with urgency as we pile into her car and head for Karen's Long Beach home.

Karen's house is filled with Serena's posters and knickknacks: castoffs that I guess Serena distributed when she moved from our large Closter house to a smaller apartment. For me, the aura hovering in Karen's home is a poignant and painful déjà vu, and I recoil in disgust. In the bedroom, black rocks are spread across her pillows—a bizarre display. Even more distressing, Karen's personality and body language have altered severely since our last visit together. She has evolved into a perfect groupie clone. In fact, she resembles Serena and the rest almost entirely in speech, attitude, and thought. We gather in the living room, and soon, mother confronts daughter. Judy G's voice is grave. "Liz has told me some very disturbing things about George that I think you should know."

Judy G. begins methodically (she is a retired teacher), but her surging emotions soon take over. The presentation becomes frantic as she relates the details of perverted sex and humiliation. During all of this, Karen doesn't blink an eye. George's blatant lack of morality and merciless exploitation don't seem to phase her in the least. "Well, George doesn't do that anymore; that's all in the past. Besides, Liz is very angry because she can't control him. To punish him, she talks behind George's back, trying to turn people against him."

Coming up against the brick wall of Karen's brainwashing, her mother's hopes are dashed instantaneously. Personally, I hadn't expected any other response; the loyalty of Group members to George is supernaturally powerful and ugly. Judy G. begins to comprehend the vise grip in which George holds his followers. Karen goes on to praise her guru, describing the wisdom she has gained. Fed up with her lack of ethics, I ask her how she can justify the violence, sex, and financial exploitation. The faithful devotee responds indifferently, "Oh I can see that George used you all to advance, but his ends are worth your sacrifice . . . Liz, I know you call this a cult, but it's not. In cults, they sacrifice animals; George explained that to us last week. We love animals."

Exactly like Serena, I sense that, no matter what evidence is presented, she will never consider George from any other perspective. Her personal convictions are rigidly final. Karen's mother wants to know how her daughter can tolerate the crippling therapy costs while she is struggling with her finances. Karen, however, has her priorities in order. "Paying George is more important than paying my electric bill. Besides, what I give now will come back later."

George's familiar Law of Reciprocity strikes again. . . .

Judy G., disheartened by her daughter's attitude, asks exactly how George has helped her, and Karen credits him with better health and more stable emotions. Whenever she is in trouble, she can always go to him for answers. Karen has just betrayed one of the Ten Commandments, (Thou shalt not put false gods before you) and her mother's eyes light up with fire, "Karen, you can't rely on another human being to tell you how to live. You can only do your best each day, hold onto God's hand, and humbly ask Him to help you."

These wise words, straight from her heart, are lost on Karen. She responds to her mother's distress in the same way my mother responds to mine, with cold eyes and a slight shake of the head as she wonders to herself, *What is wrong with these people? It's so obvious that George is right. Why don't they just give in?*

While dissension storms in the living room, I slip into her children's bedroom. Jack and Lulu, now aged seven and six, third-year veterans of The Group, are playing on the floor with dolls and trucks. I ask them what they think of George, hoping they have held onto their original feelings, but my hopes are dashed. "George is great. He loves everyone. We trust him to help us," they reply like little robots. "We like going to New Jersey."

My heart breaks. They have lost themselves too. Those innocent children, I would kidnap them tonight if I could.

When it is time to leave, Judy G. suffers terrible conflict. She has confronted the unconquerable monster, George's hold on her daughter's mind, and she realizes that she has no weapons to bring it down. Deflated, she shares her innermost feelings, "I will pray now, and every day, that God will open Karen's eyes, and she will want to leave The Group like you did, Liz."

I will pray also, and ask God for forgiveness that I ever brought Karen and her children into the devil's den.

A couple of weeks later, Judy G. receives an unexpected phone call from my mother. After they hang up, Judy phones me at my office. "Your mother just called me; she hasn't done that in years. I guess Karen told The Group about your visit. She seemed to be fishing around to see how much I knew, and finally, I lost my temper:

'Rachael, how could you do this to us? Jeannie and Liz met in the sandbox in Central Park when they were three. We've been friends ever since. We spent holidays and summer vacations together—like family. How could you send us to that sicko for therapy, when he had already seduced both you and your daughter! I trusted you, and you betrayed us.'"

They say that when you define a problem, you have fought 50 percent of the battle. Although I know instinctively that I have been persecuted and abused, often my thoughts still speak George's language—logic and reasoning he developed to justify his actions. The disparity between my heart and my mind causes great conflict.

One day, while browsing the stacks at a local Barnes & Noble, my eyes fall upon a book entitled *Cult Mind Control*, and I purchase it. The author, Steven Hassan, a former "Moonie," (devotee of the Reverend Sun Myung Moon) has concisely defined and outlined the distinct characteristics of a cult. This is my moment of epiphany because Hassan's descriptions match George's group perfectly. Soon I discover other books that touch upon the aspects of my twisted journey. Using Amazon.com's search engine, numerous volumes by accomplished psychologists, scientists, and victims of other cults, pop onto my screen. A whole new world opens up for me, and I begin to read profusely. Puzzle pieces emerge and fit together as I explore (with an open mind) spirituality, brainwashing, mind control, faulty logic, emotional blackmail, abuse of all types, etc. from the viewpoint of many others—people who, it is clear to me, make valid points. I gobble up these books voraciously, and as I do, my thinking patterns begin to change, and my conflict to subside. The testimony of experts validates what I have always known in my heart, and their words give me permission to push George's lies out of my head and bring my mind into agreement.

At the back of one of my books, I discover "Cult Information Services," a Teaneck, New Jersey-based cult awareness group, (I had no idea such resources existed!) and I contact them. I learn that similar organizations are present in many states—sources of information, counseling, and legal advice. I submit George's name and address for their database, and they offer to refer me to a lawyer who specializes in cult cases. In fact, I can meet him at their annual gathering, coming up in just a few weeks.

I attend the conference, and for the first time, meet others who have had parallel experiences to mine. A former Moonie and a woman who has just escaped a small, destructive group in Upstate New York speak during the morning lectures. If I ever questioned the nature of my group, after hearing their personal testimonies, my doubts are put to rest forever.

Just a few weeks earlier, the "Heaven's Gate" cult committed mass suicide in California, and the courageous parents of one of the victims (26-year-old Gail Maeder, from Long Island) arrive at lunchtime amid scores of TV cameras. Surrounded by blaring lights and pushy reporters, they speak for a few minutes. Standing just three feet away, I empathize with their grief over this incomprehensible crime. If you have never been inside, how can you truly understand how a normal person could follow the directives of a raving madman? I wish I could say something to ease their suffering. I know that nothing will bring back their daughter, and they may never understand why they lost her.

After lunch, I meet Herbert Rosedale, the attorney I've been looking for. A man of great status in his field, he is currently representing a high profile case involving Reverend Moon's daughter-in-law. I offer him my synopsis of The Group, and he invites me to telephone him the following week. If anyone can help me, he can.

A week later I phone, hopeful for the last time. He explains the legal reality: George can lawfully operate as a therapist, without certification. By signing my check, I have *consented* to pay him for his services. Therefore, nothing illegal has transpired. Mr. Rosedale repeats what I have read in a few books about cults: The law is not set up to validate mind control as a crime. Unless I have a bottomless pit of money to invest in an attempt to set a new, legal precedent, I have no case. George's only tangible offense is alleged assault. However, the statute of limitation is one year, and I am well over the limit. In addition,

I have no proof. Mr. Rosedale sympathizes with my feelings but sincerely recommends that I try to get on with my life.

Thankfully, it has been several months since I've set eyes on Serena or any other Sharkman. Surprising, since they only live five minutes from me, and we shop in the same stores . . . eat in the same restaurants. I dread the day when I will round the corner of a K-Mart or Pathmark aisle and run into one of them. I imagine myself exploding with rage in public, unable to contain myself, while quizzical onlookers conclude that I am certainly rude and possibly insane. I am sure that someday I will be put to the test, but I pray for the distant future.

It happens in October at Bergenfield's Colonial Diner on Washington Ave. Not a place I would expect to run into Serena; it isn't part of her regular circuit. Yet, as the waiter shows me to my table I glance up, and there she is, seated at a booth in the back corner. My heart skips, and I grit my teeth, but she smiles encouragingly, appearing happy to see me, although I can't imagine why. After all, I am the manipulative bitch who screwed her out of her $40,000 half of the business only nine months ago. Regardless, she acts as if our history was never anything but pleasant. It is creepy. I would prefer it if she were angry at me, at least that would be human, but she is a *Stepford Wife*—a "living in the moment" type of a robot, forever a student of her father.

I, however, am human, and the sight her face triggers acute anxiety. But I don't have a choice, so I force myself to approach her.

"It's really good to see you, Elizabeth," Serena smiles with apparent sincerity while rising from her seat immediately to give me a hug. I recoil at her touch; a cobra has more warmth.

"How are you?" I respond nervously, trying to calm my quaking limbs, hoping she won't notice.

"Oh, really busy. I've been flying all over the place; just got back from Orlando on business," she declares with self-importance.

"What kind of business?" I probe, observing her eyes shift as her mind seeks a diversionary statement. *Nothing has changed.*

"You lost a lot of weight," I observe.

"Yes, well you know we are all vegetarian now. We don't want to kill animals. How are your cats?"

"Oh, just fine."

"Magic died, you know," she states matter-of-factly.

When we shared the house in Closter, Serena had two cats that kept company with mine, Magic and Taz. Magic was an orange-striped male. I am genuinely surprised and saddened, he couldn't have been more than seven. "What happened?" I ask, distressed.

"It was his kidneys, something genetic. I tried several vets, here and in the city, and a lot of other things, (I know this means George shaking his head over the poor animal.) but he didn't have the courage to fight the negativity. He actually died in my arms, just last month."

"Oh, that's terrible; I am so sorry."

"Yes, it was really hard. . . ." She pauses for a moment as if considering something and then focuses directly at me, two cold marbles mounted on a plastic mask. "I had him freeze-dried," she reveals, repressing an almost whimsical giggle.

"What!?" I am horrified, repulsed, "Why? How? What is that? I never heard of such a thing!?"

As if discussing a new flavor of ice cream she is about to order, Serena continues, "I heard about it on TV, so I decided to try it."

"But, I mean, what do you do with him? Is it like taxidermy?"

"No, he's not stuffed, just all the moisture taken out."

I imagine what Magic must look like now, a flattened mat of orange fur with a tragically sunken face, like road-kill. Why? Why? Why would you want to do that to an animal who used to sleep with you, a faithful companion? How could you stand to look at this grotesque distortion and remember that he was once your friend? "Serena, that's so morbid; what does it look like?"

I continue, struggling to grasp the reality of what she is describing.

"Like beef jerky with fur." She smirks and then grins with what seems like pride.

"I mean, what do you do with him now?" I continue.

"Oh, I just keep him," she responds vaguely.

"Why? For what? Where? On your mantle as a decoration?"

"Oh, you know, I just wanted to do it." Her voice trails off.

There will be no more details forthcoming, and thankfully, with the arrival of my food, our conversation ends in a few more sentences. Before I return to my table she rises to hug me again, placing her hand meaningfully on my shoulder, assuring me of how "really good it is to see me again." She leaves the diner about five minutes later, touching me once more on my back as she passes toward the exit, murmuring softly, sincerely, for me to "take care." . . . And moments later, my head splits open with the truth—like father, like daughter, a chip off the old block; Serena means to have a try at the resurrection experiment herself.

Serena mails a videotape of her father shaking his head to a national television program: *Strange Universe*. Thanks to her efforts, George wins a position as one of five semifinalists in a contest entitled, "America's Strangest Person." A video crew gathers footage in the den during a Thursday night meeting, and in November, George makes his debut on national TV. He performs for his audience, shaking energetically while supporting, with both hands, a thirty-pound rock on top of his head. "One day, my head just started shaking on its own," he explains pompously, "I always speak the truth; it's the only thing that will survive," he announces at the end of his spiel.

That son-of-a-bitch liar, I think, cursing at the screen.

On the three-minute clip, I observe Max seated on the love seat across from George. Recognizing his familiar blue and green, plaid couch, my mind drifts into the not-too-distant past. If only the innocent-looking piece of furniture could reveal the history of crimes committed upon it. If only the audience could see what happens after the camera crew leaves and Ben emerges, even now within camera range, hidden behind that very couch.

Max Stavos speaks to the cameras, glorifying George's mission, and I spot my mother, seated on one of those uncomfortable, green, velveteen, folding chairs, directly behind him—on the other side of the universe from me—in a semitrance as usual. I am offended and appalled. The show capitalizes on George's weird habits, only to benefit their ratings. Disgusted, I think to myself, *It's all a big joke to them.* If only the viewers knew the real truth; if only I could tell them about the lives George has destroyed.

On a cold, December evening, Judy and I run into Max Stavos at the Bergenfield Dunkin' Donuts. "There's big stuff happening now," he grins, running over a long list of their accomplishments, "I'm running for New Jersey Senator as an Independent against Senator Lautenberg, and Christopher is on the ballot for Bergen County Sheriff (This is all true!). George is broadcasting a weekly radio program from his house. He purchased equipment and got an FCC license. Several out-of-state stations are picking him up. Know what else? I have my own TV show! It's on local cable every week, and George is my co-host. We've been interviewing authors and politicians—inspiring people who've achieved something in life. It's called *No Limits*. George is in the papers too."

He whips out a copy of *The Suburbanite*, our local weekly. It refers to George's work with inmates at Sing Sing Prison in Ossining, N.Y. and describes his radio show, featuring him as a benevolent, talented citizen. On the next page is an ad for Max's TV show.

"By the way," he adds, "George and Doris's divorce became official in November."

She must have gotten half of his money, I think with resentment, *my money, my mother's money, blood money . . . I hope she enjoys it.*

That night I sleep restlessly. In a dream, I run into my mother and Pauline a few blocks from my mother's Upper West Side apartment. They are walking quickly, arm in arm, giggling like girlfriends, on their way to The Group in New Jersey. They barely notice me as I approach them, and Rachael greets me lackadaisically, despite the fact that I have not seen her in almost a year. "Oh, hi Liz."

Rage and hurt escalate, choking me with pain over my mother's indifference. Seeking to strike back at them all, I turn to Pauline, threatening her, "I'm going to call your parents and tell them what you are doing—that you are in a cult destroying your life."

Unimpressed, Pauline retorts, "Well, they won't believe you. Anyway, it's not a cult." With that, she shrugs her shoulders and walks away, joking with my mother, taking her away from me.

I reach out my hand toward them as they disappear around a corner. "Don't go Mommy; please don't leave me," I cry out to the empty street.

The clock glows 3:00 A.M. when I jolt from my sleep, my body soaked with sweat.

It is December 19th, and I call my mother, as always, to invite her for Christmas dinner.

"No, Liz, I don't think so."

"What?"

"I don't want to see you."

"Why not?"

"Because you can't keep your trap shut about George. You blab to other people about his private affairs when it's none of their business."

"You'll never see me again, forever?"

"Maybe someday, but not now."

"But when?"

"I don't owe you any explanations."

I hang my head and stare at the floor, choking on the lump in my throat. "I bought you a nice Christmas gift," I mumble. "Guess I'll UPS it to you." I can say nothing more. "Well, bye Mom, I guess. . ."

Have I lost you forever?

Elizabeth is a joy in my life and the best friend I ever had. I have been more than repaid, with the richness of our friendship, for the sacrifices I made and the terror I experienced venturing into the "Devil's Den" like a fireman, and carrying Elizabeth out on my back. God has put me in many places to do many things, but this has been by far my most rewarding assignment. I will forever be honored that He selected me for this very special mission. What a wonderful testimony this story is to God's love and power, when you can find Him inside and follow your heart!

January 29

The oddly-shaped package, labeled with my mother's return address, arrives at noon. My fortieth birthday passed exactly one month ago, but I haven't heard from her since mid-November of last year—the day I presented her with a copy of this book. I knew she wouldn't take it well, and the butterflies in my stomach almost caused me to change my mind, but I didn't want her to find out from someone else that our wretched past, mine and hers, was now unashamedly exposed to the world. I endured nearly three hours of superficial conversation, but it was she who finally pushed me over the edge. "Liz, George is ready for you to come back. He told me to let you know. . . . Now I'm not supposed to share this with you," she whispered as if the walls had ears, "but I overheard him confiding in Bess that he thought it might have been a mistake to throw you out." She seemed confident that I well might accept George's magnanimous offer.

"Mom," my voice trembled with disbelief, "I'm George's nemesis. How could you or he begin to think otherwise? I am the only former member who has no problem exposing him. In fact, I am a time bomb just waiting to blow."

"Why? I don't think you really are his enemy. I remember you correcting Bess, Pauline, and the others many times, declaring, 'Be quiet and listen to this man; he's the only one who makes sense.' I know you got a lot out of your sessions with him; you told me so many times."

"Don't you get it at all!" I stated with force, ineffectively curbing my frustration. "This is Elizabeth speaking, not George's brainwashed puppet."

She gazed at me quizzically, unmoved, so I rose from my seat, finally finding the strength to retrieve my book from its hiding place under my purse and present it to her. Her pained eyes filled me with instant guilt, and when a few moments later she clutched her chest and moaned, "I'm not feeling very well," a recriminating thought hissed, *You should have respected your* *mother's privacy. Now she'll have a heart attack and die from shame, and **it will be all your fault**.* But a moment later she recovered, and I realized that despite my doubts, nothing could have stopped me from telling my story.

"Why did you hurt me like this? For attention from others? You must really hate me. Why can't you just forget the past and move on?"

Her voice descended like an iron fist and I squirmed. I betrayed my own mother by exposing her ugly secrets publicly. Only a *terrible* daughter would do such a thing! . . . Then I grabbed the wise response that Judy had given me the previous week, in case I needed it. "Mom, every word is the truth, and if you didn't want these things to be revealed, then you shouldn't have done them to me. This is my life. I lived it. It is my right to tell anyone I want."

I shed tears of regret that day, seated at my mother's rickety, dining room table piled high with manila folders, yellowed newspaper articles, and several treasured rocks, my shoes stirring patterns in the dusty red Persian rug below. I told my mother I loved her and that I was so very, very sorry—not that I regretted writing my story—but sorry that it all had ever happened, sorry that she had been part of it, sorry that George had held his first group in this very living room 22 years ago, sorry that my mother was still, to this day, one of his most avid promoters.

My package contains a small wrapped item—a juvenile scarf imprinted with teddy bears, a card indicating that this is a "Happy Birthday Gift," and a copy of George's latest book, *Focus or Dead*. A wolf's head fills the cover, staring at the reader with cold eyes. Apparently he is writing prolifically and had added three more titles to his collection since 1997. Why did she send my gift one month late? Judy proposes an explanation. "She must have waited until her connection to The Program broke, you know, the obligation to give gifts on holidays. What an atrocity for George to teach that expressing love by remembering someone's birthday hinders personal growth." Judy hugs me with genuine sadness for the twisted mind of my mother and the relationship of which I have been deprived.

"It's OK, Jude. I'm trying hard to accept her for who she is. I can't ruin the rest of my life wishing she was someone else or trying to force her to change."

President's Day, Monday, February 21

These days, life is mundane. I attend to the daily demands of business: processing website orders for *Exambusters Study Cards*, sorting Bar Mitzvah proofs, and paying bills. Sometimes I miss the excitement Judy and I experienced during my escape from The Group, but more important, I value my peace of mind. I feel safe now, and that is precious. In fact, in my three years of freedom I have thankfully never run into George. I find that strange; after all, we are neighbors.

Bob Nicholas specializes in custom framing, and we've done business for ten years. I stop in during the early afternoon to pick up some work. Considering it's a holiday, and the highways are crammed with retail shoppers, it seems strange that his store filled with gifts, antiques, and framed art is completely empty. In fact, an eerie silence hovers. Although he's usually speeding from one task to the next, and so am I, today, we are both uncharacteristically calm. We fall into light conversation and chat for several minutes, not seeming to be able to break the connection.

The bell jingles on Bob's front door, and a shopper enters. We both look up curiously. . . . My adrenaline rush is instant. It is George. Even though he is 40 feet away, with his back to me, I would know him anywhere. I begin to tremble. After years of habitual terror, I am still conditioned. Unaware of my reaction, Bob picks up the conversation. I stare hard at his face, nodding politely, hearing nothing but my roaring emotions, wondering what in the world I will do.

George meanders among the gifts, picking up items at random, inspecting them, and putting them back down. He seems to be taking an awfully long time to approach the counter, and I know he is here for a reason. George doesn't spend the massive amounts of money he robs from his followers; material things don't interest him, and he is a notorious cheapskate. Perhaps he sees me too, but he doesn't show it. I am relieved, because I need a little time. I have to stop shaking; George poses no threat, and my reaction is ridiculous. It takes a few minutes, but the sensations finally subside, replaced by a wave of calm, and I am grateful. The silence in the store, aside from Bob's voice, is almost palpable. In the next moment George advances toward us, and I must confront him. He acts as if he doesn't know me, obliging me to break the ice. "Aren't you going to say hello?" I address him with a steady confidence that he has never seen.

His face impassive, George extends a reluctant hand toward the one I have just offered. "How are you doing?" His familiar little-boy sweetness flows with light caress, yet displaying an appreciable lack of interest.

"I saw you on Max's show. It was very interesting."

"Yes it was."

"You lost a lot of weight; must be the vegetarian diet."

Actually, now 58, he looks shriveled, almost pathetic, and his upper back has developed a slight curvature. Perhaps the early onset of osteoporosis—overdue reciprocity for years of neglecting diet and exercise. I project into the future, imagining a withered old man shuffling down the halls of some nursing home, completely drained of the power he once wielded over us. The end of his life seems nearer than the beginning, and I see how temporary things really are. There is nothing else to say, so I turn and walk away, exiting the store. Neither of us says goodbye.

Walking toward my car, the reason for George's visit to Bob's store comes to me suddenly, and I rush back inside. George, thankfully, has left, but in the middle of the counter lies that familiar, velvet, rock pouch on top of George's new business card. Christopher's sketch shows his father holding a globe of energy aloft, like Atlas supporting the world. The card introduces him as *Reverend* George Sharkman. A creepy shiver runs through me and I begin trembling. Bob notices my change. "What's the matter? You're pale as a ghost."

"Oh Bob, you have no idea who that man is."

"Do you know him? What's with that guy? He seems crazy, and I felt . . . evil. He offered to buy a small bracelet, and I didn't even want to take his money. I just wanted him to leave."

"I'm glad you felt that way. He was trying to sell you his rocks, right? Well do me a favor and throw that thing away, as far away as you can."

Bob is confused and stands frozen while I spend the next half hour vomiting out details of George and The Group. I keep glancing at the rock, an ominous reminder of its master's lingering essence. When I have finished, Bob finally comments. "I can't believe you acted so calm. If he had done all of that to me, I would have wanted to put my fist through his face."

"That was not calm; it was shock and paralysis."

Bob throws the rock in the garbage.

One Week Later, 10:00 P.M.

The phone jangles on my night table, and I grab it.

"Hi, Liz; how are you?" A voice reaches through the wire. I shake my head. "Who is this?" Then a shred of familiarity reaches my brain, and I correct myself quickly. "Oh; hi, Mom."

"You mean you don't recognize me?" The voice is slightly miffed.

"Oh yeah; I do. I'm sorry; it took me a moment. . . . Did George tell you he ran into me last week?"

"I heard something. He said he didn't recognize you."

"That's bullshit; except for a few extra crow's feet, I've looked the same for fifteen years."

My mother ignores my statement. "George is a Reverend now, you know."

"I know. I saw his business card. How did he get that status? On the Internet?"

"I'm not sure, but I know he did it to save on income tax. I don't really approve. . . ."

In my life my mother is present but distant. While she chatters, my mind drifts. *Mom, I've known you all my life, but you don't know me.* I snap back to reality. "Mom, would you like to go to a movie sometime."

"OK, sure . . . ," she responds.

After everything that has happened, why do I still want to associate with her? I wonder. But I know the answer. She is still my mother and always will be. Not that I will ever forget who she is inside—that I can't trust her not to hurt me, but I can't move away, wipe the blackboard clean, and start fresh. Every day I pass George's street on the way to work. Often I spot Max's and Chris's cars on the road. They all remain nearby, and I have come to accept a familiar sight—the cars of my former comrades clustered around George's driveway on a Thursday night. I picture them inside George's den, (Bess, Nora, Pauline, Beatrice, Laura, Mom) doing what I used to do, feeling what I used to feel, reveling in what I now know to be a seat of pure evil. I don't like what they are doing, but for most of them, I believe that this is the life they choose. Perhaps some people simply aren't meant to leave a cult. But I am proud of myself. I have escaped, and I have survived.

> *You looked like father; you felt like mother.*
> *My mind told my heart, 'there is no other.'*
> *And I gave you my soul, and every ounce of control . . .*

from a song by Melissa Ethridge

It is afternoon and I haven't heard from my mother. In her apartment on the Upper West Side, several miles from Ground Zero, I know she is OK. But still, in such a heart-wrenching crisis, you need to feel sure. Rachael picks up after a few rings.

"Mom, are you OK? Michael was on a roof in Manhattan for his job and saw the towers come down. It took him hours to get home, and Judy and I were going crazy 'til he did."

"Oh, that must have been fascinating!"

"Fascinating!? Mom, there were people jumping out of windows; they were dying in agony and terror on national TV!"

My mother's perfunctory response is indifferently didactic. "George called me a little while ago. He explained that the people wouldn't have died if they had been more in touch with the god inside them. They had bad energy from negative thinking."

"Mom . . ." I don't know what to say. How could a human being have any other response than the raw shock, empathy, and pain currently shared by the entire planet? "I'll talk to you soon," I finally stammer. I hang up and wonder what insane, higher metaphysical intelligence assigned her to be my mother.

The Dream
Thursday, January 9, 2003, 8:00 A.M.

The phone rings by my bedside, as it does most mornings, and Judy's voice pulls me from grogginess. "I had a strange dream last night, Liz," she begins.

"What?"

"Well, it was about your mother. We were walking together, and she was hanging on to me for support. She was clutching her chest. I could see you in the distance, sitting in another room, but you were unaware of us. At one point, your mother reached over and kissed me on the cheek and said, 'I love you very much.' We entered a large building with many beds. Your mother was assigned one of them. I wonder what it means?"

"Wow, I have no idea."

"Your mother didn't die in the dream."

"Well, that's a relief! My mother is 82 now, but she doesn't have any heart problems that I've ever known about."

"Your mother would never kiss me. She's always been jealous and has put me and our friendship down whenever she could."

"I know. She's never told *me* that she loves me, let alone you!"

The phone rings, and my mother's voice chirps, "Hi, Liz. It's Mom."

"Hey, what's up?"

"Well, I think I might like to see your chiropractor in New Jersey," she requests with sudden and uncharacteristic timidness.

"Your back pain is that bad?"

"Yes."

"Do you have any Tylenol?"

"What's Tylenol?"

"It's a pain reliever like aspirin."

"I'll go out and buy some if I feel well enough to walk the few blocks to the Rite Aid."

Adrenalin surges. Now I am scared.

Since the summer, Rachael has been referring to a muscle she sprained "from carrying too many heavy, grocery bags. Plenty of rest will take care of it," she has assured me many times. "I've been working with the rocks, sleeping with them between my legs, and the pain is going away."

However, for several weeks she's been mentioning "some pain" frequently. To her deaf ears, I've recommended my chiropractor several times. "I think it's a pinched nerve, Mom. That happens to me all the time."

Today, if my mother has decided to take my advice, then she must be suffering a lot more than she's been letting on.

First thing Saturday morning, I call my chiropractor to set a Monday appointment for my mother. Then I call her back. "Mom, it's all taken care of."

"Oh glorious Monday," she chants almost worshipfully.

I am really scared.

Monday, January 13, arrives and I rise with purpose, calling my mother immediately. "How are you doing?" I query, afraid of the response.

"Not so good. Last night I fell in the kitchen around midnight and couldn't get off the floor. I slid on my rear end to the phone down the hall and called the super. It was close to 1:30 A.M. when he finally helped me into bed."

It's about noon when I pick up Judy and rush into Manhattan to get Mom, my heart pumping like it never has before. Not even waiting for the elevator, I take the four flights of stairs two at a time. My hand trembles as I fumble with the key to her door. I am terrified of what I will find.

My mother is sitting in the dark, in the midst of her filthy living room, waiting for me like a helpless waif. She hasn't had a shower in over a month (because she was afraid of slipping in the tub). She is skinny and pale. In fact, recently her back pain has robbed her of her appetite, and I fear that she has been starving. The last few months she has had great difficulty getting out to the grocery store and has mainly been living off a large piece of Swiss cheese and some canned kidney beans. I had no idea any of this was going on.

I gag as I enter the kitchen. The sink is filled with soiled pots and dishes half-soaking in putrid water. Her refrigerator is almost empty, and what little there is, is spoiled. The machine can no longer cool because the compressor, after some 20 years, gave out months ago. Although she gave George $18,000 in 2002, she neglected to purchase herself a new appliance. There is milk in her freezer from the year 2001 that she claims she thaws a little at a time for tea. On the icebox door is a George affirmation scratched on a slip of paper: "Talk to god—you!" It is pinned under his magnetic business card. On the edge of the bathtub I notice smeared, brown stains. My heart sinks; *they must be blood. She hurt herself at some point, perhaps badly, and never even told me.* Seeing her like this rips me apart, and I realize how lucky I am that I didn't receive a phone call from her super, who had found her on the floor, already gone, perhaps after several days. There are rocks everywhere, and she holds one as she timidly looks up to greet me. Over the past two years, the devastation of osteoporosis has distorted her spine; she has lost at least three inches. For the first time in my life, she seems small and helpless. With the support of my arm on her right side and my grandmother's cane on her left, we hobble slowly toward the elevator. After decades of defiance and abuse, Rachael's terrifying, stubborn ego has been replaced with this alien creature now clinging to me piteously.

When we arrive at the car downstairs, Judy suggests that we visit the emergency room at Holy Name Hospital in Teaneck, New Jersey. She secretly suspects that my mother's condition is something far worse than a pinched nerve. It takes about 40 minutes to get to Holy Name, and my mother's pain drives her to vomit and pass out briefly on the ride over the George Washington Bridge. Judy guides my mother into a wheelchair, and I follow numbly—petrified—knowing that something huge is happening.

The Holy Name ER is generally efficient but today, due to a surge of winter flu, there is a long wait. Connected to Mom's distress, I journey beside her as she sits in the wheelchair, wrenched with a torment that pushes her back and forth over the edge of consciousness.

It takes about 90 minutes for the triage nurse to finally call us for the intake. Judy urges my mother to be completely honest and not hold back any information, but I never could have imagined what I'm about to witness. Mom sheepishly admits that the nurse might want to make a note in the chart about her left breast. She pulls up her shirt. The nurse sucks in her breath and is speechless for a moment. "How long have you had this?" she asks, stupefied.

"Oh, I don't know. A couple of years at least."

"When was the last time you saw a doctor?"

"I can't remember. About thirty years ago, I guess."

The nurse is incredulous. "But . . . why wouldn't you go to a doctor for this?"

"I just didn't."

My mother's entire breast is a tumor. It is shriveled, cratered, and hard as a rock. It is so hideous that I can't bring myself to look at it beyond a quick sideways glance. A lightening bolt of truth stabs my mind, *This is the fruit of George.*

A couple of minutes later, the same triage nurse beckons me to step back into her office. Her personal emotions appear to have overwhelmed her. "Your mother's breast is very bad. I can't understand why, in this day and age, she wouldn't have consulted a physician."

"It's a really long story," I stammer out, despising George but knowing I could never explain.

"You know, I'm not supposed to say this, but you better be prepared. This cancer has probably spread and could be all over her body."

"Thank you, truly, for your concern." I grab her hand, grateful for the humanity that drove her to break hospital protocol. Yet what she has told me, in my heart, I already know.

My mother is ushered onto a stretcher inside the main room. Frightened patients surround us, languishing behind curtains that afford inadequate privacy. Their tiny cubicles are shared with concerned family. Judy and I take seats on opposite sides of Mom. Judy holds her hand and strokes it, reassuring her that everything will be OK and that she has come to a safe place where people will ease her pain. My mother looks up and takes Judy's hand. She murmurs, "I am so grateful to both of you. Thank you. I love you very much." She beckons Judy to lean over the bed bars and asks for a kiss. Judy and I look at each other in shock. The many beds, the destroyed breast on her chest—Judy's dream is unfolding.

Thirty minutes later, a shot of Demerol affords my mother relief from the agony that has plagued her for much too long. A series of blood tests, scans, and interviews follow, and I feel hopeful. But when a nurse queries, "Your mom has cancer?" I recognize, way before the doctor's diagnosis that is to come, that today is the beginning of the end.

It is after 10:00 P.M. when they finally find a bed and admit her to the cancer ward. She is hooked up to oxygen and given more pain medication and a sleeping pill.

The following day, Tuesday, we hear from the doctor. The cancer has spread from breast to skeleton—hence the back pain—and is beyond cure. But there are drugs to thwart its spread and buy her time. A bone scan confirms the cancer's location—two huge hot spots in the middle of her spine.

Mom is incoherent from pain killers. Looking at her wasted body and sickly pallor, I fear she won't make it through the weekend. I wonder if I've said everything to her that I need to, and if I'll still have the chance. Reality sinks in too; I must take over her affairs. Fighting through her mental fog, I query Mom about bills, income, bank accounts, etc. It seems so cold to be discussing money with her health so precarious. After decades of rejection, ("My affairs are none of your business. Just worry about yourself.") there is no resistance. Rachael gives me permission to locate her will and other documents. She swears that George is not in the will, but I remember our joint will-signing day 25 years ago, only too clearly. I am right. George, referred to as "family friend," will inherit 20%. (My will contained the same bequeathment but was changed soon after I left The Group.) He is also alternate executor. (I come first.) Wednesday evening, a small party by her hospital bed (lawyer, notary, and four witnesses) observes while she signs a new will eliminating George, and another document granting me power of attorney.

Rachael soon declares that she would like to end her relationship with George. For me, this victory is welcome, but hollow. If it weren't for this illness, she would still be there. Unlike me, she suffers no remorse over the quarter-century of irreplaceable years nor the quarter-million dollars that she invested in a lie. In her mind, it is simply time for a change.

Empowered by her decision to dump George, my mother wants to prevent him from finding her. She relishes the thought of depriving him of one of his favorite challenges—visiting the hospital room and filling it with his healing Energy. Last weekend, when my mother phoned to inform him that she would miss her regular Monday session in order to visit my chiropractor, he had ominous words. "Rachael, I'm warning you. If you follow this path with stupid doctors, you'll be the next one to die."

We ask the lawyer to call George on her behalf. The message is abrupt. "Rachael is under a doctor's care and will no longer be available for sessions." After a 25-year relationship, George responds with a single, indifferent query, "What type of doctor is she seeing?" And when the lawyer states that he is "not at liberty to reveal this information," George responds, "Oh. OK then. Goodbye," and hangs up. But defiantly, he immediately lifts his receiver again, dials Mom's Manhattan apartment and leaves a message on the machine. A week later I find it: "Rachael, it's George," his classic, little-boy voice caresses, "give me a call." Laura, the nurse, also leaves a message: "Rachael, it's Laura. Please call me. I need to talk to you. I'm very concerned about you." On the tape, I hear voices in the background. She is calling from George's office. Laura and my mother have always detested each other, and Laura's strained voice belies her true feelings. This is an abhorrent, but mandatory, assignment from George.

My mother spends the month of January in the hospital. We have many conversations about George, and she seems to have finally admitted that he is no good. According to her, he was always "out for himself." He exploited and dominated people to get what he wanted. She brings up Joe—a loss that, to this day, still brings pain. "George is greedy and loves money. He wanted your money and needed total control to get it. He believed that your bond with your boyfriend Joe might interfere with his agenda, so he set about breaking up the two of you. He convinced Joe that you were manipulating him with the Female Program."

"Do you think I was doing that?" I ask directly.

"No. George just lied to get what he wanted."

"So you were aware that he was sabotaging us."

"Yes, very aware."

"I had no idea. I was away at college and also very naive. But I need to ask you a question. Did you feel at the time that George was doing something wrong?"

"Yes, absolutely."

"What did you do to *try* and stop him? Or to warn me?"

"Nothing."

"Why not?"

"I don't know. George was too powerful, I guess." Her reply is passive and contains no regret.

"George is a murderer!" I burst out, frustrated by her lack of parental protectiveness (which I thought was instinctual).

"I wouldn't call him that," she retorts defensively.

I explode. "You sat there watching a crime being committed, and you didn't lift a finger to try and stop it. George drove Joe to such distraction and distress that he fogged out and missed all the signals from the approaching train. I'm sure that's what really happened. He really loved me, you know."

Rachael snaps back, "Well I don't know anything about this 'love' concept you refer to, I haven't experienced it myself, but I think you're over-dramatizing. Besides, George did not control the train that hit Joe."

"He didn't have to be. He just confused Joe to the point where he lost his innate self-defenses. Without them, George knew my boyfriend was simply an accident waiting to happen."

I can forgive my mother for a lot, but not for this.

During that first month, I visit the hospital as often as I can. Mom and I talk about many things, and one day, she tells me about her lump. She first felt it in her left breast during a session with George about two years ago. Laura was babbling to him about how her own breasts were asymmetrical, so my mother lifted her shirt and felt around. There she made her discovery. As the lump grew over the next several months, she wanted to see a doctor, but she was too afraid of George's inevitable wrath.

Later I find a selection of books and articles on cancer in her apartment. She has been ingesting a daily dose of some special mushroom mixture, glorified in a nutrition magazine for its anti-carcinogenic properties. She knew she had cancer for two years, but she never said a word. That hurts.

Within a few days of the will-signing it becomes clear that Rachael is never going home. In the evenings after work, for the next three months, Judy and Michael help me clean out Mom's 1,400 square-foot, Manhattan co-op apartment and put it up for sale. Mom never threw anything out, and in the beginning there is no place to walk or sit without dislodging a pile of newspapers or manila folders, fire hazards that cover every available surface. We sift through thousands of sheets of paper, mounds of clothing, and several cartons still unpacked from a move in 1978. I wear a mask to keep from inhaling the clouds of dust that billow around us as we disturb her piles. During these endless hours of examining, sorting, and discarding, I uncover hundreds of morsels of her sad life, and mine. George's artifacts are everywhere. Business cards, rocks, assigned books, and endless, psycho-spiritual musings scribbled on scrap paper. From our pre-George life I find cancelled checks that chronicle my childhood: payments to my therapist, Addy, who I had seen as a young teenager; college tuition, apartment rent, "living vitamins" . . . these innocuous slips of paper trigger poignant memories. My 8th grade graduation dress and valedictorian speech are buried in an old trunk. Announcements of my birth and my father's obituaries emerge from the bottom of a desk drawer. I find tax returns from the 1970's that list her expenses to the quack nutritionists she worshiped. But most painful and telling are the letters that I had written to her from college, right after Joe was killed by the train. In them, I talk about the huge hole his departure has left, how lost I feel, and how I believe that following George is my only salvation. My words reveal how hard I was trying to view the world through George's eyes. This included not making friends, or for that matter, trusting anyone at all, because they were all "playing games." Looking back, I see that from the very beginning, I was actively reprogramming my thoughts—brainwashing myself, based on George's instructions.

Judy, Michael, and I throw out most of the apartment's contents—over 60 filled, contractor-sized garbage bags and an equal quantity of stuffed cardboard cartons. Her whole life (and some of mine), now reduced to mounds of refuse that fill the building's basement. Even Rachael's clothing is not in good enough shape to donate. When one evening, Michael brings the clothing hamper out from the bathroom and I open the top to empty it, a dusty cloud flies into my face. I gag on it and remember what I once read—the majority of dust in a home is made up of sloughed, dead skin cells.

In early February my mother is released from the hospital and transferred to a nursing home. It is so strange; I used to visit her three holidays a year, and now I see her almost every day. We are such different people, she and I, and it is often a struggle to make conversation. So I entertain her as best I can by trying to spice up the mundaneness of my own daily doings. After a culture-filled life in Manhattan, my mother has been relegated to a virtual closet. In her semi-private room (for an outrageous price without Long Term Care Insurance), there is barely enough space for a few personal belongings. I do my best to please her, and after the way she treated me my whole life, in the beginning I wondered why. But to me, it is the right thing, the only thing, to do. I am errand girl, shopping to acquire requested delicacies such as chocolate-covered raisins or potato chips. Trying to lighten the depressing atmosphere of her new home, whenever she asks for anything, I respond, "Your wish is my demand," and she laughs, telling me I take such good care of her. When the weather is good, I take her out of jail for short drives. To her, a trip into civilization, even to the grocery store, holds a thrill similar to my visit to Disney Land when I was eight. When I am not there, she sleeps most of the time. Her fatigue is from weakness, but also I think, from boredom—an eager, educated mind, craving stimulation, trapped inside a body that no longer serves.

The majority of her fellow residents in God's waiting room have lost their sense of reality. One woman roams the halls holding a baby doll that she believes is alive. A man across from Rachael's room yells loudly, "Get the police; hurry up. Where are you officer?" for hours, until the nurses put him to bed. Most are in diapers, and the place smells of urine—even though the staff works hard to keep everything clean. Sometimes it takes three nurses to change a resident's diaper, and I hear screaming because, for whatever reason, they do not want to be touched. My mother, incontinent, is in diapers too. She is oblivious to the food stains on her clothing and face, just like a baby. The withdrawal of her well-being is slow, but steady. Heart problems have emerged, and hearing, and sight, and kidney, and bladder. Each new breakdown brings her closer to saying goodbye. The admission application for the nursing home asked whether I had burial arrangements, and where they were. So this is how it ends; I must plan a funeral. How tragic for my mother, and her neighbors; people who enjoyed decades of active life while unknowingly, they were ever approaching this heartbreaking finale. For them, no matter how they lived their lives, on this earth—there will be no second chance.

Rachael Burchard passed away at the age of 84, on May 3, 2005, after the cancer metastasized to her liver. Elizabeth and Judy were present to witness her final breath. May she rest in peace.

The Thursday after Tuesday, September 5, 2006
The End of the Beginning

I've just finished lunch at my desk when the call comes.

"Is Elizabeth Burchard there? Have you heard the news?"

"News? No."

"George Sharkman died two days ago."

"What? How?"

"I'm sorry. I don't have any more information."

Shock is immediate, but not surprise. Less than a month ago I drove past him on the street. Although only 64 he seemed feeble—struggling to move. I guess I felt his dying then. Am I sad? No. Glad? No. Terrified? Yes . . . *for George's harem*: Women close to sixty with no families, no friends, no viable employment, *and no selves*. They've served their master for almost three decades. And George had them convinced he'd never die, never abandon them. What will they do now? How will they process this inconceivable reality? With their life support system ripped away, will they crumble and die? I fear another 1997 Heaven's Gate. I remember my absolute dependence on him from which I miraculously escaped almost ten years ago. How I have struggled to reconstruct a life from the ashes of George's devastation. It has been nearly impossible. If my destiny had taken a different path . . . I shudder to imagine myself among them now . . . utterly hopeless. *There but for the grace of God go I.* I barely sleep that night; those tormented, lost women—who were my friends—infuse my being. And I can do nothing to help.

Today, George is gone one week. Since my mother passed last year, I have no direct pipeline into The Group. So Judy and I have scoured local papers for more details, but we've come up empty. I pull into my parking spot behind my office. Just another work day; "let the stress begin . . ." *But it's not*, because without warning *SHE* materializes three feet from my car door—Serena, the unwelcome phantom from my past. It's been eight years. Eyes red-rimmed from seven days of tears, lower lip trembling, she looks like a lost little girl. I know, only too well, the emotionally incestuous relationship she had with George, and I also know what it's like to lose a father. Her swollen face summons instant and profound compassion, a reflex of my humanity. Our former darkness is momentarily forgotten as her vulnerability floods me with hope. Is there a real person trapped inside Serena after all? Held captive by her father's relentless bullying since birth, will she rip the gag from her mouth and finally speak? Perhaps this monumental event will force her eyes open and she'll embrace the truth for the first time, that her father was an insane fraud who brainwashed her into believing in his immortality and godhood. After all, today the undeniable truth is here. *George lied.*

My hand trembles as I lock my car. Serena approaches stiffly to hug me. I recoil but bear it, then push her up the stairs to my office, which used to be hers too. We sit . . . a surreal deja vu.

"I know. I'm so sorry," I begin.

"How? I actually came here to tell you."

"That's very kind of you; I would have wanted to know. What happened?"

"He had a massive heart attack while driving and crashed into a telephone pole just a few blocks from his house." She pauses. "How have you been?"

"You know life: work, holidays, friends. Pretty routine. And you?"

"Still working; still single. I'm 38 now."

Serena is the same age as her father when I met him. (When she was only nine.) So many painful years have passed.

Serena's piercing, hypnotic stare is just as I remember and she focuses on my eyes. I break the gaze; I won't let her work her voodoo on me, so she reaches for more conversation. "I've become a Born Again Christian; I was baptized this year."

I'm taken off guard with this one and want to make a snide comment. *What won't she think of next?* But of course, aware of how deeply she's grieving, I stifle my impulses. "How does that fit? I thought you believed that your father was God? He did claim to be the Alpha and Omega, the only path to our salvation. *I was there.* Now instead you believe that *Jesus* is the Way, the Truth, and the Light, and He died for our sins?"

"Well, I'm open to believe anything and everything."

Typical Serena. Evasive when challenged. But I'm still curious. "What made you do this?"

"The Bible you gave me as a holiday gift the last winter we were together."

I don't remember, but *OK*. How ironic that I supplied the key to her next level of nonsense!

"I've been reading The Bible to my father this last year, and he was starting to change," she states seriously.

Now that's a picture! I laugh to myself. *Change into what? And I guess it didn't do much good because he's no longer here.* "But George said he'd live forever. How do you explain his death?"

"I asked him about a month ago, and he said that it doesn't matter. The physical body is unimportant."

I suppose George knew at some level he was on his way out, so he had to change his story. After all, *he was never wrong.* And clearly Serena feels the same. So much for hoping she'd wake up to his perverted agenda. Resurgent memories of their hypocrisy and selfishness begin to roil. With old wounds throbbing and my emotions threatening to erupt, I pray for Judy to arrive and rescue me. Thankfully, in the next few minutes she does.

"Hi, Serena. So sorry to hear about your father."

We chat casually, but soon I pick up the ball to ask some significant questions. "What happened to the resurrection of Ben, the dog?"

Serena is unfazed. "Oh, my father realized that only the soul lives forever. So, he buried Ben this summer."

"But he tried for twelve years! Wasn't that a big waste of time?"

"No. Because he learned the truth in the end."

"What of the white rock that contains Ben's soul?" I ask.

"I keep it with me always now." She pulls it out of her pants pocket and displays it in her palm.

"Oh. I haven't seen that in a long, long time." Amused at the familiar sight, I reach to touch it, but Serena pulls her hand away and clutches her treasure protectively close to her body. I remember the overpowering sacredness George infused and how the group members worshiped that holy stone. It's so ridiculous, and I imagine grabbing it and flinging it out the window, but I wouldn't be so cruel.

"Where is George now?"

"He's all around me and part of everything in the universe. He's been telling me he loves me; he'll always be with me, and everything's gonna be OK."

After all these years, I know how they think. "I know that; but I meant his body."

"Oh. He's buried in the Jewish cemetery in Westwood."

I know where that is, and later I'll take Elizabeth there if she wants. She can spit on George's grave or dance the tarantella, or maybe just yell at him for what he stole from her. She never had a chance to confront him and get closure after he threw her out.

My mind turns to his women who must be suffering right now. "What about the mission? How will it continue without a leader?"

"Each of us must carry it on within ourselves," Serena responds without a flinch, as if she had prepared for this question.

"Who's still involved?"

"Pauline (Elizabeth's college roommate), Bess (George's girlfriend), and Laura (the nurse from Columbia Presbyterian

Hospital). Also, Max (Elizabeth's assigned mate with whom she lived for eight miserable years.)"

So, only four true believers remain. Elizabeth was involved in George's heyday, when he was on the upswing. But since she left, it seems followers have peeled away un-replaced. Although George had big plans to spread his message to the planet through his magic rocks, he didn't turn out to be a successful guru; his group has been dying, along with him.

"Aren't those women terribly upset? We've been very worried about them."

"Yes, they've been calling me a lot, but I can't deal with it right now. They've been meeting, supporting each other. They'll be OK." Serena asserts this with proprietary authority. Now I remember how her father trained them to view her as second in command. I quickly analyze the real reason she's avoiding them. Serena must maintain an illusion of superiority; she can never allow them to see her vulnerable.

At this point, Elizabeth intervenes with an almost unbelievable comment. "Serena has become a Christian, you know."

This one really throws me. What are we playing here? Spiritual musical chairs? What happened to their eternal and devout dedication to her father's New Age babble? Immediately I am suspicious and intent on debunking her. "Did you have a funeral, Serena?"

"Yes. Last Sunday."

"Was there a viewing?"

"Yes."

"And all the group members went?"

"No. It was private—family only."

That's it. Any real Christian would know that people need a chance to say goodbye. Their leader was just plucked out of the universe with no warning. You'd have to be one cold son-of-a-bitch to block those tormented women from trying to find closure. Serena is one bogus Christian in my book. But be that as it may, I have more ground to cover. "You and your brother are going to be quite wealthy now. What will you do with all that money? You'll never have to work another day in your life!"

Serena reacts defensively but quickly covers with a stoic look. References to the small fortune her father vampirically drained from his enslaved prisoners are obviously still strictly forbidden.

"Well, the house anyway," I continue, "must be worth well over half a million."

"I'm thinking of moving into my father's house," she states, then changes the subject. "I have a lot of friends now."

I am not surprised. Serena was a communications major and always very social. She has a way with people that George never did. While his entourage has dwindled, apparently she has begun to build hers. But "friends" or future followers? Her father groomed Serena from birth to collect people inclined to servitude. A warning of things to come? A shiver runs through me.

Soon after, Serena rises, hugs each of us in turn, which neither of us welcome, tells us to "take care of each other" and exits. Elizabeth and I stare at the open doorway in disbelief while Serena's presence lingers.

"Did that just really happen? Bad juju," Elizabeth says.

"Yeah. Better call the exorcist—fast. . . . You know, George died at age 66 in '06. Maybe Satan called him home." We both pause a moment, then I add. "You know what's next?"

"Yeah. I think I do, although I don't think Serena knows it yet."

"Those poor desperate women. They'll do anything to get close to a piece of George, to go back and sit in his den forever . . ."

The passing of the baton. Serena is young and strong. She has been groomed from childhood by her father: charisma, secrecy, magical thinking, hypnotic manipulation, and the skill to create a substitute reality into which she can seduce unsuspecting future subjects. Serena will build upon the dregs of George's former glory—a new kingdom behind the mask of Christianity. Channeling the energy of her father's soul and his relentless insanity, she will carry his mission forward—the next generation of deception. Hail to the high priestess . . . and God help us all.

It's early evening on the first anniversary of George's death when Max enters the Closter Diner and spots me in a booth. I motion for him to sit across from me. After a year of abandonment, I have been wondering how they're all doing.

"Big anniversary today?" I offer.

"Whaddya mean?" Max is taken off guard.

"You know . . . George. He died a year ago today. Have you visited the grave? I have."

Facing my bluntness, Max is nervous. "Yes, once. Well, uh, what did you experience when it happened?"

"Experience? You mean was I upset?" I pause to think. "I've been gone for ten years. I had to disconnect. I didn't feel much of anything."

"How about metaphysical?"

"What does that mean?"

"A change in the world's energy. We all felt the shift to a higher intensity."

"No; I didn't sense that."

Max, more confident now, steps onto his pulpit. "We're a giant step closer to the ultimate choice that everybody's gonna have to make. When the energy gets too strong, all the people will be out of control. They'll have to drop their games and give in, or they'll be toast."

"Sounds like you're referring to the Apocalypse."

"The what?"

"You know—The Bible—the end of the world where only the good and faithful will be freed into happiness and joy. Christians everywhere believe in that."

"No. That's only intellectual training; this is experiential and really happening. George knew the way out."

"Listen; how are the girls? Are Laura, Bess, and Pauline still with you?"

Max narrows his eyes in suspicion. "Yes. Why do you ask?"

"Because I was really worried about them. I remember how dependent I was on George, and that he made us feel he would never leave us. Now it's obvious he lied about his immortality. I know how devastated I would have felt if I had still been in The Group last September. I might have ended up in a mental hospital."

Max appears momentarily humble. "We were devastated, and we're keeping together. In fact, we meet a few times a month to practice focusing for a couple of hours, usually here at the diner. We feel George all around. His energy has merged with the universe. In fact, I feel him now. If you were sensitive, you would know the truth."

I hesitate, but force myself to ask the pregnant question that has plagued me since George's exit. "Do you want to follow him?"

Max is confused. "Meaning?"

"Pass over to join him. You know. We always followed George in everything. He wanted it that way, and so did we."

Uncomfortable as he processes my implication, Max is then annoyed at being cornered. "No. Not at this time. Listen I'm late for a meeting. Nice seeing you." He shakes my hand, kisses me on the cheek, and swiftly exits the diner.

With a grimace of disgust, I wipe his slime from my face.

At first the caller's voice is unfamiliar, but after a few words, unpleasantly, it all comes back . . .

"Jude, guess who just called! Max. His mother—you remember Adrianna—passed away last Friday."

"How old was she?"

"88. He's holding a memorial service Sunday at Delmonico's. You know, that fancy Italian place on Broadway; I'm nervous about going."

"You don't owe him anything."

"It's not that. Maybe Pauline and some of the others will be there. I haven't seen them since George threw me out in '96."

Judy pauses for a moment. "OK. If you feel you really want to, then you should go."

"I didn't recognize him at first. 'Max who?' I said. 'Max, *your friend*.' He was annoyed."

"Friend! Has he looked up that word in the dictionary lately?"

I laugh. Judy never leaves bullshitters anywhere to hide, and that's one of the things I love about her. "Poor Adrianna. Max told me she had a series of mini-strokes about eight years ago that left her helpless. He was bringing in George regularly to reverse her brain damage. Adrianna always disliked George. I wish I could have rescued her from that repulsive scene."

"Not exactly a crime you can report to the police."

Sunday afternoon. I arrive a bit before 1:00 pm when the service will start. Parking my car, I pop a Xanax to quell my anxiety, squeeze the rosary I stowed in my purse this morning for protection, hesitate, then head for the entrance. Barely inside the door, Max rushes over, throwing his arms around me with a bear hug. I stiffen in disbelief and confusion.

"Thank you for coming; you mean so much to me." His voice quakes holding back tears.

Exactly how do I mean so much to him? I wonder. Yet, despite our history, seeing his overwhelming grief, I feel sorry for him. But then again, if he really loved his mother, he wouldn't have forced George's loathsome presence upon her against her will while she was dying. I guess our definitions of love are not the same.

Max turns to greet another guest, and I am on my own. No one else from The Group is here yet, and the room is filled with strangers. At the front a podium is flanked by two tables. The left displays a 16 x 20 portrait of his mother on an easel with three large rocks carefully placed at the base. How could it be otherwise? A surge passes through my chest. I had affection for Adrianna, a dynamic, accomplished woman, beloved by numerous friends and her large Greek family, so different from her mentally twisted son.

Soon we find seats as waiters circulate to take our lunch orders. A minister speaks words of comfort and then friends and family take turns honoring Adrianna's life and memory. Max is last, still on the verge of tears, tremulously thanking everyone for coming.

In a mirrored wall, I catch a glimpse of Pauline taking a seat at the back, followed by Laura. I tighten. They're here. I must confront them. This is why I came. To procrastinate, I begin chatting with Max's cousin seated opposite me.

"*How are you?*" The feminine voice inspires adrenalin. Serena towers over me beaming, and for a moment, I don't know her. Apparently, since her father's death, Serena has reinvented herself. This modern model is clothed in a stylish pantsuit and sports a sophisticated, trendy haircut complete with auburn highlights. Now forty, middle-aged, she's done a damn good repackaging job. Still, between the ears, nothing's changed. Same creepy, hypnotic gaze. And why is she so happy to see me, just like Max? I still don't get it. Maybe it's what I represent—a piece of her life with Daddy. She points toward Pauline. "I'm sitting over there with my boyfriend. Join us."

After more than a decade, Pauline and Laura seem basically unchanged, and they aren't particularly thrilled to see me. Serena introduces her companion whom she met on Eharmony.com. Now I get the extreme make over! Pauline reports she's a new godmother to her younger sister's first child and will be moving to Virginia this summer to help out. Having earned teaching certification last year, she'll seek an elementary school position. Looks like these girls have enlisted in The Program, that dreaded state of being George convinced us to shun; he must be turning in his grave. What happened to the endless condemnation of outsiders? Those pathetic, ignorant robots leading dead lives while we, the elite coterie of spiritual Navy Seals, pursued the only worthy mission. Now they're joining the social sheep herd. Don't they see the hypocrisy? The betrayal of their former selves? And what about George's death? He convinced them to finance his immortality, then fled in the night, a con-man made wealthy by his marks' life savings. How do their minds process this cognitive dissonance, the colossal contradiction between ingrained belief and indisputable reality?

Conversation floats and eventually dessert is served. Afterwards, while the room empties of guests, Serena and Laura peel away. Pauline and I remain, crammed at our table in the back. Busboys scurry around us, clearing away all evidence of Max's gathering. Pauline has somewhere she'd rather be, I'm sure, but that's too bad; I won't let my last chance slip away. So, emulating Barbara Walters' style on a particularly intense television interview I once saw where she ever so diplomatically interrogated a former suicide bomber, I take a shot. "I know Serena moved into her father's house and you were all seeing a lot of each other. What happened to the mission?"

"What mission?"

"*The* mission. You know, to save the world with The Energy. Wasn't that the goal that made us willing to sacrifice so much?"

Pauline is nonchalant. "Oh, that. Well, none of us has the drive George had."

Over the cliff. The obsession that defined their identities. I gape for a moment, incredulous. They're moving on as if The Energy never existed. Televisions changing stations to broadcast this season's premiere.

I collect myself. "George believed he would live forever. I assume he left without warning?"

"We didn't expect it. If I had made a list of people I thought would die, he would have been the last, even before me."

Pauline seems OK so far with my line of questioning, so I press on. "But where did he go?"

She shakes her head; she's clueless. "I don't know. I've been looking for a medium."

"Oh, to contact him?"

Pauline nods yes. For me, this just keeps getting weirder.

"What happened when he died?"

"It was horrible. I threw up for more than a day—even blood. We're still messed up." She changes the subject. "My father died last year."

"I'm sorry about your dad . . . Do I owe you an apology?" Ten years ago, after I left The Group, I expressed my remorse to Lisa, my other college roommate, for getting her involved.

"That's the farthest thing from my mind. George was the wisest man I'll ever know. Why would you say such a thing?"

"Because it didn't turn out the way you thought. I opened the door and now you've lost . . ." I stop myself. The reality is too cruel: the few hundred thousand dollars and twenty-four years she invested in a lie. Pauline is nearly fifty, a pauper starting from scratch.

The early dinner crowd trickles in and we are pushed out into the parking lot. Blocking Pauline's path of escape to her car, I continue to bend her ear. I'm not finished. In fact, I'm starting to get upset. "*Wise man?!* What about that temper? He used to throw Laura out of the room by her hair. And the sex, I felt raped, spiritually and emotionally. I'll never forget the humiliation."

She observes impassively. "That's distant past. We all evolved into collaboration, and The Energy was getting really incredible."

Pauline makes me feel like a kindergartner who foolishly strayed while she, the wiser one, went on to experience advanced study at an exclusive university.

It begins to drizzle, and the skies threaten much worse momentarily. My time is running out, and my rage at injustice kicks up a notch as more memories flood back. I wring my hands and raise my voice a bit.

"Fine, but the abuse was real. For God sakes, he hit me in the face. *You were there!*"

Pauline doesn't budge. "George realized his temper was a distraction from The Energy and afterwards, it changed. I don't really remember those things. That was long ago." She nods her head slightly to wipe away the moment, and I am permanently disqualified. Her rigid, shark eyes pierce, judging me as a piteous creature for losing control to my anger and distress. Perhaps her lack of empathy is a defense mechanism to protect her from the enormity of personal loss impossible to cope with. Yet, I sense no traumatized woman trapped behind a wall of denial. What stands before me under the troubled afternoon sky looks a lot more like cold indifference. Translated into the vernacular—she couldn't care less.

George was never immortal; he lied about everything. Most people hate being conned. Why haven't they made him accountable for his crimes? Don't they regret giving away their power to a psycho? George was a malignant narcissist, sociopath, son-of-a-bitch who exploited and abused without conscience as if people were stuffed animals in his personal toy box. Anyone can see that, *apparently, except them.* Thus, they are spared. Unlike me, there are no panic attacks, nightmares, post-traumatic stress, fits of rage, or tears of grief, followed by a series of psychotherapy sessions and anti-depressant medications. Bona fide New Agers, they live in the moment and go with the flow, devoid of conflict. They are focused, diligently working at filling the hole George left when he exited. Life's buffet lies before them. Unhampered by George's agenda, they sample choice, new items and pile their plates high. The past does not require restitution or even comprehension. The Book of George is closed and his disciples have, with reverence, placed it back on the shelf.

Lightening flashes, bringing drops of rain. There is only one thing left to say, to me, more important than anything. I look at her eyes directly for the last time. "In the end, I couldn't stand to be near George. His aura, his personal energy, repelled me. It was poisonous. But, I guess *you* were able to tolerate his presence."

She nods yes, but to her, I know I'm speaking Russian. Unexpectedly I have a vision, so powerful and profound that for a moment, I am swept out of my body into another dimension. There, starting at the top of her head, her human skin-suit unzips. Underneath, a lizard-like creature, Sigourney Weaver's *Alien*, dispassionately observes, absolutely non-human.

Thunder cracks and the sky opens in sudden, violent downpour. I quickly hug her goodbye, wish her good luck in her new life, and we rush in opposite directions to our cars. I exit the parking lot, but within two blocks, the torrential rain makes driving impossible. I pull over on a side street and dial my cell.

"Jude, I'm done."

"How did it go?"

"I didn't need the rosary. They all seemed so . . . ordinary. I'm not afraid of them any more."

"Without George they have no power. He alone summoned the evil."

"Yeah, they only channeled what they absorbed from him. Pauline told me that when George died, she threw up for 24 hours."

"I'm not surprised; he was her lifeline, her air hose."

"Oh, and her father died last year; he was about 95."

"Did she vomit for 24 hours when her real father died?"

I pause, thinking of how much I still miss my own father even after 36 years. "No." There's much more to say, but I'll save it for later.

"You've waited twelve years to see them. Did you find some closure?"

I think of the alien hiding behind Pauline's eyes and I know I did indeed find what I was looking for.

"Yes, and it wasn't what I expected."

Appendix B

Excerpt from George's cable TV interview
Aired March 2000

Host: Our guest, Reverend George Sharkman, is a unique individual. Author of the book, *Biofeedback and Beyond*, he also hosts a radio show, *BrainTalk*, and has been a counselor for the past 25 years in stress management and the practice of a special energy. In fact, he believes that this energy he's discovered may be the salvation of mankind. Welcome, George; tell us how you got started.

George: Many years ago I went into biofeedback, which teaches the patient to listen to themselves and to control their autonomic nervous system. Instead of always running to a doctor to take care of you, you can learn to take responsibility for your life. The nervous system is dominated by our primitive, Fight or Flight reactions. We live in a state of constant fear, as if we are about to be eaten by a saber-toothed tiger. Our boss, our spouse, our parents, they all trigger us like this. Inappropriate survival reactions overpower us, and instead of removing them, we make up stories to justify them. Fear is manmade. Now, when you start to relax and slow down to the speed of life, you find out that you're made of pure energy, 76 trillion cells all emitting light, and 9 trillion brain chips that we do not use.

Host: Psychologists refer to stress as positive; a little stress is sometimes an effective motivator. It sounds like you're saying it's completely unnecessary.

George: Stress is a warning that we are being insensitive to ourselves. Normally, when we have stress, we try to do something about it, but this is wrong. We simply need to stop interfering, to get out of the way. Life flows without us doing anything.

Host: How does that affect relationships?

George: Well first of all, there are *no* relationships, only a relationship with yourself. We're all trained from the day we're born to ignore ourselves. That means we don't care for ourselves and can't care for anybody else. With this Energy I've discovered we can start to know ourselves, become happy and then relate with others without tension.

Host: What type of problems do people have when they come to you for help?

George: Cancer, heart problems, headaches . . . across the board. I just started treating a woman who has been an alcoholic for 20 years. Within three sessions she was pouring her vodka down the drain. Expensive drain cleaner, hah, hah. Usually people come to see me when there's no place else to go. Then, when we start working, and the person finds they can cure it, that's when they get anxious. They're afraid of themselves, of their own greatness.

Host: There are many popular self-help gurus out there today, Deepak Chopra, Tony Roberts, etc. How do you differ from them?

George: You have to understand, most everyone can teach someone else, but if they can't teach themselves, then it's not working. The human race is on the brink of extinction. We don't take care of the planet. We kill everything around us. Every time we cut down a tree, there's less oxygen to breathe. This isn't changing, even with all the positive information being taught by people. That's why I became the Reverend of the Universal Church of Life for People, Plants, and Animals. Everything is alive and we must learn to respect and merge with it all. Scientists say that the molecules in our eyes came from the Big Bang, same as the molecules in rocks and plants.

Host: What did you experience when you were first starting out?

George: I used the biofeedback machine myself, so I could understand how to help my patients. Then one day my head started shaking on its own, very fast, as fast as light. Now when it stopped, it released an energy, a feeling, radiance. For many years people have been discovering this energy, but the problem is, they can show it to everybody else, maybe even heal a disease, but can't use it for themselves. They have to go all the way, become who they really are. Like I said before, 76 trillion cells all emitting light. When you use your brain more than 4 percent (that's all we use), then you connect to the universe and you KNOW EVERYTHING. The shaking of the head allows me to get past symptoms, problems, and anxieties. Beyond all of that, we're unity. We belong to everything and everything belongs to us. We are truly GOD inside.

    No one listens to that inner being because the mind makes so much noise. For thousands of years we've been trying to slow down our minds, but you can't slow it down when you're the one who's creating your thoughts in the first place, so instead of trying to correct the mind, we have to FOCUS *beyond* the mind. You create a mission, to go for the *greatness inside of you*. Now when you shake, it's like shaking a bottle of seltzer, it expands. Instead of being frightened, just allow it to flow out, and you'll feel wonderful. (Camera zooms in as Sharkman begins shaking his head rapidly for about a minute.) Now, if everyone watching could start shaking their heads when they feel conflict, they would activate the energy within and shift to a better place.

Host: Is that shaking natural?

George: When it first started, it was unnatural. It occurred by itself, and I was afraid, but then I allowed it so many times that I finally entered in with it, merged my life with its force. We shouldn't be afraid of anything because there's really nothing unknown. If we can just get the brain to work, we know everything. We don't need to *educate*, we need to experience. Education forces information down and interferes with the flow of energy. Actually, our school system is pointless, just babysitting.

Host: Now the whole system is based on education. We've been trained and trained since we were small children. So you're saying that anyone who wants to learn more about what you've discovered would have to un-train themselves? (George nods in agreement.) They'd have to stop, watch, and wait, which is what you advise in your book, and to become aware of how they're interfering in their lives so they can open up space for this feeling you're referring to. What you're also saying is that this feeling can expand out into everything, into other people, and they can begin to feel energy and be transmitters for it too.

George: That's right, but the best transmitter I've found so far is a rock. I focus and release the energy in the rock. The rock is alive. . . . Everything is alive because it's all made of energy, scientists have proved this in physics labs. I take a rock, shake it up, then it starts to radiate, pulsate, and change colors. If you hold the rock, it becomes your feedback system while you're growing, a connection to your true spiritual self. When you're nervous or anxious, you hold the rock and feel it pulse. These pulsations are bigger than our heartbeats. We should have our heartbeats regulated to the universe, but we don't. So the rock, which has no interfering thought process and is totally alive, has that universal pulsation and will remind you of who you truly are. Then you'll stop your nonsense — programming, games, dramas, etc.

Host: So really, what you're saying is that the problems we have could be changed by people starting to accept this energy and their potential to feel god inside.

George: Yes, and the energy is intelligent, so if we trust it, it will guide us.

Host: And we're all made of energy, so if we integrate, you're saying that we can become a great species. How did your training in martial arts help you?

George: In college, I earned a black belt in karate. Martial arts teaches you how to focus, but it doesn't get you to your own greatness. There's something bigger than the U.S. government. There's something bigger than anything man has created, and it's inside. But, you have to access it.

Host: Do you believe that people or organizations feel uncomfortable or threatened the first time they experience this energy, that they don't understand and are afraid when they realize that there's a new way, a new direction?

George: First of all, we *must* follow this new direction if we want to survive as a species. But yes, people feel threatened when they become happier because they're trained to be miserable. A person can only take a few moments of joy, and then they'll start to doubt because it's unfamiliar. They react and tighten. That's why people get sick; they're contracting all the time and eventually, their bodies break down.

Host: What did you experience many years ago, when you first discovered this energy?

George: If you look at history, all the way back to Jesus Christ, anyone who discovers something new is ostracized at first. So when I found this and started talking about it, people didn't want to have anything to do with me. They told me I was crazy. But I believed there was something more, and I didn't care what others said. I used to host biofeedback seminars. I would take the stage, look out over the audience and say absolutely nothing for fifteen minutes. The people would get so upset because of their need to have every moment of their time filled with some type of noise, that they would actually throw chairs at me. (George chuckles.) They couldn't deal with the quiet, with experiencing themselves. In quiet there's actually an enormous amount of expansion, and you can feel and hear it. There's wellness. You're never alone. When people feel lonely, that's just their thought process lying to them. If you took a microscope and looked into your body, you'd see billions of living cells and microbes. That means you have a lot of family inside. If you can externalize that and merge with everything on the outside, you're one big force with everything. Not alone but all one!

Host: We're hearing a lot about yoga, Reiki, Chi, and healers. Do you differ from all of that?

George: First of all, in meditation they talk about chakras, centers of energy. I know for a fact that there are no points of energy, we are total energy. So when I shake my head, the person feels their own totality. Our minds are small and need to classify things in parts, like post office boxes, so we can feel like we have control. With new information, we must reinterpret things. For example, arthritis. Remember we are electricity, so imagine that our electric company (the universe) sends 100,000 volts through us. Then we squeeze and tighten from the intensity. The result is pain that we interpret as arthritis or some other disease. Because man loses control, he reacts in fear. We are continuously contracting over this tremendous force we are made of and creating all kinds of diseases. Break the word "disease" into parts and we get *dis* and *ease*, really stress from lack of control.

Host: How should we relate with animals?

George: Animals are energy and intelligence. They don't think as much as we do, so they feel and understand more. We are afraid of them because they know exactly what we're thinking, just like small children. They have a crazy program: to kill for food. We see this on the Discovery Channel, shows about African lions, but when animals are touched by The Energy, they lose their aggressiveness and roll over on their backs. Animals are more caring because they don't have a thinking process that makes them doubt themselves. We're the only species that doubts. We were put here to learn from animals, but instead we are making them extinct. We have to take responsibility because we are creating this mess. We're ripping down trees to build another shopping mall and pouring pollution into the oceans and air. If we don't stop, we'll destroy our natural world. The animals will have nowhere to live and nothing to eat, and neither will we.

Host: So, can you sum up what we, as citizens, must do, and how this relates to what you're doing with energy?

George: We have to learn to take care of ourselves. My intention is to continue shaking up The Energy. You know scientists have discovered recently that our bodies regenerate all of our cells; the body is really made to live forever. In my opinion, it is only the crazy thought process that interferes with this. People don't do anything about their misery and destructiveness because they figure they'll die soon and go to heaven. Everyone's just biding their time. But I have news for them, there is no heaven to escape to. It's all here on the Earth, and people are gonna have to deal with their immortality, learn to take responsibility for their negativity, and make changes fast or else. . . . It'll be too bad for them. Soon, this energy I've discovered will finally wake everybody up to see the truth. If they've been practicing to accept the bigness, they'll be able to deal with who they really are, consciously. If they're not in practice, it's gonna be scary.

Host: Thanks George, for sharing your unique insights with us today.

Appendix C

QUESTIONS FOR DISCUSSION

Search for Spirituality
(to be discussed after reading section)
1. When you hear the word "cult," what do you picture?
2. Describe the people you might expect to find in a cult.
3. What does "spirituality" mean to you?
4. Compare and contrast spirituality to religion.

My Past: Oct. 1940 to Sept. 1977
1. How would you describe Elizabeth's relationship with her mother? her father?
2. Which life events contributed to Elizabeth's emotional vulnerability?
3. Elizabeth's mother was involved with a series of gurus. What might drive a person to seek a guru?

January to December 1980
1. Explain whether or not George handled his first meeting with Elizabeth in a professional manner. What might her emotional state have been at the time?
2. What is George's agenda with Joe, and how does that affect Elizabeth's emotional stability?
3. Does Joe's death make Elizabeth more vulnerable to George? Might she have handled George's advances differently if she wasn't depressed?
4. What are some of the things George does to create dependency?
5. Is there truth to any of George's assertions about "The Program," the state of society, social conditioning, etc.?
6. Where does he depart from rational logic into faulty logic to further his agenda?
7. How might George's childhood have affected his personality and personal goals?
8. What is the point of the headshaking, and is it a form of hypnosis?
9. Define hypnosis. What are some methods that might induce hypnosis aside from the classic swinging pocket watch?
10. Why do cults often encourage members to give up family and friends?

Fall 1984 to Summer 1987
1. Describe Elizabeth's conflict over her relationship with George.
2. How does George gather more recruits? Why is he able to use the school system?

3. How does George draw in newcomers? What are they looking for? What do they think he has to offer?
4. What is magical thinking? How does George manifest this in himself? How and why does he teach it to his flock?
5. How does he use his atypical, strange behavior and habits to gain the allegiance of his group?
6. Why does Elizabeth abandon her former plans for a career in medicine?
7. What is the purpose of pairing up group members as couples?
8. How does George create a state of isolation in his devotees' lives? Why?
9. How and why does George create a unified belief system within his group?
10. According to George, what is "The Energy" and what is its purpose? What do *you* believe The Energy is?
11. What emotional needs of members are being filled by participating in The Group?
12. How does George exploit his members for personal gain and what does he gain? How does he cover up or validate the exploitation?
13. What are some of the socially unacceptable activities that George is fostering? Is he doing anything illegal?
14. Given that the group members are adults, not minors, evaluate the following: "These people are here of their own volition and are responsible for the consequences of their choices; the cult leader isn't forcing anyone to participate."

February to December 1991
1. How does George motivate his followers to spend more time with him? What does he gain from their increased participation?
2. How does George validate shop-lifting? Where is his logic at fault?
3. Why do his devotees, responsible citizens up to this point, agree to engage in shop-lifting? Why don't they report him to the police?
4. In the Thanksgiving morning session, why does George interrogate Pauline? How and why do Pauline's peers support the interrogation?
5. What is George's attitude toward family holidays and why?
6. How and why is Serena able to take control of Elizabeth's business?
7. Why does George oppose Elizabeth's desire to leave Max?

January to December 1993

1. How has Serena's personality been shaped by her father? Given the power of her father's influence, to what extent, if at all, is she responsible for her unreasonable behavior.
2. Why does George quickly convince Elizabeth to give up Preston?
3. From the guru's vantage point, what is the true purpose for the trip to Washington, D.C.?
4. What does George accomplish by threatening to abandon his followers?
5. How and why does George treat his children differently from the rest of The Group?
6. Why, after ten years, does Lisa decide to leave? Describe the opposition (internal and external) she faces in order to accomplish this.
7. What does the guru intend to accomplish by joining the Perot group *United We Stand America*? Is this a common strategy among cults?
8. What is the difference between Elizabeth's friendship with Judy, and Elizabeth's relationships with her peers in the cult?

Saturday August 27, 1994

1. Why does George criticize Elizabeth for being upset when her mother faints?
2. Why do you think Karen's children dislike George?
3. Why does Serena fail to win back her position in the Perot group? What does this show about the difference between insiders' and outsiders' responses to George's will to control?
4. Why does Judy tell Elizabeth that God doesn't like what's going on in George's den? Why doesn't Elizabeth understand what she means? Do you agree with Judy? Why or why not?
5. Why do most of the group members accept responsibility for Ben's death?
6. How does George change after Ben's death, and why do most of the (college-educated) group members so readily follow his lead?
7. Elizabeth has trouble accepting the "Ben mission." In your opinion, why? What does she do instead?

October 1995

1. Name one or more of George's pseudo-scientific assertions. Why would educated people accept his statements without question? If one of his devotees confronted George with scientific fact, how might he handle this?
2. Why does The Group oppose Elizabeth's friendship with Judy?
3. Define the power of suggestion. How does it manifest in George's group?

4. How do the "Enoch Commandments" differ from *The Bible*'s Ten Commandments?
5. Which personal experiences and strengths make Judy an ideal person to help Elizabeth?
6. Which dysfunctional and self-destructive behaviors does Judy observe among group members while attending George's meetings?
7. Envisioning the "hand in glove" analogy, describe some complementary roles played by guru and devotee.
8. What does Judy offer to Elizabeth that is unavailable in the cult?
9. How does George try to manipulate Karen's children? In your opinion, regarding Karen's choice to expose her children to George (despite their protests,) is she a good parent? Why or why not?
10. Are the children in the same or a worse position than George's adult followers?
11. It is clear that Elizabeth doesn't want to give George any more money. So, why does she continue to attend sessions and pay him?
12. Do you find it incredible or understandable that George is able to peddle his wares in respected institutions such as Barnes and Noble Bookstores and Sing Sing Prison? Explain.
13. How is it that George is able to circulate within "normal" society without being spotted and rejected or attacked?

February 1996
1. Why is George so upset when Elizabeth visits a doctor?
2. Despite his blatant mistreatment of others, why does Serena insist on always defending her father?
3. Do you feel empathy for Elizabeth's lament, "I want my twenty years back?" Why or why not?
4. Despite the fact that Serena is a poor business partner, why does Elizabeth feel that "divorce" is not an option?
5. Why does George eject Elizabeth from the fold?

January 10, 9:00 PM
1. What price does Elizabeth pay for not returning to the cult? What does she gain? What challenges does she face now?
2. Compare objective to subjective perception. Which does Serena use to confirm that her father was able to lengthen a light bulb with The Energy? How is her reasoning in contradiction to the scientific method?
3. Describe the reasoning Serena uses to convince herself that her father has not committed any wrongdoing, despite concrete evidence to the contrary.

4. Speculate on what you would do in Serena's position and why.
5. Why isn't the legal system available to both help Elizabeth obtain restitution from George *and* prevent him from continuing his practice?
6. Why do group members, including Elizabeth's mother, take George's side when he throws Elizabeth out?
7. After Elizabeth has figured out George's con, why doesn't Elizabeth's mother embrace her daughter's discoveries?
8. Can you find fault with some of the assertions George makes during his radio interview?
9. Describe some lessons about life choices and relationships between people that you are able to take away with you after reading this book.

Cult Fundamentals

General:
1. Define cult.
2. Name some different types of cults.
3. How do they differ, and what do they have in common?
4. Compare cults to organized religion.
5. Define sociopath. Are cult leaders necessarily sociopaths?
6. Compare cult leaders to religious leaders (priests, rabbis, ministers, etc.) vis a vis personality, ethics, personal agenda, and behavior.
7. Define brainwashing.
8. What is mind control?
9. How is mind control achieved in a cult group?
10. To the cultist, what are some of the harmful effects of cult involvement?
11. List some benefits that could, in certain cases, be gained by a cultist from cult involvement?

Campus Recruitment:
1. Why do many cults recruit on college campuses?
2. What are some common methods of on-campus cult recruitment?
3. Which personality traits might make a person vulnerable to cult recruitment?
4. What life events might make a person vulnerable to cult recruitment?
5. The methodology of cult recruitment is generally considered unethical. Why?
6. What could cause you to suspect that a friend or family member has fallen under cult control?

7. In order to establish that a group is not a cult, what questions can you ask before agreeing to participate in an off-campus retreat or other group-led event?

   Myths:
Here are some common myths about cult involvement. Why are they inaccurate in many cases?
a. Only losers and weirdos join cults. If I check out a group and find normal-looking, friendly, and articulate members, then it can't be a cult.
b. This is an issue of freedom of choice. People choose to become members freely.
c. Cult members can leave any time they want to.
d. It's an issue of religious freedom.
e. He (or she) is an adult. He says he's happy. What right do I have to judge?

   Moral Issues:
1. What are some things that take place in cults that are morally wrong and/or illegal?
2. In general, are morally wrong actions also illegal? Give some examples.
3. Name some cult activities that are morally wrong but not illegal.
4. Is it fair to conclude that cult devotees generally have a weak moral character? Why or why not?
5. What is the difference between subjective truth and objective truth?
6. Cults are sometimes called "truth-twisters." How do members come to choose cult doctrine over objective truth?

REFERENCES

Analyzing Cults

Arnott, Dave, *Corporate Cults*, AMACOM, 2000.

Conway, Flo, and Jim Siegelman, *Snapping*, Stillpoint Press, 1995.

Galanter, Marc, *Cults, Faith, Healing, and Coercion*, Oxford University Press, 1999.

Gomes, Alan W., *Unmasking The Cults*, Harper Collins, 1995.

Hassan, Steven, *Combating Cult Mind Control*, Park Street Press, 1988.

Hassan, Steven, *Releasing the Bonds*, Aitan Publishing, 2000.

Hoffer, Eric, *The True Believer*, Harper Collins, 1951.

Hunt, June, *Cults (audio)*, Hope for the Heart, 1997.

Kramer, Joel, and Diana Alstad, *The Guru Papers: Masks of Authoritarian Power*, Frog, Ltd. Books, 1993.

Layton, Deborah, *Seductive Poison: A Jonestown Survivor's Story of Life and Death in The People's Temple*, Anchor Books- Doubleday, 1998.

Lifton, Robert Jay, *Destroying the World to Save It*, Henry Holt, 1999.

Muster, Nori J., *Betrayal of the Spirit*, University of Illinois Press, 1997.

Patrick, Ted, *Let Our Children Go*, Ballantine, 1977.

Singer, Margaret, and Janja Lalich, *"Crazy" Therapies—What are they? Do they work?*, Jossey-Bass Publishers, 1996.

Psychology of Mind Control and Evil

Fromm, Erich, *The Anatomy of Human Destructiveness*, Henry Holt, 1973.

Goldberg, Carl, *Speaking with the Devil: A Dialogue with Evil*, Viking, 1996.

Hoover, William L., Ph.D., *Psychology of Mind Control*, Harcourt Brace, 1995.

Milgram, Stanley, *Obedience to Authority*, Harper Collins, 1974.

Peck, M. Scott, *People of the Lie*, Simon and Schuster, 1983.

Sargant, William, *Battle for the Mind*, Malor Books, 1997.

Winn, Denise, *The Manipulated Mind*, Malor Books, 2000.

Psychology of Manipulation and Deceit

Capaldi, Nicholas, *The Art of Deception*, Prometheus, 1987.

Carter, Jay, *Nasty Men*, Contemporary Books, 1993.

Carter, Jay, *Nasty People*, Contemporary Books, 1989.

Evans, Patricia, *Controlling People*, Adams Media, 2002.

Fellows, Bob, *Easily Fooled*, Mind Matters, 2000.

Ford, Charles V., *Lies! Lies! Lies! The Psychology of Deceit*, American Psychiatric Press, 1996.

Forward, Susan, Ph.D., *Emotional Blackmail*, Harper Collins, 1997.

Forward, Susan, Ph.D., *Toxic Parents*, Bantam, 1989.

Glass, Lillian, *Toxic People*, Saint Martin's Griffin, 1995.

Green, George, and Carolyn Cotter, *Stop Being Manipulated*, Berkley Books, 1995.

Hogan, Kevin, *The Psychology of Persuasion*, Pelican, 2000.

McGraw, Phillip, *Relationship Rescue*, Hyperion, 2000.

Norwood, Robin, *Women Who Love Too Much*, Simon and Schuster, 1997.

Simon, George, *In Sheep's Clothing: Understanding and Dealing with Manipulative People*, A.J. Christopher, 1999.

Hypnotism

Bowers, Kenneth, *Hypnosis for the Seriously Curious*, W. W. Norton, 1976.

Copelan, Rachel, *Fell's Official Know-it-All Guide: Hypnotism*, Frederick Fell, 2000.

McGill, Ormond, *The New Encyclopedia of Stage Hypnotism*, Crown House, 2001.

Moine, Donald, and Kenneth Lloyd, *Unlimited Selling Power: How to Master Hypnotic Selling Skills,* Prentice Hall, 1990.

Sutphen, Dick, *The Battle for your Mind*, Speech delivered to the World Congress of Professional Hypnotists Convention, Las Vegas, NE 1999.

Debunking New Age/Pseudoscience

Ankerberg, John, and John Weldon, *The Encyclopedia of New Age Beliefs*, Harvest House, 1996.

Groothuis, Douglas R., *Unmasking the New Age*, Intervarsity Press, 1986.

Hines, Terence, *Pseudoscience and the Paranormal*, Prometheus Books, 1988.

Hoggart and Hutchinson, *Bizarre Beliefs*, Richard Cohen Books, 1995.

Hunt, June, *New Age Mentality: A New Mask for an Old Message* (audio), Hope for the Heart, 1997.

Jeremiah, David, *Invasion of Other Gods* (audio), Turning Point, 1996.

Randi, James, *An Encyclopedia of Claims, Frauds, and Hoaxes of the Occult and Supernatural*, Saint Martin's Griffin, 1995.

Randi, James, *Flim-Flam*, Prometheus Books, 1982.

Schick, Theodore, and Lewis Vaughn, *How to Think about Weird Things: Critical Thinking for a New Age*, McGraw-Hill, 2002.

Proponents of New Age and the Supernatural

Anderson, U. S., *Three Magic Words*, Thomas Nelson & Sons, 1954.

Chopra, Deepak, M.D., *Ageless body, Timeless mind*; Crown Publishers, 1993.

Cooper, Robert, *The Other 90%*, Random House, 2001.

Covey, Stephen R., *The Seven Habits of Highly Effective People*, Simon and Schuster, 1989.

Edward, John, *Crossing Over*, Jodere, 2001.

Edward, John, *One Last Time*, Berkley Books, 1999.

Fisher, Mark, *The Millionaire's Secrets*, Simon & Schuster, 1996.

Lewis, Clyde, *An Encounter with a Prophet*, Amadon Publishing, 1995.

Millman, Dan, *The Way of the Peaceful Warrior*, H. J. Kramer Inc., 1990.

Morgan, Mario, *Mutant Message Down Under*, Harper Collins, 1994.

Peck, Scott, *The Road Less Traveled*, Simon and Schuster, 1978.

Redfield, James, *The Celestine Prophecy*, Warner Books, 1993.

Robbins, Anthony, *Unlimited Power*, Ballantine, 1986.

Walsch, Neale Donald, *Conversations with God*, G. P. Putnam's Sons, 1995.

Williamson, Marianne, *A Return to Love: Reflections on the Principles of A Course in Miracles*, Harper Collins, 1992.

Good and Evil: Christian Perspective

Banks, Bill, and Sue Banks, *Breaking Unhealthy Soul Ties*, Impact Christian Books, 2003.

Cuneo, Michael, *American Exorcism*, Doubleday, 2001.

Hammond, Frank, and Ida Hammond, *Pigs in the Parlor*, Impact Books, 1973.

Goodall, Wayde, and Thomas Trask, *The Battle: Defeating the Enemies of your Soul*, Zondervan, 1997.

Martin, Malachi, *Hostage to the Devil*, Harper Collins, 1992.

Meyer, Joyce, *How to Fight the Devil and Win* (audio), Life in the Word, 1996.

Page, Sydney, *Powers of Evil*, Baker Books, 1995.

Prince, Derek, *Deliverance and Demonology* (audio), DPM, 2003.

Unger, Merrill, *Demons in the World Today*, Tyndale House, 1995.

Unger, Merrill, *What Demons do to Saints*, Moody Press, 1991.

Whyte, Maxwell, *A Manual on Exorcism*, Whitaker House, 1974.

RESOURCES

1. Jewish Board of Family Services Cult Clinic, 120 West 57th Street, 10th Floor, NY, NY, 10019-3371, (212) 632-4640

2. Cult Information Service of NY and NJ, Box 867, Teaneck, N.J., 07666, (201) 833-1212

3. www.freedomofmind.com — Freedom of Mind Resource Center, PO Box 45223, Somerville, MA 02145-0002, (617) 628-9918

4. www.ICSAhome.com — International Cultic Studies Association, PO Box 2265, Bonita Springs, FL 34133, (239) 514-3081

5. www.wellspringretreat.org — Wellspring Retreat and Resource Center, PO Box 67, Albany, OH, 45710, (740) 698-6277

6. www.NEIRR.org The New England Institute of Religious Research & Meadow Haven Retreat and Recovery Center, PO Box 878, Lakeville, MA 02347-0878, (508) 947-9571

7. www.watchman.org — Watchman Fellowship, PO Box 13340, Arlington, TX 76094, (817) 277-0023

8. www.TheCultNextDoor.com – 201-784-0001

THE AUTHORS

Elizabeth R. Burchard was born in Manhattan in 1959. In 1982, she earned a BA in biochemistry from Swarthmore College. A former high school chemistry teacher, (The Fieldston School, Bronx, N.Y.) Elizabeth has owned and operated Expressions Photography Studio, in Closter, New Jersey, since 1988. A portrait artist, she specializes in soulful black and white images of children. In addition, Elizabeth also developed *Exambusters*, a series of study aids for test preparation. Since 2000, the co-authors have lectured live and on the radio about the dangers of cult involvement.

Judith L. Carlone, born in 1952, was raised in an Italian community in Hoboken, New Jersey. After graduating from high school, she devoted herself to the entertainment business for almost two decades as a lead singer and songwriter. During that time, she also lectured at New Jersey high schools, inspiring seniors to further their educations. She is currently a licensed realtor and insurance agent. She makes her home with her husband of forty years, Michael, two cats, Teddie and Rayme, and two dogs, Toby and Alfie. The authors may be contacted at info@TheCultNextDoor.com

CPSIA information can be obtained at www.ICGtesting.com
Printed in the USA
BVOW05s1027031215

429265BV00028B/668/P